Ideology, Crime and Criminal Justice

Cambridge Criminal Justice Series

Published in association with the Institute of Criminology, University of Cambridge

Published titles

Community Penalties: change and challenges, edited by Anthony Bottoms, Loraine Gelsthorpe and Sue Rex

Ideology, Crime and Criminal Justice: a symposium in honour of Sir Leon Radzinowicz, edited by Anthony Bottoms and Michael Tonry

Reform and Punishment: the future of sentencing, edited by Sue Rex and Michael Tonry

Ideology, Crime and Criminal Justice

**A symposium in honour of
Sir Leon Radzinowicz**

Edited by

Anthony Bottoms
Michael Tonry

WILLAN
PUBLISHING

Published in association with the Institute of Criminology, University of Cambridge by

Willan Publishing
Culmcott House
Mill Street, Uffculme
Cullompton, Devon
EX15 3AT, UK
Tel: +44(0)1884 840337
Fax: +44(0)1884 840251
e-mail: info@willanpublishing.co.uk
website: www.willanpublishing.co.uk

Published simultaneously in the USA and Canada by

Willan Publishing
c/o ISBS, 5824 N.E. Hassalo St,
Portland, Oregon 97213-3644, USA
Tel: +001(0)503 287 3093
Fax: +001(0)503 280 8832
website: www.isbs.com

First published 2002

ISBN 1-903240-90-5 (cased)

British Library Cataloguing-in-Publication Data
A catalogue record for this book is available from the British Library

The portrait of Sir Leon Radzinowicz facing page xiii is reproduced by kind permission of Roger Hood

Printed and bound by T.J. International, Padstow, Cornwall

Contents

List of contributors

Sir Anthony Bottoms, previously Director of the Institute of Criminology, is Wolfson Professor of Criminology, University of Cambridge.

Clive Emsley is Professor of History at the Open University.

David Garland is Professor of Law and Sociology at New York University Law School.

Roger Hood is Professor of Criminology and Director of the Centre for Criminological Research, University of Oxford.

Dr Alison Liebling is University Lecturer in Criminology, Institute of Criminology, University of Cambridge, and Director of the Institute's Prisons Research Centre.

Seán McConville is Professor of Criminal Justice at Queen Mary and Westfield College, University of London.

Michael Tonry is Professor of Law and Public Policy and Director of the Institute of Criminology, University of Cambridge, and Sonosky Professor of Law and Public Policy, University of Minnesota.

Preface

This volume is offered in tribute to the late Sir Leon Radzinowicz, the first Wolfson Professor of Criminology at Cambridge University, and the founding Director of the Cambridge Institute of Criminology. The main papers in the volume were all first delivered at the Leon Radzinowicz Commemorative Symposium convened in Cambridge on 30–31 March 2001 and have now been revised and edited for publication. To them we have added the obituary notice from *The Independent* by Anthony Bottoms, the memorable after-dinner speech at the Commemorative Symposium delivered by Professor Roger Hood, and a complete bibliography of Radzinowicz's published works.

Leon Radzinowicz, who died in December 1999, was a larger than life figure with enormous energy and drive. His first book, *Mesures de Sûreté: étude de politique criminelle*, was published in France in 1928. His final book, *Adventures in Criminology*, a major autobiographical work of intellectual creativity and originality, was published in England in 1999. Few criminologists have been so prolific, and none have been so sustained in their scholarly productivity. And to this scholarship one must add Radzinowicz's immense organisational achievement in founding the Cambridge Institute of Criminology and his many major contributions to public life in Britain. All this from a man who first came to Britain in his early thirties as a Polish émigré who spoke fluent French and Italian, but no English. It is astonishing that within a decade he had published the first volume of his highly acclaimed five-volume *History of English Criminal Law and Its Administration from 1750*.

Because Radzinowicz is so commanding a figure in the history of British criminology, the Cambridge Institute of Criminology thought it appropriate, a year after his death, to convene a commemorative symposium to celebrate him and his work. The Symposium was organised around four themes that encapsulate Radzinowicz's major contributions to the worlds of ideas and affairs. His landmark five-volume history remains influential, widely read and widely cited. Accordingly, in exploration of the first theme – the history of English criminal justice – two papers were commissioned. The first, by Professor Clive Emsley of the Open University, examines the history of policing. The second, by Professor Seán McConville of Queen Mary and Westfield College, London, examines a neglected topic the English penal system's treatment of Irish political offenders.

The second theme, the history and development of criminological thought, expressed particularly in Radzinowicz's book *Ideology and Crime*, also resulted in two papers. The first, by Professor David Garland of New York University, examines some aspects of *Ideology and Crime*, considers their salience at the beginning of the twenty-first century, and suggests the main features of a final, new, chapter of that book as Garland imagines Radzinowicz might have written it. The second, by Professor Sir Anthony Bottoms of the Cambridge Institute of Criminology, picks up on themes of the relations between crime and morality that are sketched in *Ideology and Crime*, and relates them to recent developments that help us understand why people comply with the law and, implicitly, why they do not.

The third theme focused on one of Radzinowicz's most enduring legacies in criminal justice policy, the creation of the so-called 'dispersal system' for high security prisoners in England, arising out of the report of a subcommittee of the Advisory Council on the Penal System, chaired by Leon Radzinowicz. The complex development of the dispersal system since the early 1970s – sometimes through troubled times – is charted by Dr Alison Liebling of the Cambridge Institute of Criminology.

The fourth theme celebrated Leon Radzinowicz's immense contribution to the institutional development of criminology as a subject of study in British universities. Professor Roger Hood of Oxford University, Radzinowicz's close friend and long-standing intellectual collaborator, contributes an important paper on the influence of systematic criminological knowledge on policy.

The commemorative symposium was convened by the Cambridge Institute of Criminology to celebrate the life and achievements of its founding Director, but the Institute was keen to share the occasion with friends and colleagues from universities and research organisations elsewhere in the British Isles. We were therefore delighted that so many senior colleagues, representing (among others) most of the major criminology institutes and departments in the United Kingdom, were able to join us for the symposium, and to share in what proved to be a successful and constructive occasion. The following were present: Graham Allen, Estella Baker, John Baldwin, Sharon Bergin, Keith Bottomley, Anthony Bottoms, Stephen Boxford, Mary Bowen, Elizabeth Burney, David Butterworth, Maureen Colledge, Stanley Cohen, Tim Cook, Patrick Crate-Lionel, Adam Crawford, John Croft, Paul Crosland, Roy Darlison, Malcolm Davies, Jennifer Davis, Gavin Dingwall, Michael Doherty, Andrew Dowden, David Downes, Anthony Duff, Colin Dunningham, Clive Emsley, David Faulkner, David Garland, Loraine Gelsthorpe, Adrian Grounds, Frances Hepworth, Frances Heidensohn, Alex Hicks, Roger Hood, Tim Hope, Julie Horney, Michael Hough, Carolyn Hoyle, Gareth Hughes, Martin Innes, Barrie Irving, John Jackson, Geoffrey Jones, Susanne Karstedt, Vicky Kemp, Helen Krarup, Alison Liebling, David Livesey, Ian Loader, Amanda Matravers, Sarah McCabe, Seán McConville, Hugh Mellor, Priscilla Mitchell, Jade Moran, Rod Morgan, Tadashi Moriyama, Martin Narey, Barbara Natasegara, Ken Neale, Nicky Padfield, Jon Olafsson, Pam Paige, Peter Raynor, Charlotte Read, Sue Rex, Colin Roberts, Paul Rock, Gerry Rose, Judith Rumgay, Andrew Sanders, Joanna Shapland, Anthony Smith, David Smith, Richard Sparks, John Spencer, Stephen Stanley, Heather Stewart, Pamela Taylor, David Thomas, Michael Tonry, Bryan Turner, Dirk van Zyl Smit, Andrew von Hirsch, Humphry Wakefield, Nigel Walker, Donald West, Linda Whitebread, Brian Willan, Per-Olof Wikström, David Windlesham, Peter Young and Richard Young.

No conference such as that, nor any book such as this, could occur without the assistance and participation of many people. Our greatest gratitude is to Sara Harrop who almost single-handedly handled the arrangements for a two-day residential conference attended by, at various times, more than a hundred people, and did it with such grace and efficiency that proceedings flowed from event to event seamlessly and easily. She has with equal efficiency and exemplary care overseen the development of this book. We are also grateful to Professor Andrew von Hirsch who played a principal role (with Professor Bottoms) in planning the conference and who, along with Professor Susanne Karstedt of the University of Keele, offered commentary on Professor Hood's paper.

When he retired from his professorship, Radzinowicz was the subject of a *Festschrift* volume, *Crime, Criminology and Public Policy: Essays in Honour of Sir Leon Radzinowicz* (Heinemann Educational Books, 1974), edited by Roger Hood. It is a sign of his extraordinary accomplishments and stature that, a quarter of a century later, his memory and his influence remain so vital that what is in effect a second *Festschrift* seemed called for. We have entitled this volume *Ideology, Crime and Criminal Justice*, in deliberate reference to Leon Radzinowicz's influential *Ideology and Crime* (which two of the papers take as their starting point), and also in homage to Radzinowicz's immense contributions to the history and the contemporary development of criminal justice in England.

Finally, it is fitting that we should record our own special word of gratitude. In succession, we have both had the great good fortune to direct the Institute of Criminology. In doing so, we have been conscious of the very sound foundations that Leon Radzinowicz laid for the Institute, creating as he did a new subject and a new department within one of Britain's leading universities. We offer this volume to his memory, in admiration and gratitude.

April 2002

Anthony Bottoms
Michael Tonry

Sir Leon Radzinowicz (1906–1999)

Sir Leon Radzinowicz: an appreciation*

Anthony Bottoms

Leon Radzinowicz was a man of formidable energy and intellect. More than any other single person, he was responsible for the successful establishment of academic criminology in Britain in the postwar era. He also played an active and distinguished part in the shaping of penal policy in England from 1950 to 1972, and he was a commanding figure on the international stage in the fields of criminology and criminal justice.

He was born Leon Rabinowicz in Lodz, Poland in 1906. (He changed his surname in the 1930s.) His father was a doctor, a cultured man of substantial means. This background afforded the young Radzinowicz a significant degree of financial independence, which was of special significance when prudence required emigration from Poland in the late 1930s.

In the prewar era, educated Polish society was significantly Francophone. Radzinowicz's fluency in French was such as to enable him, immediately on leaving school at 18, to register as a student in the Faculty of Law at the Sorbonne. After a year in Paris, he transferred to the University of Geneva, where his interest in criminology was first kindled. At that time, European criminology was dominated by the Italian Positivist School, the doyen of whom was Enrico Ferri. Radzinowicz taught himself Italian in order to be able to read directly the work of the positivists. On graduating from Geneva, it then seemed natural for him to move to Rome for doctoral studies, and he acquired a

*Reprinted by permission from *The Independent*, Obituaries, 1 January 2000.

doctorate of law under Ferri's guidance in only 12 months. A French version of his doctoral thesis was published immediately in Paris in 1928, containing a glowing preface by the Italian maestro.

From Rome, the young scholar returned to Geneva as a *Dozent*. Not long afterwards, he visited Belgium to make a special study of the penal system there. His book on the Belgian system was published in 1930, and led to the award of a royal decoration, the Chevalier de l'Ordre de Léopold. He was still only 24.

There followed a return to his native Poland, but here, though he pursued important avenues of research, storm-clouds began to gather as the Nazi influence spread. Radzinowicz pointed out the dangers of the new ideological tendencies, and developed a strong concern for human rights, which was to remain ever afterwards a key element in his intellectual approach. But in the Poland of the 1930s, he felt himself increasingly perceived as 'a nuisance, indeed a kind of criminological dissident'.

In the 1930s, criminal justice in England was internationally famous, for example because of the probation and borstal systems. The Vice-Minister in the Polish Ministry of Justice suggested to Radzinowicz in 1936 that a report on the English system would be valuable. Formal backing from the Ministry was obtained, and Radzinowicz immediately set out for England, at his own expense, to fulfil this task. He intended to return to Poland, but circumstances dictated that he never lived there again.

In England, Radzinowicz was put in touch with a legal academic at Cambridge, J.W.C. Turner of Trinity Hall. Turner was a remarkable figure who, unusually for his time, regarded criminal law as a subject worthy of serious academic study. He was generously welcoming both to Radzinowicz and to his subject (criminology being then unknown in Cambridge). By 1940, Turner had persuaded the Cambridge Faculty of Law to establish a 'Committee to Consider the Promotion of Research and Teaching in Criminal Science', and soon afterwards the Faculty created a tiny Department of Criminal Science, led by Turner and Radzinowicz. Leon Radzinowicz had at last found his permanent intellectual home.

From 1940 until his retirement in 1973, Radzinowicz threw himself body and soul into the development of criminology at Cambridge. This work had two main aspects: his own research, and institutional developments (including the encouragement of the research of colleagues). In both spheres, there were notable successes.

For his own research, Radzinowicz selected as his primary topic the history of English criminal justice. As he saw it, criminology is, ultimately, an applied science or it is nothing. The English heritage of official reports (or 'Blue Books') in the sphere of criminal policy therefore fascinated him, for in these sources one could find not only proposals for legislation, but often much information on subsequent practical effects. He set out upon the gargantuan task of writing a multi-volume history of English criminal justice from 1750 to the twentieth century, encompassing legal, administrative and ideological developments.

The task was indeed accomplished, though much more slowly than was originally anticipated because of Radzinowicz's mounting administrative commitments and public duties. Volume 1 (*The Movement for Reform*) appeared in 1948: it focused particularly on the eighteenth-century capital statutes and their implementation, and the movement for reform of the system up to 1830. This volume immediately consolidated Radzinowicz's already high intellectual reputation: it won him a Cambridge LLD, a fellowship at Trinity College, and the James Barr Prize of the Harvard Law School.

Volumes 2 and 3, on policing and prosecution, were published in 1956; they were followed in 1968 by Volume 4, in which the themes of both the reform of the capital laws and the spread of professional police forces were followed to their culminations in the 1860s. The final volume appeared in 1986, jointly authored with Professor Roger Hood of Oxford: it covered developments in crime and the penal system in the Victorian and Edwardian eras. Radzinowicz's *History of English Criminal Law* is by any standards a superb intellectual achievement: about 2,600 pages of text, extremely carefully researched, yet always presented very lucidly. It is a *magnum opus* to which scholars will refer for many decades yet.

His personal scholarship was not confined to English historical topics. In particular, he drew upon his Continental European background to produce *In Search of Criminology* (1961), a survey of European and North American scholarship at that time, and *Ideology and Crime* (1966), an outstandingly lucid history of the development of criminological ideas since the eighteenth century.

But personal research consumed only a small part of Radzinowicz's energies. In the Department of Criminal Science, one or two empirical research workers were recruited, and research on, for example, sexual offences and the results of probation was undertaken. An influential book series of criminological monographs was successfully launched.

Then in the late 1950s came the decisive breakthrough. The government made overtures to London and Cambridge Universities concerning the possible establishment of the first interdisciplinary university-based Institute of Criminology in Britain. Cambridge's response was positive, London's lukewarm. The Wolfson Foundation provided vital initial funding. Leon Radzinowicz was elected as the founding Wolfson Professor of Criminology at Cambridge in 1959, and appointed as the founding Director of the Institute of Criminology in 1960. Research and teaching in the subject expanded rapidly, under the guidance of some very able assistant directors of research recruited by Radzinowicz.

The establishment of the Institute was a major opportunity, but there were also significant difficulties to be met. Some in Cambridge were sceptical about the intellectual respectability of criminology as a subject. Criminologists outside Cambridge did not always wish the Institute well, and Radzinowicz's preference for applied criminology came to be regarded as deeply suspect by younger radical scholars in the late 1960s. He was always aware of the potential for the Institute to fail. He chose to meet these difficulties by demanding of himself, and the staff of the Institute, high standards and a tough workload, and by being on occasions vigorous in the defence of his approaches. Hence, he was sometimes unpopular.

But in retrospect, his achievement was enormous. By the time of his retirement, the Cambridge Institute of Criminology was securely established, and it has acted as a prototype for the successful establishment of criminology in many British universities. Many of today's leading criminologists, in Britain and elsewhere, initially learned their craft in the Cambridge Institute of the 1960s and 1970s. And the Institute Library, whose establishment and development was especially close to Radzinowicz's heart, became one of the leading research libraries in the subject in the world. Fittingly, it was renamed the Radzinowicz Library of Criminology at the time of his retirement.

Astonishingly, he found time and energy for much, much more. He was a member of the Home Office Advisory Council on the Treatment of Offenders from 1950 to 1964, and of its successor council from 1966 to 1972. Within the latter, he chaired the subcommittee, reporting in 1968, which led to the establishment of the present so-called 'dispersal system' of maximum-security adult prisons in England.

He was, additionally, a member of two Royal Commissions: the hugely influential Royal Commission on Capital Punishment (1949–53), and the ill-fated Royal Commission on the Penal System (1964–6), which Radzinowicz quickly realised was making little progress. (It was dissolved, largely at his instigation, in 1966.) On the international stage, at various times he played significant roles in criminal justice issues in both the United Nations and the Council of Europe, and from 1962 onwards he was a visiting professor in several different universities in the United States.

Honours were showered upon him. He was knighted in 1970, and in 1973 he was elected both a Fellow of the British Academy and an honorary foreign member of the American Academy of Arts and Sciences. In 1974, a substantial *Festschrift*, written by colleagues and former students from all over the world, was presented to him. To his great pleasure, he was appointed an honorary Queen's Counsel in 1999.

He remained mentally very active until his death. In 1988, he published a well-documented account of the foundation and development of the Cambridge Institute, and in 1999 (no less than 70 years after the publication of his doctoral thesis) he completed *Adventures in Criminology*, a fascinating series of autobiographical essays about his career. From his retirement home in Philadelphia he kept in active contact with many friends from around the world, always delighting them with his wit, his shrewdness and his interest in their affairs.

(Leon Radzinowicz, criminologist: born Lodz, Poland, 15 August 1906; Lecturer, University of Geneva 1928–31; Lecturer, Free University of Warsaw 1932–6; Assistant Director of Research, Department of Criminal Science, Cambridge University 1946–9; Director, Department of Criminal Science, 1949–59, Wolfson Professor of Criminology, 1959–73; Director, Institute of Criminology, 1960–72; Fellow of Trinity College, Cambridge, 1948–99: Kt 1970; FBA 1973; QC 1999; married 1933 Irene Szereszewski (marriage dissolved 1955), 1958 Mary Ann Nevins (one son, one daughter; marriage dissolved 1979), 1979 Isolde Klarmann (née Doernenburg); died Philadelphia, Pennsylvania, 29 December 1999.)

Recollections of
Sir Leon Radzinowicz*

Roger Hood

It is 28 years since Sir Leon retired from the Wolfson Chair and the Directorship of the Cambridge Institute of Criminology – which he had founded and put on the map so effectively. He went to live in America nearly twenty years ago with his charming wife Isolde, who sends her very best wishes to you and her regrets for not being able to travel at this time. I guess that many of you would not have met him, and certainly very few would have known him at all well. So I would like to share with you some of my personal knowledge, recollections and insights gained over forty years: first as Sir Leon's research student, later as a colleague at the Cambridge Institute, and then as collaborator, co-author and close friend.

He had reached an age when virtually all his contemporaries were dead and, as he wittily said, he had more doctors than friends. But when I saw him last, a mere ten days before he slipped away, his interest in the Cambridge Institute, his thirst for information about developments elsewhere, especially in the careers of the 'young lions' as he called them (although of course many had already become 'old lions'), and his passion for the subject to which he had devoted his life, burned as fiercely as ever. I had been ordered to bring my laptop. More work might have to be done!

He cared not just for the subject of criminology but also for its subject matter. He was deeply imbued with what he called 'social liberalism'. He believed that it is possible to move towards a system of criminal

*Presented originally as an after-dinner proposal of a toast to the memory of Sir Leon Radzinowicz QC, LLD, FBA in Cambridge, 30 March 2001.

justice that is less repressive, less cruel, more respecting of the rights of citizens, more responsive to a calm reflection on the findings from well-conducted research. On the other hand, he was no libertarian senti-mentalist. He had no illusions about crime and the damage it caused: no illusions about the problem of recidivism. Nor was he fearful of recognising that imprisonment has to have a place in the armoury of society's means to restrain offenders. Yet he believed it was vital to recognise that attempts to control crime mainly through the penal system could easily slide into a policy of social repression.

What was he like as a person? Stocky, dynamic, with electrifying eyes and a commanding personality. He knew he was a 'grand seigneur' and played the part convincingly. He loved good suits from Savile Row and hand-made shoes and he travelled by taxi and always stayed in the best hotels. A patron of good restaurants, he nevertheless hated vulgar extravagance and greed. While he admired those who succeeded in life, especially in public and intellectual life, he despised pomposity. He had extraordinary antennae when it came to assessing people and could spot a phoney a mile away. He took a personal interest in a wide variety of people from all walks of life and was adored by many of the ordinary people with whom he came into contact from taxi drivers to waiters. They, like so many others, were magnetised by his personality.

Working with him, as I had the privilege to do for many years, I became in awe of his enormous energy, his extraordinary memory, his powers of composition and attention to detail, his artistic sense and flair for his adopted language, his lively wit, sense of fun and conversational brilliance.

He was immensely generous and supportive while at the same time being extraordinarily demanding. Only your best would do: you had to be on your toes all the time. Sloppiness in work and sloppiness of manners, laziness, pretentiousness, lack of preparation were all anathema to him. All of this did not make him an 'easy man' to get on with. But he had no desire to be easy-going. Indeed, when asked by a fellow member of the Royal Commission on Capital Punishment to define a psychopath he found it amusing to give himself as an example. But he meant it only partly as a joke, for he was proud to be a person with an unusual degree of determination and desire to succeed. He demanded just as much from himself as he demanded from his colleagues. He expected the same high standards of scholarship and professional conduct. One knew that he placed giving an honest opinion and the pursuit of what he thought was right above trying to avoid hurt feelings and one had to learn to expect not only praise but some very severe criticisms if one did not keep up to the mark. He admired and was loyal to those who stood up for themselves and their beliefs, even if he did not agree with them. That was probably because he was fiercely independent himself.

It has been said that he was authoritarian, even ruthless, as the first Director of the Institute in Cambridge. Certainly the style he brought to the task is not what we have become used to these days – when everyone is on first-name terms. It was formal, indeed distant as became a continental Professor (and those of you who have visited German Law Schools will know what I mean). I remember when the announcement of his knighthood was made at a law faculty dinner on 31 December 1969. On leaving the Hall one of my senior colleagues remarked: 'It makes no difference to me, I always call him "Sir" anyway!'

He loved excitement. I hope I may be allowed to repeat a story some of you have heard before. One evening he took me to Bookbinders, the famous seafood restaurant in Philadelphia, where he was well known and always sat in a booth in the bar area. The owner came to greet us:

'I'm so sorry Sir Leon but there are no booths available.'

Leon's eagle eye spotted an empty booth, next to one at the far end, where four men were sitting.

'What about that one?'

'Not for you, Sir Leon.'

'Why?'

The owner leaned forward to whisper: 'It's Little Tony Scarfo' – a well-known Philadelphia gangster who had been in the news amid a spate of gangland executions.

Leon feigned deafness: 'WHO?'

'Little Tony Scarfo!'

'WHO?'

'SHUSH! Little Tony Scarfo and his men,' came the hoarse whisper from the anxious owner.

'I don't know him. What can he do to me?'

'It's not safe,' pleaded the owner.

'Nonsense,' said Sir Leon. 'It's just the right booth for us.'

Leon sat with his back to Little Tony, who was dressed in an immaculate white suit, with his lieutenant, his lawyer and his 'shooter' (surveying all, hand across chest) in attendance.

I was constantly asked in a loud stage whisper:

'Roger, what are they doing now? What did they say?'

What could I do? I feigned deafness too!

He taught me how to drink a large strong Beefeater Dry Martini and then, after a long apprenticeship, how to drink two large Dry Martinis. They never seemed to have any effect on him, but if they were not full, cold and perfectly made he would send them back! And he taught me another valuable lesson. If one wants to produce work up to the best of one's ability, one can't dance at several weddings at the same time.

We began working closely when I moved from the Institute in Cambridge to Oxford and we embarked on Volume 5 of the *History of English Criminal Law*. It was an immensely exciting and rewarding experience. He was tremendously hard working and had an extraordinary memory. We had many battles as I resisted (as we all do!) his determination to cut, indeed savage, some of the lengthy drafts I had distilled from our research assistants' voluminous extracts. He turned out to be right, of course. They were much better when more concise and to the point. When the writing stage began we sat together composing every sentence. Every three sentences written had to be read back aloud several times, then every paragraph, page, section and chapter: amendments, refinements and additions being made constantly. It's a technique that I commend to you. But no wonder when he was asked how we had managed to write such a large volume together he said: 'Roger didn't have a knife and I didn't have a gun so we were able to survive!'

It is not a cliché, but a reality to say that we shall never see his like again. He spoke fluent French, German, Italian, Polish of course, and had been fluent in Russian. He understood completely, and had personal experience of, the modern development of our subject in its international, historical and contemporary contexts, from Enrico Ferri onwards. He came to this country from his native Poland when aged 32 with a tremendous reputation and many publications behind him. He mastered English and made himself within a relatively short space of time the foremost historian of English criminal law and penal policy. The first massive volume of *The History*, published in 1948, was, as Lord Macmillan wrote, 'a truly Herculean task', opening up for the first time the social and political history of criminal law. But there was much more than this: his many essays on penal policy; his early ventures into empirical studies of the relationship between economic conditions and crime and other topics; his involvement in public life, notably as an influential member of the Royal Commission on Capital Punishment and the Advisory Council on the Penal System; his international influence in the United Nations, the Council of Europe, and as a teacher and adviser around the world.

But perhaps most of all he will be revered for having had the courage, energy and determination to ensure that criminology in this country gained a foothold of academic respectability, a subject that deserved to be taken seriously. Many others have played their part. But without Sir Leon Radzinowicz we would all have greater mountains to climb.

He would have been extraordinarily gratified by this event.

So, please join me in drinking a toast to the memory of an illustrious scholar, a true pioneer and a unique personality.

Part I
Theory

Chapter 1

Ideology and crime: a further chapter

David Garland

Introduction

In 1965, Leon Radzinowicz delivered the James S. Carpentier Lectures to an Ivy League audience in uptown Manhattan. The venue was Columbia University Law School – a great and venerable institution that my colleagues at New York University now think of, fondly, as the second best law school in the City. Back in 1965, however, Columbia was the unchallenged centre of legal education in New York, and the Carpentier Lectures were a prestigious occasion that bestowed considerable honour upon both the lecturer and the subject of his lecture.[1] The following year these Columbia lectures were published as a short book entitled *Ideology and Crime: A Study of Crime in its Social and Historical Contexts*.

When I took my first class in criminology in 1974, as a student in the newly formed Department of Criminology at Edinburgh University (headed by Derick McClintock, who had worked with, or for, Radzinowicz for 25 years) *Ideology and Crime* was at the top of the reading list. If the point of an introductory text is to give an accessible overview of the subject *and* to convince the reader of the subject's importance in the wider scheme of things, then *Ideology and Crime* did its job brilliantly.

In 1965, a person taking a cool, hard look at criminology would probably have described the subject as a fledgling sub-discipline with a dubious history, uncertain scientific credentials, and a very tenuous claim to academic respectability (see Martin 1988; Garland 1997). Needless to say, this was not the image evoked by *Ideology and Crime*. In

Radzinowicz's urbane, polished prose, criminology is portrayed not as an upstart subject, scrambling to claim a place in the academy, but as a central current in mankind's struggle for enlightenment, a crucial element in the formation of a modern civilisation, a humanistic science connected to the very heart of cosmopolitan culture.

As Radzinowicz tells it, criminology's story is set amid the grandeur of European culture, in an age of scientific progress and social reform. And, in the process of telling this story, using all his considerable powers of language and imagery and historical allusion, Radzinowicz ensures that the prestige of these noble origins is effectively transferred to the struggling new subject. In the span of this short book, and in an impressive feat of rhetorical power and historical conjuring, criminology's status and significance come to take on world-historic dimensions.

This is institution-building raised to a fine art – firing the imagination as a preliminary to raising the funds and building the buildings. It seems likely from the circumstances that Radzinowicz's appointment as a Carpentier Lecturer had been the result, at least in part, of urging by members of the New York Bar Association, who were at that time campaigning to establish an 'Institute of Criminology and Criminal Justice' in New York City and who had already commissioned Radzinowicz to produce a short report on that subject (Radzinowicz 1965). If so, his sponsors must have been delighted by his bravura performance.

Ideology and Crime opens with a characteristically arresting passage:

The first modern penal ideology [which he calls 'the Liberal Position' or 'classicism'] was forged during that memorable turning point in human affairs, the eighteenth century, and tempered in the fires of more than one revolution. It was forged in Europe at a time when Europe was the centre of the world. Its precursors were French philosophers at a time when France was the centre of Europe. Negatively it was part of the revolt against many ancient abuses, positively it was part of a new view of man in relation to himself and to society.

(Radzinowicz 1966: 1)

Undergraduate readers coming to this story for the first time could be forgiven for being swept away by Radzinowicz's magisterial prose and fully convinced of the subject's world-historic importance. And why not? Government ministers, major philanthropists, charitable foundations and university authorities were also moved by claims such as these. Indeed, in the catalogue of causes that produced the Cambridge Institute of Criminology and the criminological establishment that has emerged in Britain over the last 40 years, Radzinowicz's rhetorical skill, his historical vision and his demonic energy must certainly figure as forces that played a key role.

Ideology and Crime remains today my favourite historical introduction to criminology. To describe it as a history of criminology isn't exactly correct, however. Rather, it is a succinct outline of the intellectual and political frameworks that have shaped penal policy and practice from the eighteenth century to the present day – or rather, to the day before yesterday, since the penal landscape of 1965 is very different from the one that we now confront, as Radzinowicz himself would later point out.

My own work, for what it is worth – and without being much aware of its debt to Leon Radzinowicz – has adopted a rather similar approach. Rather than write a history of ideas, I have tried to examine the dialectic between criminological concepts and criminal justice institutions, tracing the criminological assumptions that have become embedded in our penal practices, examining the political and cultural commitments that structure our patterns of crime control (Garland 1985, 1997, 2001). My early exposure to *Ideology and Crime* seems to have made a lasting impression.

Radzinowicz's uplifting, unashamedly Whiggish account of 'The Liberal Position' is followed by an analysis of 'The Determinist Position' that emerged in the nineteenth century in the wake of Lombroso's discoveries. Whereas Radzinowicz treats the Liberal Position as a foundational contribution to the architecture of modern criminal justice, he regards the Determinist Position with considerably more ambivalence. Radzinowicz may have been a student of Enrico Ferri and trained in the Italian positivist school, but, as he tells us in his memoir, he had by 1936 'ceased to be a positivist'.[2] Accordingly, *Ideology and Crime* credits the positivist school with inaugurating the scientific study of crime and criminals, and of establishing the importance of individualised treatment and reform. But it also notes that 'much could be said about the fallacies, the inconsistencies, the absurdities to be found in the positivist ... theses' (Radzinowicz 1966: 56).

The third and final framework that *Ideology and Crime* describes is the one with which Radzinowicz himself is most closely identified. If the framework that emerged in the eighteenth century was essentially a political one, and the nineteenth-century framework was a scientific (or pseudo-scientific) one, the framework that emerges in the twentieth century is an action framework, a problem-solving orientation geared not to political principle or to scientific method but instead to the practical needs of governmental institutions. The heroic age of criminology was over. The twentieth century was not the Age of Reason, nor the Age of Science. It was the Age of Administration, and in Radzinowicz's vision it had a criminology to match.

'The Pragmatic Position', as he calls this modern mentality, is the 'method of treating each problem as it arises ... instead of approaching them all on the basis of some single principle' (Radzinowicz 1966: 101). It is peculiarly English, or perhaps Anglo-American, in its emphasis on practical reasoning, in its avoidance of philosophical principle and theoretical commitment, and in its embrace of compromise positions that are conceptually incoherent but institutionally effective.

The underlying (and surprisingly Hegelian) argument of *Ideology and Crime* is that the great dialectic of history has, after a centuries-long struggle between classical thesis and positivist antithesis, produced a distinctively pragmatic criminology that is at once a historical synthesis and a higher form of practical reason. In the closing oration of his Columbia lectures, Radzinowicz returns to the grand narrative with which he had opened his peroration:

> The first flush of enthusiasm for liberty and justice that followed the period of the Enlightenment was bound up with a philosophy of natural progress and individual achievement. It hardened, nevertheless, into the bleak and rigid codes of the Classical School of criminal law.
>
> The equally enthusiastic attempts of 'social Darwinism' to apply the findings of natural science ... to the understanding of the socially unfit depended on an incongruous marriage of the pseudo-scientific with the pseudo-philosophical. The offspring was a narrow social aggressiveness.
>
> Now [he said, summing up the present and its non-ideological ideology] we distrust philosophizing and [we] call for facts ...
>
> (Radzinowicz 1966: 127–8;
> my interpolations in square brackets)

The era of administrative criminology had arrived. Twentieth-century criminology, or at least Radzinowicz's version of it, had absorbed the lessons of eighteenth-century liberalism and nineteenth-century determinism but was enthralled by neither. It was a sober, realistic, non-ideological approach that distrusted philosophical doctrines and political dogmas, preferring to rely upon empirical evidence, institutional needs and piecemeal solutions. In that respect, it was, of course, perfectly attuned to the Fabian-style social engineering that was the hallmark of the British welfare state.[3]

The links between Radzinowicz's preferred penology and the politics of the welfare state are not fully developed in these Columbia University lectures. Perhaps he considered these ideas to be too socialistic for his upscale American audience. But the connection is made perfectly explicit elsewhere. In a booklet published the year before his Carpentier Lectures, entitled *Criminology and the Climate of Social Responsibility*, Radzinowicz had pointed to the links between the progressive penal measures of the postwar period and the welfare state values that underpinned them.

This 1964 booklet, which began life as a lecture to the Howard League, opens by summarising a recent wave of progressive measures and the 'reforming zeal' that had brought them about. He must have decided that the grand historicism that he had in store for the New York lawyers would fail to strike the right note with the Howard League stalwarts, because he adopted an altogether more homely idiom in his speech to them. After setting out the enormous gains that had recently been made, he summed up the situation thus: 'Yes', he said, 'the reforming oven has been for some time at full blast, producing bread and pastry to satisfy all kinds of taste' (Radzinowicz 1964: 5). In the Radzinowicz library of criminological metaphors, America is the experimental laboratory of criminological science and Britain is its Hovis bakery.

When Radzinowicz writes in 1964 and 1966 about the Pragmatic Position and about the socio-liberal compromise which it entails, his assumption is that this approach had grown out of the struggles of the previous centuries and was a solid historical achievement. But by the time of his last book in 1999, he had come to think of this formation as very much more tenuous than it had seemed a third of a century before. As he put it in *Adventures in Criminology*, 'schemes of criminal policy with a ... socio-liberal bent are very fragile historical constructs indeed' (Radzinowicz 1999: 116). The erosion of the socio-liberal position, the historical shift to a more conservative, more authoritarian, framework in criminal policy, is also the subject of an article Sir Leon published in 1991, with the resounding title 'Penal Regressions'. If a Whiggish narrative of civilising progress had served, for most of his long career, to capture Radzinowicz's understanding of penology's historical trajectory, the events of the 1980s and 1990s forced him to reconsider this historical vision.

As it happens, these 'penal regressions' and the erosion of the 'socio-liberal compromise' have been the central focus of my own recent work, and are dealt with at length in my book, *The Culture of Control* (Garland

2001). What I intend to do, in the remainder of this essay, is to add a coda to 'Penal Regressions', extending the analysis that Sir Leon began in that article. Or perhaps I should be a little more audacious, and think of it as a draft of a fifth and final lecture to add to the four that Radzinowicz delivered in 1965 – though of course today he would deliver them not at Columbia but at New York University for the status reasons to which I subtly alluded in my opening remarks.

So, following his lectures on the Liberal Position, the Determinist Position and the two lectures on the Pragmatic Position, a final, updated lecture can be added – entitled, perhaps, 'The Control Position'. My version of this lecture will endeavour to adopt the same aphoristic, broad-brush style that Radzinowicz used in the originals, and will refer to recent developments in the USA as well as the UK. The intention is to convey a framework of thought and action, and not to worry too much about empirical exactitude.

'Lecture Five: The Control Position'

What changes have occurred in the period between *Criminology and Climate of Social Responsibility* (Radzinowicz 1964) and 'Penal Regressions' (Radzinowicz 1991)? How ought we to describe the penal ideology that has taken shape over the last thirty years and which currently prevails?

First, we should not exaggerate the extent of change. The field has not been transformed from end to end, nor has the criminal justice state been completely made over. What has happened is that criminal justice institutions have altered their emphases and the field of crime control has expanded in new directions, as state agencies and civil society have adapted to the growth of crime and insecurity that accompanied the coming of late modernity.[4]

At the structural level, change has been a matter of assimilating new elements in the system (such as the victim, crime prevention, restorative justice); altering balances and relations (between punishment and welfare, state provision and commercial provision, instrumental means and expressive ends, the rights of offenders and the protection of the public); and finally changing the criminal justice system's relation to its environment (above all its relation to the political process, to public opinion and to the crime-control activities of civil society).

The institutional and cultural changes that have occurred in criminal justice are analogous to those that have occurred in the welfare state more generally. Talk of the 'end of welfare' and the 'death of the social' –

like talk of the demise of rehabilitation – should be understood as a kind of counter-rhetoric, not as empirical description. The infrastructures of the welfare state have not been abolished or utterly transformed. They have been overlaid by a different political culture and directed by a new style of public management (Pierson 1994). In the process they have become more restrictive and means-tested, more determined to control the conduct of claimants, more concerned to transmit the right incentives and discourage 'dependency'.

Like the criminal justice reforms of the last twenty years, current social policies are shaped by the perceived dysfunctions and pathologies of our welfarist institutions. The solution has become the problem. Penal-welfarism shares the fate of the welfarist social arrangements that brought it into existence. Its destiny is not to be dismantled, but to become the problematic terrain upon which new strategies and objectives are continually built.

The new culture of control

One might sum up this complex process by saying that although the structures of control have been transformed in some respects, the most significant change is at the level of the culture that enlivens these structures, orders their use and shapes their meaning. The cultural co-ordinates of crime control have gradually been changed, altering the way that penal agents think and act, giving new meaning to what they say and do. This new culture of crime control has three key elements: (a) a recoded penal-welfarism; (b) a criminology of control; and (c) an economic style of reasoning (see Garland 2001: chapter 7). Here I have time to describe only the first of these three – but it is the element that corresponds most closely to what Radzinowicz means by a 'penal ideology', so it seems appropriate to focus upon it here.

What do I mean when I talk about the 'recoding' of penal-welfarism?[5] Something along the following lines: in the day-to-day practices of criminal justice, there has been a marked shift of emphasis from the welfare to the penal axis. In the course of these developments, both 'penal' and 'welfare' modalities have changed their meaning. The penal mode, as well as becoming more prominent, has become more punitive, more expressive, more security-minded. Distinctively penal concerns such as less eligibility, the certainty and fixity of punishment, the con-demnation and harsh treatment of offenders and the protection of the public have all been given much higher priority.[6]

The welfare mode, as well as becoming more muted, has become more conditional, more offence-centred, more risk conscious. The

9

offenders dealt with by probation, parole and the juvenile court are now less likely to be represented as socially deprived citizens in need of support. They are depicted instead as culpable, undeserving and somewhat dangerous individuals who must be carefully controlled for the protection of the public and the prevention of further offending. Rather than clients in need of support they are seen as risks who must be managed. Instead of emphasising rehabilitative methods that meet the offender's needs, the system emphasises effective controls that minimise costs and maximise security.

Rehabilitation redefined
Where rehabilitative interventions are undertaken today their character is rather different than before. They focus more upon issues of crime control than upon individual welfare, becoming more 'offence-centred' than 'client-centred'. The offence is no longer taken to be a superficial presenting symptom; it is instead the thing itself, the central problem to be addressed. Where once the individual's personality or social relations formed the object of transformative efforts, that object is now offence behaviour and the habits most closely associated with it. The point is no longer to improve the offender's self-esteem, develop insight or deliver client-centred services, but instead to impose restrictions, reduce crime and protect the public. These shifts in practice, together with a renewed stress on less-eligibility concerns, prompt treatment programmes to hold themselves out as being for the benefit of future victims rather than for the benefit of the offender. It is these future victims who are now 'rescued' by rehabilitative work, rather than the offenders themselves.[7]

Rehabilitation no longer claims to be the overriding purpose of the system, or even of traditionally welfarist agencies such as probation and parole. It is now one aim among others, delivered as a specialist provision, and no longer accompanied by any great amount of idealism or unrealistic expectation. The rehabilitation of offenders is no longer viewed as a general all-purpose prescription, but instead as a specific intervention targeted towards those individuals most likely to make cost-effective use of this expensive service. It is treated as an investment rather than a standard entitlement, and like all investments, is closely monitored and evaluated to ensure that it produces returns.

In that respect, the 'What Works' movement currently influencing penal policy in the UK bears the marks of the post-Martinson scepticism and reflexivity: it is not a return to rehabilitative optimism. Whether the offender is being punished or being treated, the key concerns are now to protect the public by reducing the risk of further victimisation and to do so with a minimum of resources. If the official aim of penal welfare was the promotion of social solidarity, the overriding concern today is, quite unashamedly, the efficient enhancement of social control.

Probation repositioned

For much of the twentieth century, probation was a core institution of criminal justice. Extensively used, in the vanguard of penal progress, it was the exemplary instance of the penal-welfare approach to crime control. In today's world, probation occupies a position that is much more conflicted and much less secure. Over the last thirty years, probation has had to struggle to maintain its credibility as the ideals upon which it was based have been discredited and displaced.

Under pressure from government, probation has tightened its procedures, highlighted its supervisory capacities, downplayed its social work affiliations, intensified its controls and represented itself as a community punishment. 'Intensive probation orders' have been developed, involving heavier restrictions and reporting requirements; and probation supervision has increasingly been 'blended' with more explicitly penal measures, such as curfews, partial custody and fines. As one English Chief Probation Officer put it, 'The Probation Service has absorbed the politics of punishment, entered the market place, mirrored the private sector [and] taken its managers through a grand renaming ceremony' (Wallis 1997: 91). But even after all this upheaval, the courts and the public remain unconvinced that probation is a 'real' punishment and a credible means of control.[8]

The reinvented prison

In the penal-welfare system, the prison functioned as the deep end of the correctional sector, dealing with those offenders who failed to respond to the reformatory measures of the other sectors. In theory if not in practice, the prison represented itself as the last-resort terminus on a continuum of reformatory treatment. Today it is conceived much more explicitly as a mechanism of exclusion and control.[9] Treatment modalities still operate within its walls, and lip service is still paid to the ideal of the rehabilitative prison. But the walls themselves are now seen as the institution's most important and valuable feature.

The old penal-welfare ideal of the permeable prison, of the open prison that lowers the barrier between custody and the community, of reintegrating prisoners and their families by means of home leaves and paroles and day release – these ideals are now much less in evidence. Instead the walls have been fortified, literally and figuratively. Perimeter security has been enhanced, and early release is more restrictive, more strictly controlled, more closely supervised.

11

The prison–community border is heavily patrolled and carefully monitored to prevent risks leaking out from one to the other (Sparks 2000). Those offenders who are released 'into the community' are subject to much tighter control than previously, and frequently find themselves returned to custody for failure to comply with the conditions that continue to restrict their freedom. For many of these parolees and ex-convicts, the 'community' into which they are released is actually a closely monitored terrain, a supervised space, lacking much of the freedom that one usually associates with 'normal life'.

Like the pre-modern sanctions of transportation or banishment, the prison now functions as a form of exile, its use shaped less by a rehabilitative ideal and more by what Andrew Rutherford (1996) calls an 'eliminative' one. It serves as a kind of reservation – a quarantine zone in which purportedly dangerous individuals are segregated in the name of public safety. Large-scale incarceration functions today as a mode of economic and social placement, a zoning mechanism that segregates those populations rejected by the depleted institutions of family, work and welfare, and places them behind the scenes of social life.[10]

In the same way, though for shorter terms, local prisons and jails are increasingly being used as a repository for the mentally ill, drug addicts and poor, sick people for whom the depleted social services no longer provide adequate accommodation.[11] Most recently, 'zero tolerance' and 'quality of life' policing have begun to extend this coercive zoning, using aggressive arrest practices to exclude 'disorderly' individuals from public spaces wherever they are seen as interfering with commercial interests or the 'quality of life' demanded by more affluent residents (Harcourt 1998). Private security forces have long done the same thing for private or commercial space.

The new individualisation and punishment-at-a-distance

In the penal-welfare framework, the offending individual was centre stage: the primary focus of criminological concern. Sentencing was to be individualised to meet the offender's particular needs and his or her potential for reform. Biographical accounts were assembled. Social and psychological reports were prepared. The individual characteristics of the offender were, in theory if not always in practice, to be the key determinant of all penal action. In vivid contrast, the individual victim featured hardly at all. For the most part, he or she remained a silent abstraction: a background figure whose individuality hardly registered, whose personal wishes and concerns had no place in the process.

In contemporary penality this situation is reversed. The processes of individualisation now centre increasingly upon the victim. Individual victims are to be kept informed, to be offered the support that they need, to be consulted prior to decisionmaking, to be involved in the judicial process from complaint through to conviction and beyond. Victims' impact statements are introduced in court in order to individualise the impact of the crime, to show how the offence affected this particular victim, in all her particularity, in all her human specificity. This process has gone furthest in the USA, where several states now permit individual victims to make recommendations to the judge prior to sentencing and to put their views to the parole board prior to the release of 'their' offender, but similar developments are also evident in the UK.[12]

Meanwhile in the latest wave of sentencing laws, the offender is rendered more and more abstract, more and more stereotypical, more and more a projected image rather than an individuated person. 'Just deserts' sentencing begins to have this effect, particularly where standard sentences are routinely imposed. Sentencing guidelines take the process further. Mandatory minimum sentences go all the way, completely undoing any element of individualisation at the point of sentencing.[13]

These methods of fixing sentences well in advance of the instant case extend the distance between the effective sentencer and the person upon whom the sentence is imposed. The individualisation of sentencing gives way to a kind of 'punishment-at-a-distance' where penalty levels are set, often irreversibly, by political actors operating in political contexts, far removed from the circumstances of the case. The greater this distance, the less likely it is that the peculiar facts of the case and the individual characteristics of the offender will shape the outcome. The treatment of offenders thus becomes increasingly less individuated at precisely the moment when the victim is brought into full human focus and given an individual voice.

The society–offender relation

The penal-welfare approach proceeded as if the interests of society and the interests of the offender could be made to coincide. Rehabilitating offenders, reforming prisons, dealing with the roots of crime – these were in the interests of everyone. Money spent on treating the offender and improving social conditions would be repaid by falling rates of crime and a better integrated society. The treatment of offenders was a positive sum game. Today the interests of convicted offenders, in so far as they are considered at all, are viewed as fundamentally opposed to those of the public.

This declining respect for the rights of offenders and the near-absolute priority given to public safety concerns can be seen quite clearly in the growing practice of disclosure and notification. In today's information society, criminal justice agencies come under increasing pressure to share their information with members of the public, particularly where this concerns security risks and potential dangers. Community notification laws and paedophile registers are prominent instances of the new willingness to disclose information that would once have been confidential (Finn 1997; Hebenton and Thomas 1996). So too is the practice of correctional agencies (such as the Florida Department of Corrections) that now post Internet websites giving details of all the prisoners who are released from their custody: their offence, their prison sentence, their new address and so on.[14] This new practice is in sharp contrast to the thinking embodied in the Rehabilitation of Offenders Acts that were passed in the 1960s and 1970s, which made it illegal to disclose information about an ex-offender's criminal record after a certain time had elapsed.[15] The assumption today is that there is no such thing as an 'ex-offender' – only offenders who have been caught before and may strike again. 'Criminal' individuals have no privacy rights that could ever trump the public's uninterrupted right to know.[16]

Finally, one sees this shifting balance (in the society–offender relation) in the way that 'stigma' has taken on a renewed value in the punishment of offenders. In the penal-welfare framework, stigma was viewed as a harmful and unnecessary aspect of criminal justice. Stigmatising an offender was liable to be counterproductive in so far as it lessened the offender's self-esteem and his or her prospects of reintegration. Correctional institutions such as juvenile justice, children's hearings, probation and reformatories were carefully designed to avoid stigmatising effects. And even prison regimes came to abandon the use of demeaning symbols such as the convict haircut or the broad stripe uniform. Today stigma has become useful again. Doubly useful in fact, since a public stigma can simultaneously punish the offender for his crime and alert the community to his danger. Community notification schemes, paedophile registers, community service workers dressed in distinctive uniforms, chain gangs in the southern states of the USA and 'scarlet letter' penalties requiring offenders to proclaim their criminality with signs and pictures – all of these involve the public marking of the offender. Whether for punitive effect or public protection, the deliberate stigmatising of offenders is once again a part of the penal repertoire (Brilliant 1989; Karp 1998).

As the offender's perceived worth tends towards zero, victims' interests expand to fill the gap. One sees this in the changed attitude towards minor offences and what used to be called 'crimes without victims'. Today there is no such thing as a victimless crime. If no one in particular is harmed by the conduct in question, this does not prevent the invocation of a *collective victim* – 'the community' and its 'quality of life' – that is deemed to suffer the ill effects that must always flow from prohibited behaviour, however trivial. Public drinking, soft drug use, graffiti, loitering, vagrancy, begging, sleeping rough, being 'uncivil': these cease to be tolerable nuisances or pricks to the middle-class conscience and become the disorderly stuff upon which serious crime feeds.

In current police thinking, in the new city ordinances that are everywhere being passed, and in the world of commercialised private security, victimless crime is a thing of the past (Ellickson 1996). Every minor offence, every act of disorderly conduct – particularly if committed by poor people in public spaces – is now regarded as detrimental to the quality of life. In the high-crime society, tiny crimes are viewed cumulatively and 'the community' is the collective, all-purpose victim. The public's fears and insecurities, its heightened awareness of the problem, its scepticism about liberal policies, its lack of concern for the offenders themselves – all of these have prompted us to find victims where there were once only violations.

Conclusion

So how would Sir Leon conclude this final lecture? Probably by delivering some shrewd, trenchant observations that displayed his customary realism and the wisdom that derives from a long-term perspective. Probably by urging greater effort and determination by those who carry on in his tradition. Perhaps he might have said something along the following lines:

> A pretty bleak picture, I think you will agree. And one that must appear discouraging to criminologists and penal reformers alike. The oven of penal reform no longer burns at full blast. The forward march of penal progress is temporarily halted. The forces of reaction have taken charge. But if the last thirty years have taught me anything – and I hope you will allow that even an old dog can learn a few new tricks – it has taught me that there is no Hegelian dialectic of penal change, no Whig story of penal progress.
>
> This, my friends, is not an altogether bad thing. The penal ideologies and crime control practices of the present day should not be regarded as our destiny, our predetermined historical fate. Our criminal justice arrangements are the outcome of human actions and institutional decisions and the never-ending struggle

between contending points of view. Social, economic and cultural conditions certainly set limits to what can be achieved, as my historical work has tried to show. But they do not determine that outcome with any inevitability or finality. As that great Frenchman Raymond Aron once remarked, the point of our work is to make history intelligible – not to do away with it altogether.

Notes

1 The James S. Carpentier Lectureship was established at Columbia Law School in 1903 by General Horace W. Carpentier in honour of his brother. General Carpentier expressed the desire that the lecturers be 'chosen for pre-eminent fitness and ability' and that 'this lectureship will be made so honorable that nobody, however great or distinguished, would willingly choose to decline this invitation.'

2 This emphatic abandonment of his positivist past is perhaps why Sir Leon takes me to task in a footnote in *Adventures in Criminology* (Radzinowicz 1999: 198 fn 9) for alleging that, in the 1960s, the Cambridge Institute was viewed as being associated with a 'positivist' approach. Having settled his account with the real Positivist School, he would not accept the attribution of the term, even in a watered down form. Perhaps he was being a little touchy – the Institute certainly *was* viewed in these terms, and I was careful to put the term 'positivism' in quotation marks to indicate my own doubts about the use of that term. What is revealing is that he should continue to care so much.

3 Radzinowicz emphasises criminology's social utility, its bipartisan political credentials, and its ability to enhance the efficiency and effectiveness of criminal justice processes. But these governmental virtues are somewhat modest in comparison to the vaulting ambition of the nineteenth-century founders of criminological science, who promised to unlock crime's causes and cures – a promise that a more astute Radzinowicz took care to avoid. One might surmise that it was precisely because his was a peculiarly unheroic criminology, detached from grand theory and great ambition, that Radzinowicz felt the need to invoke the subject's illustrious past in order to enhance its otherwise modest present-day status.

4 Radzinowicz had much to say on the postwar growth of crime and its relationship to the organisation of modern society, long in advance of other commentators. See Radzinowicz (1966: chapter 3) and Radzinowicz and King (1977: chapter 1) for comments on the effect of affluence, mobility and welfarism on crime, and the importance of thinking in terms of situational opportunities as well as individual dispositions.

5 Like Radzinowicz's concept of 'the socio-liberal compromise', the term 'penal-welfarism' refers to the hybrid system of legal and social reasoning

that governed criminal justice policy in the US and the UK for most of the twentieth century. For details, see Garland (1985 and 2001).

6 On penal austerity in England and Wales, see Sparks (forthcoming). On 'no frills' prisons in the USA, see Finn (1996).

7 The Labour Government Home Secretary Jack Straw and his Conservative predecessor Douglas Hurd agree on this. In a recent speech, Straw quoted Hurd (now Chairman of the Prison Reform Trust) on the victim-related purpose of reform in prison: '[W]e can hardly be insensitive to the opportunities which the provision of well-targeted education in prison offers. As your Chairman wrote in an article in yesterday's *Daily Telegraph*, "it is inextricably linked to the future safety of the citizen" ' (Straw 1998).

8 On the 'credibility' of probation as a punishment in the UK, see Rees and Williams (1989) and Brownlee (1998). On the failures and credibility problems of US probation, see the Reinventing Probation Council (1999).

9 The Labour Government Home Secretary recently defined his prison policy in these terms: 'First, our policy must be fundamentally about protecting the public. Assessing risk, reducing risk, and managing risk after release are the key elements of the task' (Straw 1998).

10 On the social, economic and penological functions of the American ghetto, see Wacquant (2001).

11 See Gunn *et al* (1991). One of the recurring features of neoliberal societies, where public services and socialised provision are minimised, is that the jail acts as an expensive institution of last resort, filling up with individuals who were denied care elsewhere. The New York City jail system has the largest tuberculosis treatment unit in the USA, and one of the largest HIV treatment programmes. There is a huge irony in this, and not much cost-effectiveness.

12 Britain's Labour government recently announced that a new advisory panel that will guide the Court of Appeal in its guideline sentencing decisions will include victims among its members. See Home Office (1998).

13 Even 'mandatory' sentences leave room for discretion – most often at the point of prosecution. Individuation may occur at that point, though the prosecutors' concerns differ significantly from those of the judge, and are more often directed to securing a conviction rather than doing justice or obtaining the sentence that best fits the individual's needs and deserts. Radzinowicz strongly opposed these shifts towards mandatory sentencing and published several articles deploring this trend. See Radzinowicz and Hood (1981).

14 See, for example, the following website: http://www.dc.state.fl.us/ InmateReleases/inmatesearch.asp

15 On the current status of these laws, see Home Office (1999).

16 The fact that 'Sarah's Law' was not passed in the UK in the summer of 2000, despite strong public support, suggests that liberal voices are more powerful in the UK than they are in the USA. But the course of that debate – with its emphasis upon public safety, its overstatement of the dangers involved, and the crusading, vengeful role that was ascribed by the media to

the victim's survivors – was so strikingly similar to the script established in the wake of Megan Kanka's death in the USA that it would seem only a matter of time before Britain has a version of Megan's law with its community notification provisions enacted into law.

This is the unchanged text of a talk delivered at the Radzinowicz Commemoration Symposium in March 2001. The 'lecture' that forms the second part of the talk is a slightly revised excerpt from Chapter 7 of my book, The Culture of Control *(OUP 2001).*

References

Brilliant, J. (1989) 'The Modern Day Scarlet Letter: A Critical Analysis', *Duke Law Journal*, 1357–85.

Brownlee, I. (1998) *Community Punishment*. London: Longman.

Ellickson, R.C. (1996) 'Controlling Chronic Misconduct in City Spaces: Of Panhandlers, Skid Rows, and Public-Space Zoning', *Yale Law Journal*, 105, 1165–248.

Finn, P. (1996) 'No-Frills Prisons and Jails: A Movement in Flux', *Federal Probation*, 60, September, 35–44.

Finn, P. (1997) *Sex Offender Community Notification*. Washington, DC: National Institute of Justice, Office of Justice Programs.

Garland, D. (1985) *Punishment and Welfare: A History of Penal Strategies*. Aldershot: Gower.

Garland, D. (1997) 'Of Crimes and Criminals: The Development of Criminology in Britain', in M. Maguire, R. Morgan and R. Reiner (eds), *The Oxford Handbook of Criminology*, 2nd edn. Oxford: Oxford University Press.

Garland, D. (2001) *The Culture of Control: Crime and Social Order in Contemporary Society*. Oxford: Oxford University Press.

Gunn, J., Maden, T. and Swinton, H. (1991) *Mentally Disordered Prisoners*. London: Home Office.

Harcourt, B. (1998) 'Reflecting on the Subject: A Critique of the Social Influence Conception of Deterrence, the Broken Windows Theory, and Order-Maintenance Policing New York Style', *Michigan Law Review*, 97 (2).

Hebenton, B. and Thomas, T. (1996) 'Sexual Offenders in the Community: Reflections on Problems of Law, Community and Risk Management in the U.S.A., England and Wales', *International Journal of the Sociology of Law*, 24, 427–43.

Home Office (1998) *Press Release*, 5 January 1998.

Home Office (1999) *The Rehabilitation of Offenders Act 1974: A Consultation Paper*. London: Home Office.

Karp, D. (1998) 'The Judicial and Judicious Use of Shame Penalties', *Crime and Delinquency*, 44, 277–94.

Martin, J.P. (1988) 'The Development of Criminology in Britain: 1948–1960', in P. Rock (ed.), *The History of Criminology in Britain*. Oxford: Oxford University Press.

Pierson, P. (1994) *Dismantling the Welfare State*. New York: Cambridge University Press.

Radzinowicz, L. (1964) *Criminology and the Climate of Social Responsibility*. Cambridge: Heffer.

Radzinowicz, L. (1965) *The Need for Criminology*. London: Heinemann Educational Books.

Radzinowicz, L. (1966) *Ideology and Crime: A Study of Crime in its Social and Historical Contexts*. London: Heinemann Educational Books.

Radzinowicz, L. (1991) 'Penal Regressions', *Cambridge Law Journal*, 50, 422–44.

Radzinowicz, L. and Hood, R. (1981) 'The American Volte-Face in Sentencing Thought and Practice', in C. Tapper (ed.), *Crime, Proof and Punishment: Essays in Memory of Rupert Cross*. London: Butterworth.

Radzinowicz, L. and King, J. (1977) *The Growth of Crime: The International Experience*. London: Hamish Hamilton.

Rees, H. and Williams, E.H. (1989) *Punishment, Custody and the Community*. London: LSE.

Reinventing Probation Council (1999) *Broken Windows Probation*. New York: Manhattan Institute.

Rutherford, A. (1996) *Criminal Policy and the Eliminative Ideal*. Southampton: Institute of Criminal Justice, University of Southampton.

Sparks, J.R. (2000) 'Risk and Blame in Criminal Justice Controversies', in M. Brown and J. Pratt (eds), *Dangerous Offenders: Criminal Justice and Social Order*. London: Routledge.

Sparks, J.R. (forthcoming) 'Penal Austerity and Social Anxiety at the Century's Turn: Governmental Rationalities, Legitimation Deficits and Populism in English Penal Politics in the 1990s', in L. Wacquant (ed.), *From Social State to Penal State*. New York: Oxford University Press.

Straw, J. (1998) *Making Prisons Work*. The Prison Reform Trust Annual Lecture, December.

Wacquant, L. (2001) 'Deadly Symbiosis: When Ghetto and Prison Meet and Merge', *Punishment and Society*, 3 (1).

Wallis, E. (1997) 'A New Choreography: Breaking Away from the Elaborate Corporate Dance', in R. Burnett (ed.), *The Probation Service: Responding to Change*. Oxford, Probation Studies Unit, Oxford University.

Chapter 2

Morality, crime, compliance and public policy

Anthony Bottoms

I am very pleased to have the opportunity to contribute to this symposium in commemoration of the life and work of Sir Leon Radzinowicz. I count it a signal honour to have been elected to the Wolfson Professorship of Criminology here in Cambridge, the chair to which Leon Radzinowicz was appointed as the founding holder, and which he subsequently occupied with such distinction. In addition to this institutional connection, I was privileged also in recent years to become one of Leon Radzinowicz's friends. Now that he is no longer with us, I miss those meetings and long telephone calls when he would be genuinely interested in my activities and well-being, but also shrewdly pertinent in his questions, the whole laced with a wonderful sense of humour. He cared passionately about the progress of the work in the Institute of Criminology, which he had striven so hard to establish successfully (see Radzinowicz 1988); and in the years when I was the Institute's Director (1984–98), he was always a great source of support and encouragement.

The subject that I have chosen for my contribution to this symposium is 'Morality, Crime, Compliance and Public Policy'. I shall begin with some observations on this topic derived from a rereading of Leon Radzinowicz's Carpentier Lectures of 1965, published as *Ideology and Crime* (Radzinowicz 1966). I shall then try to sketch some reasons why the normative or moral dimension (in both its positive and its critical sense) is of central importance for criminology. The third section of the paper turns to the subject of legal compliance, a topic on which I am currently working (see, for example, Bottoms 2001); in this section, the normative dimension of compliance is emphasised and, I hope, clarified.

Finally, some implications of the foregoing analysis for issues of public policy are briefly considered.

Ideology and Crime

Threading through *Ideology and Crime*, sometimes in subtle rather than in boldly stated comments, are some important themes about morality, crime and public policy. By way of introducing this discussion, I want to highlight two such comments, one concerning the Italian positivists and the other the classical school.

Positivism

In discussing the work of his own teacher, Enrico Ferri, Radzinowicz emphasises what he refers to as Ferri's 'negation of the concept of criminal responsibility as grounded in the tenet of free will' (Radzinowicz 1966: 51). The criminological positivists adopted an essentially deterministic position on the causation of crime, applying to criminal behaviour what they understood to be the methods and the working assumptions of the natural sciences. From such a perspective, there was little place for traditional doctrines of free will, as espoused both by Christian thought and by the principal writers of political philosophy of the Enlightenment. Enrico Ferri did not flinch from the policy implications of this positivist world-view. As Radzinowicz points out, Ferri devoted substantial sections of his book, *Criminal Sociology*, 'to criticism of the traditional concept of criminal responsibility and of the various attempts to adapt and preserve it' (p. 51; see also Ferri 1905/1917: Part III). That traditional concept of criminal responsibility was, of course, based upon the view that an individual who chooses, by his own free will, to commit a crime is morally responsible for that act; but, by contrast, where for any reason – such as duress, infancy or mental incapacity – the individual's moral responsibility is reduced or absent, that fact has to be taken into account by the law. Ferri wanted to sweep all this away, replacing it with the principles of what he called 'social responsibility and legal responsibility'. As Leon Radzinowicz (1966: 53) explains, the central implication of Ferri's proposed principles was that:

> it [is] not the business of criminal justice to assess and to measure the moral guilt of an offender, [but it is] its function to determine whether he was the perpetrator of an act defined as an offence, and, if so, to apply to him the measures of 'social defence', calculated

having regard to his personality and circumstances, to restrain him from committing further crimes.

For present purposes, I want to highlight two central issues that arise from Radzinowicz's discussion of Ferri's positivism. The first concerns the point, obvious enough from the preceding comments, that criminological theories and explanations can have very distinct and direct consequences for public policy.[1] This close interrelationship between criminology and public policy was a central preoccupation for Leon Radzinowicz, and I shall return to it at the end of this paper.

Second, and perhaps more fundamentally, Ferri's struggles with the concept of criminal responsibility illuminate a wider difficulty that confronts any version of strict scientific positivism when it is applied to human affairs. That difficulty can be simply stated: it concerns the question of how, if at all, from a positivist perspective one can give any serious weight to moral judgements. For example, writing a few years after Ferri, and much influenced by the so-called 'logical positivism' of the Vienna Circle, the young English philosopher A.J. Ayer famously took the view that a moralist's assertions 'cannot possibly be valid, but they cannot be invalid either' (Ayer 1936/1971: 153). Ayer further stated that 'sentences which simply express moral judgements do not say anything. They are pure expressions of feeling ... They are unverifiable for the same reason as a cry of pain or a word of command is unverifiable – because they do not express genuine propositions' (Ayer 1936/1971: 144).

I am not a moral philosopher, and I do not intend to pursue here the difficult question of the nature of moral judgements.[2] I simply want to note the implications of a world-view that prioritises science as a road to truth, and then says that science has no place (or, at best, a very secondary place) for concepts of moral judgements and moral responsibility ('sentences which ... express moral judgements do not say anything'). The subtext, the implicit derogation of moral discourse, is not hard to discern. That was the subtext of the criminological positivists, and it was a view that was, for quite a few years, to have adverse consequences for criminology as a discipline.[3] To his credit, Leon Radzinowicz quite quickly rejected such a view (see Radzinowicz 1999), a point that was not always appreciated by his later critics.[4]

Classicism

The second example of a discussion of the moral order that I want to take from *Ideology and Crime* concerns the classical school – writers such as

Montesquieu, Voltaire and above all Cesare Beccaria. On the first page of his very valuable little book, Leon Radzinowicz comments that 'negatively, [the classical school] was part of the revolt against many ancient abuses; positively, it was part of a new view of man in relation to himself and to society'.

Radzinowicz rightly emphasises the many deficiencies of criminal law and procedure in most European countries in the eighteenth century. It was, he comments, 'the dark side of successful despotism, of arbitrary authority in sovereign, church, or aristocracy' (pp. 1–2). A number of writers, influenced by Renaissance and Enlightenment appeals to Reason, found themselves in opposition to the old order, and in revolt against the unquestioning acceptance of tradition and the status quo. These writers found 'easy targets in the inefficiency, corruption and sheer chaos of existing institutions' (p. 4).

In other words, these authors of the classical school were able to attribute little by way of legitimacy to the criminal justice and criminal procedures of the (mostly autocratic) European states and statelets in which they lived. Their own critical writings then helped to reduce that legitimacy further in the eyes of other subjects. Coupled with the more general political critiques of Enlightenment philosophers, all this had profound consequences not only for criminal justice, but also for politics more generally, for example in the American and French Revolutions and beyond. I shall return to this theme of legitimacy, or the lack of it, later in this paper. For the moment, it is sufficient to note that, if and when one asserts that a given authority lacks legitimacy, this is *ipso facto* an assertion that, in the eyes of at least a significant group of its citizens, that authority is the subject of moral criticism.

But Radzinowicz's account of the classicists makes it clear that, although they began as the moral critics of one set of authorities, over a period of time some of their principles became the accepted orthodoxy for subsequent legal authorities. In fact, in some states their new principles even became part of the everyday moral discourse of ordinary people. Nowhere is this better illustrated than in the United States, where to this day one can observe the pervasive moral influence, in many (though of course not all) contexts, of the eighteenth-century principles enunciated in the Constitution and the Bill of Rights.

These reflections highlight a very important distinction of great relevance for criminologists considering issues of morality, namely the distinction between positive morality and critical morality. This distinction, first used by the nineteenth-century utilitarians, was helpfully revived by H.L.A. Hart forty years ago (see MacCormick 1981: chapter 4). Hart defined 'positive morality' as 'the morality actually accepted and shared by a given social group'; by contrast, he suggested that 'critical morality' refers to 'the general moral principles used in the criticism of actual social institutions including positive morality' (Hart 1963: 20). Radzinowicz's account of the classical school makes it clear that the adherents of this school began by offering a powerful challenge, based in critical morality, to the then existing autocratic criminal justice systems of many eighteenth-century European states; but, in due course, classical and neoclassical principles very often became part of the positive morality of later nation-states. A clear implication of Radzinowicz's analysis is that criminologists interested in morality must – if their work is to be comprehensive – consider questions both of positive and of critical morality.

Criminology and the normative

I have just referred, in a deliberately low-key manner, to 'criminologists interested in morality'. As I move to the next stage of my argument, I want to be bolder and to claim that, if they are to be true to their calling, all criminologists have to be interested in morality. To substantiate this claim, it is best to begin with the concept of 'positive morality', as defined above.

In their origins, crimes are acts that are proscribed by societies as a way of marking out conduct considered to be impermissible. Anthropological studies show that all known human societies develop rules of conduct, some of which rules are prohibitions. The distinguished anthropologist Meyer Fortes, a contemporary of Radzinowicz at Cambridge,[5] devoted what proved to be his last publication to the topic of 'Rules and the Emergence of Society' (Fortes 1983). Fortes began by pointing out that 'wherever we encounter them, ... humans are invariably social, or better stated societal beings' (p. 1); that is to say, they live in groups and societies. Emphasising also the universality of rules[6] within human groups and societies, Fortes went on to make the strong claim that:

> The capacity and the need to have, to make, to follow and to enforce rules are of cardinal importance for human social existence ... For without rules there can be neither society nor culture; and what I am arguing is that it was the emergence of the capacity to make, enforce, and, by corollary, to break rules that made human society possible.
>
> (Fortes 1983: 6).

Inevitably, the rules (including the prohibitions) in any given emerging group or society will be based on the developing social norms (or positive morality) of the group in question, since a norm is, in dictionary definition, 'a principle or standard ... that reflects people's expectations of behaviour ... and serves to regulate action and judgment' (Longman 1984). But, of course, these social norms do not emerge from nowhere; they are intimately related to the ongoing life and tasks of the group in question. To take an example from a contemporary anthropological study of traditional justice, Joan Ryan's (1995) research among the Dene people in Northern Canada shows that they had, over a long period, developed many rules intended 'to keep the community functioning in an orderly way' (p. 103). These included 'resource rules' (relating to ways of obtaining food, the sharing of food once obtained, etc.); rules for family life; and rules for the governance of the Dene people as a whole. Even in recent times, however, these traditional rules have not been written down by the Dene people (or by other indigenous Canadian peoples), with the result that 'many Canadians deny, or do not believe, that indigenous people had laws' (p. 144). Ryan's study clearly demonstrates the falsity of this view.

In contemporary urban life, our tasks and preoccupations are of course often very different from those of our rural ancestors. But rules of many kinds are still required to enable us to live our lives in an orderly way: rules of buying and selling, rules of the road, rules against violence, rules for family life, and so on. All of which raise some important further issues.

First, while it seems obviously true that in an organic, rural society the rules (including the prohibitions) of a given social group will be based on its evolving social norms, that is not necessarily the case in a more differentiated society. Here, rather than prohibitions arising out of positive morality, they may on occasion not reflect positive morality at all, but rather may be imposed by those in power in the hope of securing obedience through deterrent calculation. Even in such a case, however, sometimes (though not always) the fact of the prohibition, and citizens' evolving response to it, can influence the development of a new strand of positive morality. Something very like this seems to have occurred in relation to drinking and driving: in Britain there is now substantially greater moral disapproval of such behaviour than was the case thirty or so years ago when it was first made a criminal offence.

Second, as the drink-driving example illustrates, rules or laws, once they are in force, are responded to by citizens (both those who obey and those who do not). As Fortes (1983: 40) emphasises, the distinctive feature of rule-related behaviour is that 'the actor ... knows that the rule exists, and must be conformed to for normal social relations to be sustained'.[7] But in conforming to the rule (if that is what he or she chooses to do), is the actor acting normatively, or in response to some other motivation?

Exactly this question has been tackled at some length in the important work of Jon Elster (1989a) on social order. Elster is a methodological individualist who, unlike Fortes, starts from the proposition that 'there are no societies, only individuals who interact with each other' (p. 248).[8] From this perspective, Elster believes that, in considering why individuals behave in ways that sustain social order, it is sensible to begin with the 'logically most simple type of motivation: rational, selfish, outcome-oriented behaviour' (p. 37). Yet after a technically very impressive discussion, Elster concludes ('with some reluctance', because of the loss of parsimony in explanation) that the maintenance of social order cannot be adequately explained by using rational self-interest as a sole motivational assumption (p. 250). In particular, he convincingly develops the twin arguments, first that social norms of various kinds independently motivate individuals' order-related behaviour,[9] and secondly that such norms are 'autonomous', in the sense that they cannot be regarded as merely rationalisations of self-interest (Elster 1989a: chapter 3).

These various considerations highlight two points: first, that the initial formulation and the subsequent operation of prohibitions (including the criminal law) in any society is necessarily at least in part linked to issues of positive morality; and, secondly, that normative factors play an important role in citizens' responses to those prohibitions. As Hans Boutellier (2000: 2–3) has recently pointed out, much of this is actually fairly obvious if one spends any time in courtrooms, and it is often equally obvious in public debates and public consciousness about crime. It is, however, frequently much less apparent in the criminological journals, perhaps particularly those publishing what Boutellier calls 'control-oriented criminology', where the criminal event may often be treated in a technical manner, with its moral significance being reduced to a token nod towards the formal provisions of the criminal law. I shall return to this point at the end of this paper.

If the preceding arguments are correct, they constitute strong reasons why criminologists must necessarily take seriously issues relating to 'positive morality'. But what about 'critical morality', that is those moral principles used in criticism or defence of actual social institutions?[10] Here, of course, we shift the nature of the discourse. 'Positive morality' refers to the morality 'accepted and shared by a given social group', and the study of positive morality is therefore necessarily largely psychological and sociological (or anthropological), being focused on describing and explaining beliefs, behaviour and social institutions in the group(s) in question, including individuals' responses to prohibitions. But if we are to use moral principles to criticise or defend actual social institutions, we must ask questions of a rather different kind. We no longer describe and explain beliefs, behaviour and institutions; instead we ask 'what ought to be the case?' In other words, we move into the territory of the academic disciplines of ethics and political theory.

But although the type of intellectual enquiry is different, the inescapability for criminologists of an engagement with critical morality ultimately stems from the same sources as the necessity to address positive morality. Positive morality is, I have argued, necessarily entailed in the study of both rule-formation and the maintenance of social order, topics that the criminologist cannot properly eschew. Following Fortes (see above), a distinctive criterion of rule-related behaviour is that the actor knows 'that the rule exists and must be conformed to for normal social relations to be sustained'. But in a given situation, the actor(s), while indeed knowing all this, may nevertheless feel that the rule in question is unfair in some way, or is outdated and has lost what moral justification it might once have had. (Beccaria, and the other writers of the classical school in the eighteenth century, were clearly motivated by both of these considerations.) Hence the actor(s) may challenge the rule, perhaps forcefully. But if the rule is to be challenged, then those who wish to mount the challenge must necessarily try to develop some coherent normative principles to support their case; conversely, those who wish to defend the existing rule will also need to supply some principled justification for the rule. Thus, the debate has moved inexorably into the intellectual territory of ethics and political theory, and criminologists – if they are serious in their intellectual quest – have little option but to follow it there.

So why have criminologists so often – as Boutellier (2000) has pointed out – neglected the moral dimension of their subject? There are perhaps two principal reasons. The first, now of declining significance but once very powerful, stemmed from the dominance of positivism within criminology, and positivism's derogation of moral discourse (see above). The second reason is a little more complex. 'Morality' is often presented – not least by self-proclaimed moralists – as if it were an abstract and transcendent category, largely unrelated to the character of, and developments in, particular human societies. Such a view is not (or at any rate, not fully) compatible with the evidence from the social sciences (including social anthropology); especially with the benefit of historical hindsight, we can see how moral views about, say, lending money at interest, sexual behaviour or ethnic relations have changed in the light of economic, technological or socio-political developments in particular societies. Thus, social scientists have often chosen to prioritise analyses of social structures, social institutions, social practices, etc., and to pay little explicit or specialised attention to questions of social morality (either sociologically or analytically). In principle, however, there is no reason at all why careful philosophical or theological discussions of moral principles (and the justifications for them) cannot be combined with social-scientific analyses of the ways in which particular moral principles have developed, and have been practised, or not practised, in given societies or within specific social groups. Thankfully, there is now a growing appreciation in the relevant academic circles that this kind of intellectual bridging exercise is both appropriate and necessary.

Normative aspects of legal compliance

Jon Elster, in his study of social order, concludes that 'we will never have any general theory of collective action' because the variety of potentially interacting motivations is 'simply too large' to be encompassed in such a theory (Elster 1989a: 205). He goes on to suggest that, in this situation, social scientists should instead focus upon 'small and medium-sized mechanisms that apply across a wide spectrum of social situations' (p. 205); or, alternatively stated, 'plausible, frequently observed ways in which things happen' (p. viii; see also Elster 1989b). According to Elster (1989a: 205), if this alternative focus were to be adopted, 'the world would be a better-understood place'. Advocacy of the explanatory importance of the concept of social mechanisms has been taken further by Hedström and Swedborg (1996), who argue specifically for 'explanations that systematically seek to explicate the generative mechanisms that produce observed associations between events' (p. 281).

There is much good sense in these observations. In this section, I propose to utilise the concept of a 'social mechanism' (particularly in Hedström and Swedborg's sense of an explanatory 'generative mechanism'), and to link it with a theme that emerged in the preceding section, namely that of 'rule-related behaviour'. More specifically, I am interested in *attempting to understand and explain more fully the basic social mechanisms*[11] *that might be involved when an individual complies with the law* in a given society. With the important major exceptions of Travis Hirschi's (1969) control theory and John Braithwaite's (1989) theory of reintegrative shaming, most theoretical work in criminology has not been much concerned with legal compliance, but has – for understandable reasons – focused instead on lawbreaking. Yet compliance is clearly a topic of considerable importance for criminologists, not least because so much applied criminology is concerned to try to identify programmes that will lead to successful crime reduction – that is, to greater compliance with the law. Moreover, and of special interest for the purposes of this paper, it can be argued that moral or normative factors potentially have an important role to play in helping to secure legal compliance. To explore this potential normative contribution to compliance is primarily an exploration in the outworking of positive morality – that is to say, it is an examination of how 'the morality actually accepted and shared by a given social group' works out in practice in helping to shape individuals' obedience to the law.

In approaching this topic, I shall first outline what I believe to be the principal mechanisms of legal compliance, then discuss more specifically the normative contribution to compliance, and finally consider normative compliance in relation to varied social contexts.

Legal compliance: an overall framework

Figure 1 presents a suggested outline characterisation of the principal mechanisms underpinning legally compliant behaviour. The framework is explicitly focused on what Frank Parkin has called compliance 'as viewed from below' (Parkin 1982: 79) – that is to say, compliant behaviour from the point of view of the ordinary person, outlining the principal reasons why he or she might comply with the law.

It will be seen from Figure 1 that four principal mechanisms of compliant behaviour are suggested. These are loosely derived from Percy Cohen's (1968: chapter 2) characterisation of the potential bases for social order, but I have no space here to discuss this derivation more fully.[12] For similar reasons, the four mechanisms of compliance are here introduced only in summary or 'headline' fashion.

The first type of compliance is instrumental/prudential compliance, based on rational calculations of self-interest (that is, Elster's (1989a) 'rational, selfish, outcome-oriented behaviour'). Questions of incentives and disincentives are, of course, central in considering this kind of compliance, and criminologically speaking this takes us straight to the large literature on criminal deterrence (for recent reviews of literature in this field, see Nagin 1998; von Hirsch *et al* 1999).

Another kind of compliance is based on constraint. Some constraints that might induce compliance are physical. Some of these are based on

---

A. **Instrumental/prudential compliance**
1. Incentives
2. Disincentives

B. **Constraint-based compliance**
1. Physical constraints
   (a) Physical restrictions on individuals leading to compliance:
       (i) natural; (ii) imposed
   (b) Physical restrictions on accessibility of target, availability of means to commit crime, etc.
2. Social-structural constraints

C. **Normative compliance**
1. Acceptance of or belief in social norm
2. Attachment leading to compliance
3. Legitimacy

D. **Compliance based on habit or routine**

Figure 1   *An Outline of the Principal Basic Mechanisms Underpinning Legally Compliant Behaviour*

the corporeality and biological characteristics of human beings, either natural (if I am asleep, I cannot burgle) or imposed (if I am locked in a prison cell, I cannot attack persons outside the cell). Physical constraints may also, however, be based on the physical characteristics of the intended target of the crime, and/or the physical availability of appropriate means to commit the offence. For example, if I try to break into well-defended bank vaults using only crude equipment, my non-commission of the full crime of burglary owes nothing to my lack of motivation and everything to the physical constraints in the situation. Hence the development of 'target-hardening', weapon-removing strategies and other kinds of so-called 'situational crime prevention' that seek to reduce the effective opportunities to commit particular crimes. (For a review of situational crime prevention, see Clarke (1995); for a discussion of ethical perspectives on situational crime prevention see von Hirsch, Garland and Wakefield (2000).)

But some constraints that may induce compliance are not physical, but rather are based on social relationships and social structures. Such constraints are particularly evident where power is very unequally distributed within a given social group. Some tricky issues arise in distinguishing compliance based on social-structural constraint from compliance based on disincentives, but these issues are not central to my present argument.

In addition, it is important to distinguish carefully between compliance based upon social-structural constraint and the third kind of compliance, namely normative compliance. Social-structural constraint is focused upon inhibitions arising from the particular social circumstances, whereas normative compliance – although it is also socially based – is a more voluntary form of compliance. Normative compliance is also, by definition, necessarily related to one or more social norms, which means, as noted earlier, that it relates to actors' responses to 'a principle or standard ... that reflects people's expectations of behaviour ... and serves to regulate action and judgment'. We are therefore here centrally in the realm of morality, the realm of the 'ought', but I shall postpone a full discussion of the varieties of normative compliance until the next subsection.

Finally, and to complete the main headings of Figure 1, there is compliance based upon habit or routine, which is the most 'automatic' of the four mechanisms of compliance. This kind of compliance, of course, may depend heavily on prior life experiences such as socialisation, and I shall have more to say about it in the subsequent discussion of normative compliance.[13]

Before moving on, however, it is important to emphasise the interconnectedness of the four kinds of compliance that have been outlined in Figure 1. This interconnectedness takes two forms: biographical and interactional.

By biographical interconnectedness, I mean that virtually everyone has at some stage in his or her life complied with the law for all four of the reasons spelt out in Figure 1; the four mechanisms are therefore biographically interconnected in the sense that they are familiar to us all, and are linked within what Richard Wollheim (1984) has usefully called the 'thread of life' that each one of us experiences. Moreover, it is not an uncommon experience to find that our compliance might typically be of a different kind in different social contexts – for example, normative compliance might be the main reason why we do not commit intra-family crimes, but our compliance with the law while driving might be more governed by instrumental/prudential considerations.[14] However, this biographical interconnectedness does not necessarily entail any interactional interconnectedness. By this latter term, I mean a true interaction within the categories of Figure 1, whereby one mechanism

31

of compliance might, within a particular set of circumstances, be specifically influenced by another of the mechanisms of compliance (or by factors closely associated with it).

It is clear that true interactional interconnectedness can and does occur. One example is from the field of situational crime prevention, where the existence of an obviously well-defended target (designed to produce constraint-based compliance) can also act as a rational disincentive to the potential offender. For present purposes, however, perhaps the most salient example of interactional interconnectedness comes from the field of deterrence, where it is now well established that, as I have put it elsewhere[15] (Bottoms 2001: 104), *deterrence works best for those persons who have strong ties of attachment to individuals, or to social groups or institutions, in a context where those individuals, groups or institutions clearly disapprove normatively of the behaviour at which the deterrent sanction is aimed.* (In the language of Figure 1, note that this proposition links together, in part, aspects of mechanisms A2 (disincentives), C2 (attachment) and C1 (acceptance of/belief in norm – in this case by the group that is important to the subject).) Those interested in the details of the empirical support for this proposition are referred to the research literature on deterrence (see especially the recent overview by Daniel Nagin 1998); here, I shall simply illustrate the general finding from one important series of research studies, that of Sherman (1992) and his colleagues on domestic violence in the US.

Sherman and his colleagues measured subsequent reoffending rates for those who were arrested for the original domestic violence incident, and those who were not, within the context of an experimental research design which ensured that arrests were (with appropriate safeguards for special cases) decided upon on a statistically random basis. In three cities, the data suggested that unemployed suspects became more violent if arrested, but employed suspects did not; in one of those cities similar effects were found for unmarried versus married suspects. Thus, arrest inhibited subsequent violence to a greater extent in the employed/married group. Sherman (1992: 17) reasonably concludes that these consistent patterns, observed (with minor variations) across several sites, support the hypothesis that the effects of intendedly deterrent criminal sanctions 'depend upon the suspect's "stakes in conformity", or how much he has to lose from the social consequences of arrest'. Phrasing the results in this way, however, carries the risk of making the compliance sound purely instrumental, whereas in fact it has the mixed normative/instrumental character set out in the italicised phrase in the preceding paragraph. The compliant subject does indeed comply for instrumental reasons, because of what he fears he will lose. But what the subject has to lose, from what Sherman interestingly calls 'the social consequences of arrest', arises, it would seem, from the facts that (a) he regards himself as having a significant attachment to the individual/ social group/social institution in question (it is important to him), and (b) that the individual/social group/social institution has certain normative expectations about how people should behave (see von Hirsch *et al* 1999: 40), and may censure the subject if he breaches those expectations.[16] Where such normative factors are not present, instrumental compliance is weaker.

Many discussions in the field of crime policy have not taken seriously enough this kind of interactional interconnectedness between the principal mechanisms of legal compliance; there is instead a tendency, among both policymakers and scholars, to think in separate 'boxes' about different kinds of compliance. (There are, however, some honourable exceptions to this generalisation: see for example Wikström (1995).) It is, in my view, especially important to draw attention to such interconnections when discussing moral or normative compliance, because normative compliance is probably, among all the mechanisms shown in Figure 1, the one that in practice interacts with the other mechanisms the most frequently and with the greatest practical effects.[17] In other words, among the principal mechanisms underpinning legal compliance, normative compliance can be said to occupy a pivotal position.[18]

The normative contribution to compliance

It is time, therefore, to examine the concept of normative compliance more fully. Figure 1 suggests that there are three subtypes of normative compliance: first, that based on acceptance of or belief in the norm in question; second, normative compliance resulting from attachment to an individual, or to a social group or institution; and third, normative compliance resulting from legitimacy. Each of these must be considered in turn.

Acceptance of, or belief in, a social norm (for example, a norm against assaulting others, or taking their property without their consent) is the most obvious way in which normative factors may be linked to legal compliance. If we truly believe that a given kind of conduct is wrong, there are obvious moral reasons why we should not engage in it. Of course, those who believe particular actions to be wrong do not always refrain from committing them, as history amply illustrates. Nevertheless, for policy purposes it seems reasonable to assume that, statistically, a group of persons who sincerely believe in the immorality of a given action will (other things being equal) be less likely to engage in that action than will a group of people who do not hold that belief; and there is good empirical support for such a proposition (see, for example, Braithwaite 1989: 48). In principle, therefore, persuading people about the correctness of certain moral principles makes good sense as a contribution to crime prevention.

Of course, as parents, schoolteachers and churches have long recognised, we initially derive most of our normative beliefs from early socialisation experiences. Such socialisation may produce a habitual, unthinking avoidance of given types of conduct, which would come into the fourth category of compliance in Figure 1.[19] But such habitual compliance may also contain a valuable latent normative content. Suppose, for example, that a white male child (C) has been socialised into beliefs about respecting other human beings, even when they seem different from ourselves, and about the consequent wrongness of unprovoked assaults and bullying. C might not think about such things very much, but just accept them. Then suddenly, in his early teens, some of C's friends become disaffected with another youth, who happens to be black, and they decide to subject him to racist taunts and a beating-up, for no reason other than their dislike of him. C is encouraged to join in, but, having thought about it, declines on the grounds that the action is morally wrong. His habitual compliance, resulting from his early socialisation, then becomes normative compliance based on moral belief. Hence, good socialisation may have valuable long-term effects in producing normative compliance, even though the norms may not, for much of the time, be consciously articulated by those who have been subject to such socialisation.

This first subtype of normative compliance (compliance based on acceptance of or belief in a social norm) might reasonably be described as 'normative self-policing'. Although, of course, it takes place within a social context, in the end it is the individual's own explicitly formulated acceptance or belief that ensures the compliance. In this regard, the first subtype of normative compliance differs from the second and third subtypes, which are based more directly on social interactions.

The second subtype is described in Figure 1 as attachment leading to compliance. 'Attachment' is, of course, a concept with an established pedigree in criminological theory through Hirschi's (1969) control theory. It can perhaps most easily be explained by a simple example, that of D, a persistent alcohol-related offender in his twenties who falls in love with a non-criminal woman, E. E, committed to non-criminal values but also to D, urges him to abandon his criminality and curb his drinking. D says that, for her sake and with her support, he will try to do so. In this example, it is the attachment (or social bond) that is central to D's intended desistance from crime; and the desistance is clearly largely of a normative character, stemming from E's social values and her expectations of behaviour among those close to her. (One should note, however, that for D there is probably here also an additional prudential element in his intended compliance, namely the fear that E may withdraw her affection if he does not change. This is a further illustration of the proposition, previously discussed, that deterrence works best when applied to individuals who are attached to significant 'stakes in conventionality', as Nagin (1998: 70) puts it.)

As the above example clearly illustrates, if the mechanism of attachment is to promote normatively based compliance, it is vital that the attachment is to a person or persons holding non-criminal values. For this reason, attachments to, say, criminal peers or criminal gangs can and do have precisely the reverse effect.

In the example just given, the attachment leading to compliance is to an individual. But attachments (social bonds) to social groups or institutions can also lead to normative compliance. For example, we know that different secondary schools have significantly different rates of offending among their pupils. This is partly because of differences in the kind of pupils on the register (some schools receive many more 'at risk' children than others); but even when these pupil intake differences are controlled for, differential delinquency rates between schools remain. It would seem, therefore, that some schools are better than others at preventing delinquency (and other undesirable behaviour) and at promoting compliance. What is their secret? The research on this question is still limited, but Michael Rutter and his colleagues have suggested that, on the available evidence, one important answer seems to be that the schools with the better behaved children tend to have an 'ethos' comprising some mixture of the following factors:

good models of teacher behaviour (with respect to time keeping, personal interactions, and responsivity to pupil needs); appropriately high expectation of pupils with helpful feedback; interesting, well-organised teaching; good use of homework and monitoring of progress; good opportunities for pupils to take responsibility and show autonomy, with a wide range of opportunities for all to experience success; an orderly atmosphere with skilled, noncoercive classroom management; and a style of leadership that provides direction but is responsive to the ideas of others and fosters high morale in staff and pupils.

(Rutter, Giller and Hagell 1998: 233)

In other words, schools of this type seem to provide both social expectations and social support, which tends to produce a sense of belonging and engagement in their pupils. And this, one may reasonably infer, engenders compliant behaviour through normative attachment to the school and its values.[20] Indeed, it is very interesting that Rutter and his colleagues use the term 'ethos' to describe the 'school climates' to which they refer; 'ethos', of course, comes ultimately from the same linguistic root as 'ethics'.

The third subtype of normative compliance is that based on legitimacy; or, more fully, compliance resulting from obedience to the wishes of a recognised legal or social authority, that person or body being recognised as legitimate. Legitimacy is a characteristic that may or may not attach to those in positions of power. It is important to recognise that compliance based on legitimacy consists of more than mere lack of resistance to the demands and orders of the authorities: that would constitute compliance as a result of social-structural constraint, or perhaps compliance through disincentives, based on fear of the consequences should the subject disobey. By contrast, compliance based on legitimacy is properly to be counted as a subtype of normative compliance, because it is based on a degree of moral assent to the right of the person in power to hold that power; moreover, as David Beetham (1991) has pointed out, a fully legitimate authority figure is one who conforms to the formal rules governing his/her office, who is administering a regime that is justifiable and fair according to the accepted moral standards of the society in question, and who commands the willing support and consent of his/her subordinates (see Figure 2).[21]

Legitimacy is a topic that was for long neglected by criminologists. During the last decade, however, it has enjoyed an important renaissance, due originally to the work of Tom Tyler (1990). Using data from a panel study of Chicago citizens' encounters with the police and courts, Tyler concluded that people are often as much if not more concerned about the processes by which they are treated as about the outcomes. Of particular importance in the area of process are questions of procedural fairness ('Has their case or situation been treated in a fair way? Are like cases treated similarly?' and so on), and also issues about the manner of their treatment (e.g. 'Are they accorded respect by police in on-street encounters?'). Tyler's argument is that people view their encounters with authority as 'information about the group that the authority represents' (Tyler 1990: 175). Hence, every transaction with an authority figure raises questions that extend 'far beyond those connected with the issue to be decided' (p. 175); to the citizen encountering the police officer (or prison officer, or whoever), that official is not simply

Criteria of legitimacy	Corresponding form of non-legitimate power
1. Conformity to rules (legal validity)	Illegitimacy (breach of rules)
2. Justifiability of rules in terms of shared beliefs	Legitimacy deficit (discrepancy between rules and supporting shared beliefs, absencve of shared beliefs)
3. Legitimation through expressed consent	Delegitimation (withdrawal of consent)

Figure 2 *Beetham's dimensions of legitimacy*
Source: Beetham (1991: 20).

dealing with a particular matter in a routine transaction, he/she is also in a real sense representing, through her demeanour and behaviour, the whole public service to which she belongs. Issues raised in such transactions include 'neutrality, bias, honesty, quality of decision, and consistency' (p. 175), and these are all issues that can raise the moral questions of fairness and respect (see above). In short, we can postulate from Tyler's work that ordinary everyday encounters between legal authorities and citizens can have crucial implications for the nature of the power relations involved, and to the validity of the officials' claims to justified authority – that is, to legitimacy (for a fuller discussion in the context of prison life, see Sparks and Bottoms 1995). Where the legal authority is regarded as legitimate by the citizen, compliance in the immediate encounter is more likely to ensue. Indeed, there are even some hints in the literature that treatment by the authorities that is regarded as legitimate might enhance subjects' longer-term compliance with the law, but further replication studies are needed before this evidence can be regarded as firm.[22]

I indicated earlier that the first subtype of normative compliance (based on belief) could be described as resulting from *normative self-policing*, or what some might call normative self-control. The second subtype (based on attachment) has often been noted, in the criminological literature, as a major example of what is usually called *informal social control*; while the third (legitimacy) has been shown to vary according to the way in which *formal social control* is exercised. The three subtypes of normative compliance are therefore distinct, but potentially complementary. Those who wish to enhance legal compliance through normative mechanisms therefore have an interesting variety of possibilities to consider.

In this and the previous subsection, I have tried to provide a kind of map of the complex terrain of legal compliance. As I indicated earlier, one of the most important and influential attempts by a criminologist to explore this field has been Hirschi's (1969) control theory.[23] It may therefore be useful, in concluding this discussion, to compare directly Hirschi's approach with that postulated in Figure 1.

For Hirschi (1969: 16), 'delinquent acts result when an individual's bond to society is weak or broken'. The centrality, within this formulation, of the idea of a 'bond to society' clearly indicates that control theory has a strong normative dimension. Hence, it is not surprising that two of Hirschi's four 'elements of the bond' (namely, *attachment* and *belief*) have been utilised directly, in the preceding discussion in this paper, as two of the subtypes of normative compliance.

Hirschi's two other 'elements' are *involvement* and *commitment*. 'Involvement' refers simply to 'engrossment in conventional activities', so that the actor 'cannot even think about deviant acts, let alone act out his inclinations' (Hirschi 1969: 22). In the language of the preceding discussion, compliance is here a byproduct of engagement in conventional activities, arising from the natural physical constraint of the human condition, which means that one cannot be in two places at once (that is, B1(a)(i) in Figure 1). As for 'commitment', this is described by Hirschi (1969: 20–1) in the following way:

> The person invests time, energy, himself, in a certain line of activity – say, getting an education, building up a business, acquiring a reputation for virtue. When or whenever he considers deviant behavior, he must consider the costs of this deviant behavior, the risk he runs of losing the investment he has made in conventional behavior ... [Thus] the concept of commitment assumes that the organization of society is such that the interests of most persons would be endangered if they were to engage in criminal acts.

So stated, it is clear that 'commitment' is a kind of rational/prudential compliance, and in his elaboration of this concept, Hirschi is articulating the insight – not yet, in 1969, well developed in the deterrence literature – that deterrence works best with those who have strong stakes in conventionality (see preceding discussion).

In summary, therefore, Hirschi's theoretical formulations are fully compatible with the conceptualisation suggested in Figure 1. Figure 1 does, however, also include some modes of compliance not discussed within Hirschi's control theory, and the fourfold categorisation of instrumental/constraint-based/normative/habitual is arguably more straightforward and parsimonious than the use of concepts such as 'commitment' and 'involvement'.

Normative compliance, the social context, and the life-course

All three subtypes of normative compliance can and do vary according to differential social circumstances. Exposure to a different culture from that in which one was initially socialised may cause moral beliefs to change; attachments to individuals and to social groups and institutions may, in different social circumstances, sometimes flourish and some-times wane, with consequences for behavioural compliance; and legitimacy is well known to be a variable matter (Beetham 1991), so that even a well-loved leader may lose much legitimacy with a single ill-judged act.

Criminality is also an individual act that is socially influenced. This is strikingly illustrated in some recent research by Wikström and Loeber (2000). Criminologists studying criminal careers have shown that those who subsequently become persistent offenders tend to be characterised by a number of individual 'risk factors' that can be identified at an early age (about 8–10 years): these factors include impulsivity, low intelligence, poor school performance, poor parenting and so on (see generally Farrington 1997). In general, a higher number of 'risk factors' increases the probability of becoming a delinquent, although risk factors can also be offset by 'protective factors' – for example, a good, supportive home may reduce the risks of criminality for an impulsive child with low intelligence. Wikström and Loeber's research, however, suggests that in certain social contexts the whole concept of 'individual risk factors' might be of limited applicability. For most of the boys they studied in Pittsburgh, the probability of becoming a delinquent did indeed increase sequentially with an increasing number of individual risk factors. But for those from the most deprived and most stigmatic social areas (lower-class boys from public housing areas), delinquency rates were high, even among those with no individual risk factors. For boys from these disadvantaged areas, there was also very little increase (and no statistically significant increase) in the delinquency rate as the number of individual risk factors increased (Wikström and Loeber 2000: table 6). The obvious inference is that some social contexts are so all-encompassing, and so destructive in their normative consequences that they can wipe out the effects of factors that would, elsewhere, be of considerable significance.

Normative decisions, and criminality, may vary not only according to the social context, but also in their character as one proceeds through life. It is, for example, very well known that age is one of the principal correlates of (non-white-collar) criminality, with the age group 15–25 being at the greatest risk. The reasons for this pervasive statistic remain a subject of controversy among criminologists, but one important contributing reason is very likely to be the fact that adolescents and young adults are obliged to wean themselves from the normative context (including the normative attachments) in which they were reared, and they may then face prolonged uncertainty (and shifting social and moral alliances) before they then construct their own preferred, settled lifestyle as adults.

Some criminologists have developed further this 'dynamic life-course' model of criminality. Sampson and Laub (1993) carried out an important reanalysis of the Gluecks' classic data set and this showed the usual complex *mélange* of factors of importance in the first 15 years of life (structural background, individual difference factors, family, school, delinquent peers, etc.). Thereafter, however, matters were not set in stone. In particular, there is evidence from this study (supported by other studies) that, even after an offender has embarked on a delinquent career – and perhaps a career of persistent criminality – attachment to pro-social bonds can be of potentially great importance in preventing recidivism. A strong marriage to a non-criminal partner, or attachment to a new work situation or leisure interest that really engages the attention, can alter the trajectory of a criminal career, certainly in part for normative reasons (see further the recent overview of the literature on desistance by Laub and Sampson 2001). Typically, as Neal Shover (1996: 127) comments, such attachments 'provide both a reason to change and "social capital" for doing so'. Indeed, processes such as this can occur (as a result of the influence of the social environment on normative choices) even when the initial engagement with the conventional moral environment predates any wish to change one's criminal habits. As one of Shover's research subjects, who secured employment in a small business, put it: 'The guy [employer] liked me from the jump. And that's when I hooked up with him. And I went straight a long time *without the intentions* of going straight … That was one turning point in the later part of my career' (Shover 1996: 127, emphasis in original). Initial constraint-based compliance (Hirschi's 'involvement') here eventually transmutes into attachment-based normative compliance.

Taking the analysis of this section as a whole, then, we can reasonably conclude: first, that normative compliance has three subtypes; second, that all three subtypes can be influenced by social circumstances, sometimes very pervasively as shown in the Wikström/Loeber research; third, that moral choices constantly recur in the life course, and that even persistent offenders may sometimes desist from crime for normative reasons; and fourth, that, unsurprisingly, such desistance seems to be greatly assisted by a favourable social context, which allows pro-social normative attachments to flourish within conditions of legitimacy. In short, therefore, normative compliance really does have to be taken seriously in criminological analysis. This point is reinforced when we consider also the previous discussion about the interactional dimensions of compliance. It will be recalled from that discussion that deterrence works best when people have higher 'stakes in social conformity'. Stakes in social conformity are, of course, enhanced when people have attachments to non-criminal individuals and social institutions, and when they regard the legal authorities as legitimate. It follows – though this is a point that is hardly ever noticed by policymakers – that an enhancement of normative compliance through attachments and legitimacy can also be expected to produce, as a by-product, an enhanced effectiveness for deterrent sanctions.

Necessarily, however, the discussion in this section has provided only a skeletal conceptual framework for an understanding of compliance, and of normative compliance in particular. At the discussion following the oral presentation of this paper at the Radzinowicz Symposium, it was reasonably asked how the framework presented might be applied to a well-known issue in legal compliance, namely why females so consistently – and in so many different social contexts – conform to laws more fully than do males.[24] Similar questions could equally reasonably be raised concerning the application of the suggested framework to other important and unresolved questions of legal compliance, such as why Japan enjoys a low crime rate, at any rate for the most common kinds of street crime (on which see, for example, the literature review by Park 1997). These questions are obviously of potentially major significance for future work, but equally clearly they are beyond the scope of the present paper. However, if the conceptual framework on compliance presented in Figure 1 has merit, then it should in principle be usable – in conjunction, of course, with appropriate empirical evidence – in tackling important questions of this kind. Whether or not the framework will stand up to this kind of scrutiny must, of course, at this stage be regarded as a completely open question.

Criminal policy and the normative dimension

Given Leon Radzinowicz's well-known views on the close inter-relationship between criminology and public policy, it would clearly be inappropriate to conclude this paper without some discussion of the implications of the foregoing analysis for issues of criminal policy. Necessarily, however, in the space available, my comments will have to be brief and broad-brush.

It would of course be possible to focus on the three suggested sub-types of normative compliance – belief, attachment, legitimacy – and to make specific suggestions for possible crime-reductive approaches based on an anticipated enhancement of these mechanisms of compliance. That kind of discussion, however, is best left to a different kind of paper.[25] Here, I want instead to focus on three points of a rather more general character.

First, an implication of the foregoing analysis is that morality is always practised within a specific social context, and that moral standards can change. A consequence of this is that intendedly crime-reductive policies of a normative kind need to pay close attention to the normative understandings of the society in which they are being proposed – for if they do not, they run the serious risk of being judged to be irrelevant by the very people at whom they are principally targeted. That is true not only for the substance of moral prohibitions, but also for the form in which they are couched and the reasons that are proffered as to why they should be obeyed. Given the social transformations seen in Britain – and other western nations – in the last half-century, this means that we almost certainly cannot now revivify normative compliance by Victorian-style *de haut en bas* moral preaching, nor by attempting to breathe life into traditional kinds of social attachment such as the localised extended family headed by a patriarchal male figure. These social forms belong to an earlier, more hierarchical, more gendered and less secularised social world, in which morality was seen principally to derive from traditional rules and the wisdom of established authorities. Hans Boutellier (2000) – drawing on the work of Emile Durkheim – describes this as an 'authority model' of social morality, and he goes on to argue, in my view correctly, that to attempt now to 'restor[e] the authority model, as is advocated in many arguments in favour of stricter normative standards, means a regression to [a social] model that is structurally obsolete'.

It is important to emphasise, however, that to argue in this fashion is not to argue for the irrelevance of the normative in contemporary criminal policy. Rather, what we have returned to here is the distinction between positive and critical morality. The critical morality of the 1960s and 1970s was very negative about many aspects of the 'authority model' of social morality in which its advocates had been reared. Given the erosion of that framework, the task now is to develop and consolidate, from recent critiques, a new positive morality for our times. The core of that new positive morality can probably already be seen in such matters as our heightened awareness of the dangers of drink-driving (see earlier discussion), and what Simon Blackburn (2001: 135) has described as our 'increased sensitivity to ... sexual difference, to gender, to people different from ourselves in a whole variety of ways'. Hans Boutellier (2000: 156–7) consequently argues for 'moralizing our culture', not in terms of the obsolete authority model, but 'based instead upon the moral meaning of respect for others'.[26] It is a thesis worthy of the most careful consideration and debate.[27]

My second comment concerns the process of making critical moral observations about aspects of current criminal justice policies. It should be obvious from the foregoing analysis that such criticisms are necessary if moral progress in the delivery of criminal justice is to be made (which is not, of course, to say that all critical-moral observations about the criminal justice system are necessarily justified). It is perhaps par-ticularly encouraging, therefore, when forceful criticisms of this kind are made from within official frameworks rather than simply by outsiders. One recent British example of this is the Macpherson Report (1999), which has caused the police service seriously to re-examine its attitudes and practices as regards the victimisation of ethnic minority com-munities, and also to confront the significant legitimacy deficit that these attitudes and practices have created, over time, among members of ethnic minority communities. A further example has now been provided by the Director-General of the English Prison Service (Martin Narey), who early in 2001 argued forcefully, in a speech to the annual Prison Governors' Conference, that the state of a few English prisons raises serious moral issues, and indeed that the Prison Service has in the past been guilty of a degree of 'moral neglect' (Mr Narey's words) in relation to such 'failing prisons' (Narey 2001).

Both Macpherson and Narey have been the subject of some criticism for their remarks, including covert criticism from within the police service and the prison system respectively. But on reflection, this is not at all surprising, for if one is challenging established practices (as both Macpherson and Narey were), that challenge is almost bound to be seen as uncomfortable by some people. In a striking passage, Neil MacCormick draws attention not only to the great potential societal value of the work of the good critical moralist, but also to the vulnerability of this role:

> If the critical moralist does his work well and persuades his fellows of the greater rationality of his view, the effect over time must be a change in the positive morality. This, however, can be a risky job. Of critical moralists, the two most notable in Western history were executed, one by hemlock and the other by crucifixion.
>
> (MacCormick 1981: 54)

Both Macpherson and Narey have been prepared to use explicitly moral language in their criticisms, and this makes their comments stand out from much of what I described previously (following Boutellier) as 'control-oriented criminology'. It is this kind of criminology, and the criminal justice practices that accompany it, that are the subject of my third and final comment.

As all informed observers know, criminal policy in this and many other countries often seems increasingly to be attracted by technical and managerialist approaches to tackling crime. These technical and managerialist approaches include such things as situational crime prevention, CCTV, electronic tagging, risk assessment scores, offending behaviour programmes and the like. Each of these in its own way makes perfectly good sense, and in most of these instances the empirical evaluations have demonstrated many positive aspects of the workings of the particular scheme. There is, however, a potential downside, and that downside is one that reminds us very much of the Italian positivists' incomprehension of the moral realm.[28] If we place our primary faith in technical solutions, then a mindset can quickly develop whereby any other kind of purported solution is treated as second-rate. Thus, there is already hard evidence available from prison research suggesting that attendance at an offending behaviour programme has become a kind of Holy Grail for decisionmakers concerned with reductions in security classification, or early release from a longer sentence.[29] That is to say, such decisionmakers are much more willing to make a decision favourable to the prisoner on the evidence of attendance at an offending behaviour course than on any amount of softer evidence from the prison staff who have observed the prisoner most closely on a day-to-day basis. In a not dissimilar way, there is a significant body of empirical research evidence supporting the value of resettlement programmes after prison as a promising approach to crime reduction (see, for example, Haines 1990) – and indeed it should be obvious, from my earlier discussion of attachment, why such approaches seem to be promising. But the Home Office's version of 'evidence-led policy' seems – at present anyway – to find it much harder to accept this kind of research evidence than that arising from, say, the rather limited amount of research on electronic tagging. If the analysis of this paper is right, then public policy on crime needs to take seriously all four potential main mechanisms of legal compliance and the ways in which they interact with each other. Of the four, as I have argued previously, the normative dimension is in some ways pivotal, since it is the dimension which interacts most frequently and with the greatest practical effect with the other mechanisms. Yet – and this is the current danger – the normative dimension is also the one that is least obviously deliverable by technical and managerialist approaches. It is a danger that we should be alert to, so that we can reduce its potentially damaging effects.[30]

Notes

1 For a fuller discussion of Ferri's role in relation to Italian criminal policy, see Radzinowicz (1999: chapter 1). As Leon Radzinowicz points out, Ferri came 'very close to achieving [the] truly extraordinary triumph' of the enactment in Italy of a positivist Penal Code (p. 19). In the end, however, this project foundered because of the advent of Mussolini's dictatorship.
2 It should be noted that in an introduction to a 1946 reissue of his book, Ayer acknowledged that the treatment of ethical matters had been 'presented in a very summary way' (Ayer 1936/1971: 27). He also observed (p. 26) that criticism of his approach to ethics had been 'directed more often against the positivistic principles on which the theory had been assumed to depend than against the [emotive theory of values] itself', and that the one does not necessarily entail the other. For a discussion of emotivism in ethics see, for example, Hudson (1983: chapter 4).
3 As Boutellier (2000: 37) puts it: 'from a scientific perspective, a moral approach to social issues was long considered inappropriate, and excluded as it were from the scientific discourse'.
4 See, for example, Radzinowicz's (1999: 76) description of how, in the 1930s in Poland, he became for 'the first time … acutely conscious that the lofty principles of "social defence" could be effortlessly distorted into cruel patterns of "social aggression"'.
5 Meyer Fortes (1906–83) was William Wyse Professor of Social Anthropology at Cambridge from 1950 to 1973. During the early years of the life of the Institute of Criminology, he was an active member of Institute's Committee of Management.
6 In an important footnote, Fortes (1983: 40) clarifies the concept of 'rules'. '[I]n my usage rules are emic elements, and like Wittgenstein I include under the same rubric elements that would more usually be described as customary norms or, as Piaget does, in a juridicial terminology … In every

case, my emphasis is on the actor's apprehending the rule and intentionally conforming to – or of course, flouting – it'. He contrasts this with 'an etic or observer's usage', as when a biologist 'writes of "a rule governing [animal] behaviour selected during evolution for its adaptive outcome", ... equating "rule" with "internal mechanisms" '.

7 As Fortes (1983: 40) notes, this feature is entailed by his treatment of rules as 'emic elements' (on which see note 6 above).

8 For a full discussion of methodological individualism, see Bhargava (1992). Elster (1989a: 105) claims, ultimately unconvincingly in my view, that one can 'define, discuss and defend a theory of social norms within a wholly individualist framework'.

9 Elster differentiates 'social norms' from other concepts such as 'private norms': see Elster (1989a: 100–5). Given his individualistic methodological approach (see note 8 above), Elster's definition of a 'social norm' is somewhat unusual; it is 'the propensity to feel shame and to anticipate sanctions by others at the thought of behaving in a certain, forbidden way' (Elster 1989a: 105).

10 I have here added the words 'or defence' to Hart's original definition of critical morality, since principled defensive responses to 'the general moral principles used in the criticism of actual social institutions' clearly belong to the same kind of intellectual discourse as the original criticisms. See also MacCormick (1981: chapter 4), especially at p. 54.

11 The qualifying adjective 'basic' is quite important here. What follows is indeed an attempt to identify the main *basic* mechanisms of legal compliance, using the term mechanisms to mean 'generative mechanisms'. Even if this attempt is judged to have merit, however, it will by definition not preclude the possibility of more complex mechanisms of compliance, arising from interactions between some of the basic mechanisms. See further below, on 'interactional interconnectedness'.

12 Cohen (1968: 21) suggests that 'there have been four main types of theory to explain the existence of social order'; these he goes on to describe as 'the coercion theory', 'the interest theory', 'the value-consensus theory' and 'the inertia theory'. See also Wrong (1994: 8–9).

13 For a brief discussion on the relationship of habitual/routine compliance to the other main kinds of compliance, and why it is nevertheless appropriate to delineate it as a separate mechanism of compliance, see Bottoms (2001: 93–4). More generally, note the profound comment by Barry Barnes (2000: 28) that 'one of the strangest features of social theory is that mundane routine social action has long presented it with one of its most serious challenges'.

14 Persistent offenders, by definition, conform with the law less often than most people, but they also may be influenced to conform differentially in different social contexts. Thus, for example, Donald West's study of persistent petty offenders – one of the first research studies carried out in the Cambridge Institute of Criminology – showed that they sometimes had

'crime-free gaps' in their record, which 'tended to coincide with sheltered circumstances, such as residence in an institution, periods of military service, or, most frequent and most important, the establishment of a relationship with some stronger personality, someone able and willing to provide continuous sympathy and practical support' (West 1963: 50). See also the further discussion in the later subsection of this paper entitled 'Normative compliance, the social context and the life-course'.

15 The formulation in the text is a slightly revised version of my previous formulation, in order explicitly to include ties of attachment to individuals.

16 See also the perceptual deterrence research on tax evasion by Klepper and Nagin (1989a, 1989b), utilising survey techniques in which respondents were questioned about their perceptions of the risks of committing an offence described in a crime vignette, and about their own behaviour if they found themselves in that situation ('scenario-based surveys'). A majority of the middle-class respondents in the survey were willing to contemplate a degree of tax evasion where the potential penalty was a financial civil enforcement action by the tax authority (such sanctions are never made public). But, for the same sample, if the tax evasion also potentially involved a criminal prosecution (with its attendant publicity), then any non-zero probability of detection was sufficient to deter. As Nagin (1998: 71) puts it: 'our respondents were generally willing to consider tax non-compliance when only their money was at risk ... [but] if the evasion gamble also involved putting reputation and community standing at risk, our middle-class respondents were seemingly unwilling to consider' non-compliance.

17 For some further examples of the normative dimension interacting with other mechanisms of compliance, see Bottoms (2001: 106–7).

18 The discussion about interactional interconnectedness (in the preceding three paragraphs) of course opens up the possibility of identifying, in due course, more complex generative mechanisms of compliance (see note 11 above for the distinction between 'basic' and 'complex' mechanisms). As a first step, however, it seems of primary importance to identify correctly the basic mechanisms of compliance, and to indicate in broad terms some possibilities of interaction between them. No more than that is attempted here.

19 See the helpful comment by Fortes (1983: 7): 'Fully internalised rules are generally followed automatically (not, be it noted, unconsciously), but that they are recognised rules is made explicit in the fact that breach or mistakes are noted, perhaps only by polite correction ... but in socially more critical matters by [more serious interventions]'.

20 For a further relevant example, see my reinterpretation of Ian Sinclair's (1971) classic study of probation hostels, in Bottoms (2001: 95–7).

21 Criticising Max Weber's account of legitimacy, Beetham (1991: 11) makes the following important point: 'A given power relationship is not legitimate because people believe in its legitimacy, but because it can be *justified in*

terms of their beliefs. This may seem a fine distinction, but it is a fundamental one. When we seek to assess the legitimacy of a regime, a political system, or some other power relation, one thing we are doing is assessing how far it conforms to their values or standards, how far it satisfies the normative expectations they have of it' (emphasis in original).

22 See Paternoster *et al* (1997), but note also the possible limitation of this research commented on in Bottoms (2001: 114, n 11).

23 As is well known, later in his career Travis Hirschi produced another major text in theoretical criminology, in co-authorship with Michael R. Gottfredson (Gottfredson and Hirschi 1990). On the relationship between Hirschi's two major theoretical statements, see, for example, Taylor (2001). For assessments of Hirschi's (1969) original control theory, see, for example, Kempf (1993) and Le Blanc and Caplan (1993).

24 The questioner indicated that he had in mind feminist analyses, such as that by Pat Carlen (1988), who explicitly uses Hirschi's control theory (Carlen 1988: 11, and chapters 4 and 5).

25 For those interested, I did attempt such a discussion in the final part of an unpublished paper recently commissioned by the Home Office: see Bottoms (2000).

26 This dichotomy sounds straightforward, but it should be noted that it is not always easy, in practice, to tell the difference between the two models. For example, the new (post-1998) youth justice policy in England and Wales contains elements of what Muncie (1999: 169) has called 'responsibilization', that is provisions designed to encourage young people to be responsible for their own behaviour, and parents to be responsible for the behaviour of their offspring. 'Responsibilization', especially as it is applied to parents, has been widely read as attempting to revive an obsolete authority model, but it could be interpreted (at least if implemented in certain ways) as attempting to foster an enhanced moral respect for others.

27 Boutellier additionally develops an important 'victimalisation thesis', arguing that in the contemporary world victimhood (the harm and suffering caused to the victim) constitutes the principal new ground of legitimation for the criminal law, following the decline of the 'authority model'. This thesis, Boutellier contends, explains the increasing attention paid to the victim within the criminal justice process during the last half-century. I hope to discuss this thesis more fully in a forthcoming paper on restorative justice in contemporary societies.

28 Though one must make an important qualification here concerning offending behaviour courses, which do often contain a significant normative element within the formal course content.

29 On security classification, see the Cambridge PhD research by David Price (2000), summarised in the editors' 'Concluding reflections' in Bottoms, Gelsthorpe and Rex (2001: 234–5). On early release, see Hood and Shute (2000) on parole decisions, and Padfield and Liebling (2000) on the work of 'discretionary lifer panels'.

30 I am grateful to Per-Olof Wikström for helpful comments on a draft version of this paper.

References

Ayer, A.J. (1936/1971) *Language, Truth and Logic* (first published 1936; Pelican Book edition 1971). Harmondsworth: Penguin Books.

Barnes, B. (2000) *Understanding Agency: Social Theory and Responsible Action.* London: Sage.

Beetham, D. (1991) *The Legitimation of Power.* London: Macmillan.

Bhargava, R. (1992) *Individualism in Social Science: Forms and Limits of a Methodology.* Oxford: Clarendon Press.

Blackburn, S. (2001) *Being Good: A Short Introduction to Ethics.* Oxford: Oxford University Press.

Bottoms, A.E. (2000) 'Morality, Crime and Crime Prevention: A Discussion Paper'. Unpublished paper commissioned by the Home Office in connection with the Cabinet Office review of crime policy, headed by Lord Birt. Copy lodged in the Radzinowicz Library, Institute of Criminology, University of Cambridge.

Bottoms, A.E. (2001) 'Compliance and Community Penalties', in A.E. Bottoms, L.R. Gelsthorpe and S. Rex (eds), *Community Penalties: Change and Challenges.* Cullompton: Willan Publishing.

Bottoms, A.E., Gelsthorpe, L.R. and Rex, S. (eds) (2001) *Community Penalties: Change and Challenges.* Collumpton: Willan Publishing.

Boutellier, H. (2000) *Crime and Morality: The Significance of Criminal Justice in Post-modern Culture.* Dordrecht: Kluwer Academic.

Braithwaite, J. (1989) *Crime, Shame and Reintegration.* Cambridge: Cambridge University Press.

Carlen, P. (1988) *Women, Crime and Poverty.* Milton Keynes: Open University Press.

Clarke, R.V.G. (1995) 'Situational Crime Prevention', *Crime and Justice: A Review of Research*, 19, 91–150.

Cohen, P. (1968) *Modern Social Theory.* London: Heinemann Educational.

Elster, J. (1989a) *The Cement of Society: A Study of Social Order.* Cambridge: Cambridge University Press.

Elster, J. (1989b) *Nuts and Bolts for the Social Sciences.* Cambridge: Cambridge University Press.

Farrington, D.P. (1997) 'Human Development and Criminal Careers', in M. Maguire, R. Morgan and R. Reiner (eds), *The Oxford Handbook of Criminology*, 2nd edn. Oxford: Clarendon Press.

Ferri, E. (1905/1917) *Criminal Sociology* (translation of the French edition of 1905). Boston: Little, Brown.

Fortes, M. (1983) *Rules and the Emergence of Society*, Royal Anthropological

Institute of Great Britain and Ireland Occasional Paper No. 39. London: Royal Anthropological Institute.

Gottfredson, M.R. and Hirschi, T. (1990) *A General Theory of Crime*. Stanford, CA: Stanford University Press.

Haines, K. (1990) *After-Care Services for Released Prisoners: A Review of the Literature*. London: Home Office.

Hart, H.L.A. (1963) *Law, Liberty and Morality*. London: Oxford University Press.

Hedström, P. and Swedborg, R. (1996) 'Social Mechanisms', *Acta Sociologica*, 39, 281–308.

Hirschi, T. (1969) *Causes of Delinquency*. Berkeley, CA: University of California Press.

Hood, R. and Shute, S. (2000) *The Parole System at Work: A Study of Risk-Based Decision-Making*, Home Office Research Study No. 202. London: Home Office.

Hudson, W.D. (1983) *Modern Moral Philosophy*, 2nd edn. London: Macmillan.

Kempf, K.L. (1993) 'The Empirical Status of Hirschi's Control Theory', in F. Adler and W.S. Laufer (eds), *New Directions in Criminological Theory*, Advances in Criminological Theory, Vol. 4. New Brunswick, NJ: Transaction Publishers.

Klepper, S. and Nagin, D. (1989a) 'Tax Compliance and Perceptions of the Risks of Detection and Criminal Punishment', *Law and Society Review*, 23, 209–40.

Klepper, S. and Nagin, D. (1989b) 'The Deterrent Effect of Perceived Certainty and Severity of Punishment Revisited', *Criminology*, 27, 721–46.

Laub, J.H. and Sampson, R.J. (2001) 'Understanding Desistance from Crime', *Crime and Justice: A Review of Research*, 28, 1–69.

Le Blanc, M. and Caplan, A. (1993) 'Theoretical Formalization, a Necessity: The Example of Hirschi's Bonding Theory', in F. Adler and W.S. Laufer (eds), *New Directions in Criminological Theory*, Advances in Criminological Theory, Vol. 4. New Brunswick, NJ: Transaction Publishers.

Longman (1984) *Longman Dictionary of the English Language*. Harlow: Longman.

MacCormick, N. (1981) *H.L.A. Hart*. London: Edward Arnold.

Macpherson Report (1999) *The Stephen Lawrence Inquiry: Report of an Inquiry by Sir William Macpherson of Cluny*, Cm 4262. London: Stationery Office.

Muncie, J. (1999) 'Institutionalized Intolerance: Youth Justice and the 1998 Crime and Disorder Act'. *Critical Social Policy*, 19, 147–75.

Nagin, D. (1998) 'Criminal Deterrence Research at the Outset of the Twenty-First Century', *Crime and Justice: A Review of Research*, 23, 51–91.

Narey, M. (2001) Director-General's Speech to the Prison Governor's Conference, 5 February 2001; available online at www.hmprisonservice.gov.uk/news/newstext.asp/201.

Padfield, N. and Liebling, A. (2000) *An Exploration of Decision-Making at Discretionary Lifer Panels*, Home Office Research Study No. 213. London: Home Office.

Park, W.-K. (1997) 'Explaining Japanese Low Crime Rates: A Review of the Literature'. *Annales Internationales de Criminologie*, 35, 59–88.

Parkin, F. (1982) *Max Weber*. Chichester: Ellis Horwood; London: Tavistock.

Paternoster, R., Brame, R., Bachman, R. and Sherman, L.W. (1997) 'Do Fair Procedures Matter? The Effect of Procedural Justice on Spouse Assault', *Law and Society Review*, 31, 163–204.

Price, D.E. (2000) 'Security Categorisation in the English Prison System'. Unpublished PhD thesis, University of Cambridge.

Radzinowicz, L. (1966) *Ideology and Crime*. London: Heinemann.

Radzinowicz, L. (1988) *The Cambridge Institute of Criminology: Its Background and Scope*. London: HMSO.

Radzinowicz, L. (1999) *Adventures in Criminology*. London: Routledge.

Rutter, M., Giller, H. and Hagell, A. (1998) *Antisocial Behavior by Young People*. Cambridge: Cambridge University Press.

Ryan, J. (1995) *Doing Things the Right Way: Dene Traditional Justice in Lac La Martre, N.W.T.* Calgary: University of Calgary Press and the Arctic Institute of North America.

Sampson, R.J. and Laub, J.H. (1993) *Crime in the Making: Pathways and Turning Points through Life*. Cambridge, MA: Harvard University Press.

Sherman, L.W. (1992) *Policing Domestic Assault*. New York: Free Press.

Shover, N. (1996) *Great Pretenders: Pursuits and Careers of Persistent Thieves*. Boulder, CO: Westview Press.

Sinclair, I. (1971) *Hostels for Probationers*, Home Office Research Study No. 6. London: HMSO.

Sparks, J.R. and Bottoms, A.E. (1995) 'Legitimacy and Order in Prisons'. *British Journal of Sociology*, 46, 45–62.

Taylor, C. (2001) 'The Relationship between Social and Self-Control: Tracing Hirschi's Criminological Career', *Theoretical Criminology*, 5, 369–88.

Tyler, T.R. (1990) *Why People Obey the Law*. New Haven, CT: Yale University Press.

von Hirsch, A., Bottoms, A.E., Burney, E. and Wikström, P.-O. (1999) *Criminal Deterrence and Sentence Severity*. Oxford: Hart Publishing.

von Hirsch, A., Garland, D. and Wakefield, A. (eds) (2000) *Ethical and Social Perspectives on Situational Crime Prevention*. Oxford: Hart Publishing.

West, D.J. (1963) *The Habitual Prisoner*. London: Macmillan.

Wikström, P.-O. (1995) 'Self-Control, Temptations, Frictions and Punishment: an Integrated Approach to Crime Prevention', in P.-O. Wikström, J. McCord and R.V.G. Clarke (eds), *Integrating Crime Prevention Strategies: Propensity and Opportunity*. Stockholm: National Council for Crime Prevention.

Wikström, P.-O. and Loeber, R. (2000) 'Do Disadvantaged Neighborhoods Cause Well-Adjusted Children to Become Adolescent Delinquents? A Study of Male Juvenile Serious Offending, Individual Risk and Protective Factors, and Neighborhood Context', *Criminology*, 38, 1109–42.

Wollheim, R. (1984) *The Thread of Life*. Cambridge: Cambridge University Press; reprinted New Haven, CT: Yale University Press, 1999.

Wrong, D. (1994) *The Problem of Order: What Unites and Divides Society*. Cambridge, MA: Harvard University Press.

Part 2
History

Chapter 3

Gentlemen convicts, Dynamitards and paramilitaries: the limits of criminal justice

Seán McConville

Leon Radzinowicz and the study of history

Of his scholarly endeavours Leon Radzinowicz loved history best, and it is the basis of his enduring reputation. He relished the survey, the collection of information, the sifting and evaluation, and the polishing of a narrative that carried the reader along in English made as clear and concise as could be: no jargon, no needless obscurities. He had little or no interest in closed-shop historiographical debates. His five-volume *A History of English Criminal Law and Its Administration* shows that he had many times entered the empty place or the hopeless thicket, and found a way through both. He knew the necessity and enjoyment of attending to detail, the pursuit of strings of leads and connections, and the never-ending quest for colour, vigour and insight in presentation.

Radzinowicz deeply valued the English empirical approach for personal and political as well as scholarly reasons. It is hard to imagine a bleaker prospect than the Europe from which he came in 1938 – the grim and darkening international horizon in part the product of philosophical idealism and political and cultural romanticism. In the common law and its procedures he saw a solid, enduring part of democracy's defences against tyranny, and in the empirical method – broadly considered – a potent challenge to grand social and political theory, a solvent for a certain type of morality which had been grafted onto politics. His approach to history reflected this: a study of criminal and penal policy and its administration, proceeding from the collection and evaluation of information to the shaping of a narrative and the drawing of con-clusions. Yet his choice of area and topic was no rush to the comforting certainties and exclusions of institutions. Correctly, he saw criminal and penal policies and their administration close to the heart of the democratic process – symbol, rhetoric and practice.

History is always written for the day, and Radzinowicz's first volume of the *History of English Criminal Law* (published in 1948) was prepared amid the trauma of the war and that mixture of loss, exhaustion and hope which characterised postwar reconstruction. The long campaign to abolish the death penalty epitomised with a particular intensity the liberal humanism which he explored in those years. Radzinowicz was firmly of the abolitionist camp, and that first volume traced the con-voluted course of the doctrinal, legal and political debate over one hundred and fifty years. He saw nothing incompatible with the scholarly enterprise in this engagement in policy debates, and through his membership of the 1949–53 Royal Commission on Capital Punish-ment, and many subsequent lectures, articles and essays, made a powerful contribution to the ending of capital punishment in the United Kingdom (*Royal Commission* 1949–53; Radzinowicz 1999: 252–68).

For a novice penal historian like myself, starting out in 1970, Radzinowicz's work was simply the best, most accomplished, and written to the highest standards: only perhaps Holdsworth (*A History of English Law*) exceeded it in scope, and certainly not in literary merit. In contrast to a number of fairly superficial chronicles, generally based on secondary sources – sometimes the apologias of professionals or the abbreviations of campaigners – Radzinowicz provided an example which one could follow with confidence, while hardly ever reaching the breadth of his scholarship, his penetration and elegance in style. It is only fair to add, perhaps, that as interest in criminal and penal history stirred and revived, a number of accomplished works of scholarship were published in the following decades.

Although I was a research student at the Cambridge Institute of Criminology in the early 1970s I got to know Sir Leon and to spend time with him only in the last twenty years or so. Our conversations ran the usual gamut, from the personal and professional to current affairs. He was intensely interested in politics in all its variety, which to the end he discussed in a shorthand manner showing complete familiarity with national and international developments and their various nuances. His life's work had been, in large part, a study of politics and ethics in the context of the legal and penal processes. He was well-informed about the situation in Northern Ireland and its impact on Anglo-Irish relations. In 1979, as the conflict entered another bloody and brutal phase, Radzinowicz and his close colleague, Roger Hood, examined the nineteenth-century history of the political offender in Europe – where he or she, at least in theory, was seen as a creature apart from the ordinary criminal. They contrasted this with the treatment of the Chartists, two groups of Irish offenders (the Fenians and the Dynamitards) and the female suffragists. Despite a provision in the 1877 Prison Act easing conditions for those sentenced for sedition (largely a dead letter) and ameliorations made necessary by prisoners' health or by political expedience, the traditional English line remained intact – the politically motivated offender would have no 'special exemption from the criminal law and its mode of enforcement' (Radzinowicz and Hood 1979: 148).

Examining different groups of Irish political offenders over a more extended timescale, I draw rather different conclusions to those of Radzinowicz and Hood. Indeed, had they published their essay ten years later they would have found a much-changed penal regime for political offenders in Northern Ireland, and quite different politics in place (McEvoy 2001: 361–9). British constitutional doctrine insists that in a democracy the criminal process must in its operation (as distinct from policy-setting) be separated from the executive and politics. The history of Irish political offenders – some of whom, let us remember, committed crimes of exceptional brutality, violence and destruction – shows what a fragile thing this doctrine is, and with what ease and speed it can be swept aside. It also shows how great a challenge the conscionable offender can pose to the democratic structure; how punishment rather than being an infliction may be an opportunity for the militant to justify and intensify the political struggle; and how a liberal democracy may be faced with seemingly insoluble dilemmas. But expediency is not always inferior to principle and may at times even have a certain moral grandeur. Its pragmatism and ironic detachment were, after all, what ensnared Leon Radzinowicz so thoroughly in the British political enterprise.

Given his interests and knowledge of the field, Sir Leon was enthusiastic and encouraging when I embarked on a study of the conscionable offender in the English penal process. He had been animated and vexed by Mrs Thatcher's April 1981 simplistic 'A crime is a crime is a crime' response to demands for the restoration of special category status by political offenders in Northern Ireland (O'Malley 1990: 60). While sharing the deep concerns of all constitutional politicians about the seemingly intractable problems posed by paramilitary activity and the politics of Northern Ireland, he clung to an older view of the political offender and did not see criminalisation as an appropriate or practical policy. Time proved him to be correct in this assessment.

From time to time I had the immense benefit of discussing with Sir Leon the work from which this short essay is drawn. He occasionally commented in detail on my drafts and made a number of suggestions on approach and the eventual shape of the publication. His encouragement was no light thing – no mere exercise in politeness – and one received it always mixed with questions, objections and exhortations to make further improvements. His intellectual style was always combative, made palatable by the charm and humour with which he laced his remarks.

History, politics, punishment and Irish affairs are therefore entirely appropriate ingredients to contribute to a volume commemorating this remarkable man. Had he been able, like Tom Sawyer, to be present at his own obsequies, or to peruse this volume, it is as certain as could be that his delight at the honour would be mingled with a number of modest proposals for improvements – and some of those would undoubtedly hit their mark.

Finding a book

What follows is drawn from a wider historical project which has been under way for some years (McConville 1981 and 1995). This particular topic – the punishment of conscionable offenders – was not part of the original research agenda, a history of penal ideas and administration in England. In writing about 'ordinary' offenders and their imprisonment, however, various apparently exceptional cases, challenges to policy and procedure – and stubborn resistance to change – thrust themselves forward. Still I continued, regarding these as anomalies and exceptions, obstacles in my path, interesting if lengthy footnotes at best. Eventually, however, it could not be gainsaid that the conscionable offender had to be addressed in any study of the mainstream, since he or she periodically and repeatedly confronted and redirected penal policy. For the conscionable, trial and imprisonment can be the continuation of politics – and sometimes war – by other means. He or she questions the very nature of criminality, the reach of the criminal law, and tests current scales of culpability and desert. Frequently these offenders have turned the doctrine of deterrence on its head: martyrs consecrate protest movements – especially those which embrace violence. Special laws have had to be brought in, and many questions of justice and equity posed. Having tested criminal and penal administration in many ways and tested conventional doctrines of equity, political and other con-scionable offenders returned to freedom, frequently fortified in their cause, their moral stature enhanced, their movements reinforced. Sometimes – certainly not always – as free men and women they became significant contributors to penal policy debates and threw their experiences into wider political and ethical discussions, helping to reorient our views of the ordinary offender.

Forced by these important and inescapable considerations to recognise that this group of offenders offered a distinctive and potentially productive approach to penal policy, I planned a new volume, to deal with Irish political offenders alongside other conscionable lawbreakers from about the middle of the nineteenth century until after the First World War. This span of time marked the rise and establishment of representative popular democracy. Much of that data has now been collected. It includes overzealous imperialists, Chartists and other labour and union groups, rates-resisters, female suffragists and conscientious objectors, as well as smaller and perhaps less well-known groups such as anti-vaccinationists, anti-educationalists and a variety of religious offenders, from those who broke the ritual laws of the Church of England to the public order offences of the early Salvation Army.

Once the data had been ordered and preliminary steps taken in their shaping into a narrative, an awkwardness arose. It was a problem of accommodation: these tenants would not live together. Irish political offenders refused to be squeezed into a couple of chapters in a book dealing with conscionable offenders at large for two main reasons – the sheer volume and variety of trouble they caused, and the fact that the politics of the Anglo-Irish conflict over a period of some 75 years could not be subsumed into issues of English domestic policy and administration: that was what the whole ruckus was about. There is also the fact that although Anglo-Irish politics are essentially not very complex, they are very complicated and no scholarly approach can sidestep those complications. So with daunting ease two books grew out of one, fairly naturally and logically.

Among the issues that attract me to this material, sprouting from the mass of data from whichever angle it is contemplated, are the following: How does a penal system based on stigma, shame, submission and the demonstrable moral failure of the offender cope with those who insist that their virtue is tested, validated and magnified by their ordeal, and that the odium of criminality is cast upon their captors? What happens to a system of administration the structure of which assumes the pliability and obedience of the outcast, isolated and despised offender, when this assumption meets the fact that outside groups sustain, cherish and glorify such a person? How far does the model of representative popular democracy justify the criminalisation of those who act outside its processes and what happens when that electorate splits on sectional lines? Starting at a time when the franchise, though reformed, was hardly representative, and coming forward to a time when it was more though hardly fully representative, is there any weight in the notion that as the dogma of the popular mandate solidifies and is embedded in professional politics, tolerance of the conscionable offender declines and official and political discretion are restricted? Does this then lead to change by crisis? What part does punishment play in the reinforcement of a political movement, and when punishment is sought, what response can the structure of law usefully make? Wrapping many of these together – how does a society with reasonably democratic values, including the rule of law, deal with those who have broken the law, sometimes with extreme violence, but whose crimes have not been motivated by personal malice or gain or stained by moral turpitude? History, as always, is contemporary.

Irish political offenders

These issues can be illustrated and presented in at least an introductory manner by briefly examining the passage through the criminal and penal process of three groups of Irish revolutionists – the Young Irelanders of 1848, the Dynamitards of the 1880s and the IRA of 1919–21.

The Young Irelanders

This small group of self-appointed leaders of an unorganised and ravaged peasantry, and some urban would-be Jacobins, came together in the late 1840s – partly in reaction to the increasingly dictatorial leadership of Irish constitutional nationalism by Daniel O'Connell, the great Catholic Emancipist. They were spurred into action by the awful events of the famine years in Ireland, and drew inspiration and energy from the '48ers – the revolutionary upsurge which swept across Europe in that year – particularly the February Revolution in France (Duffy 1883; Davis 1987).

The supposed leader of this movement was William Smith O'Brien. He was a self-conscious member of the old Irish aristocracy and his associates in the leadership of the Irish Confederation (their militant alternative to O'Connell's Loyal Repeal Association) were educated and professional men. They had rudimentary organisational powers, were strong on rhetoric, fierce on honour, and talked themselves over the cliff into revolutionary actions which were both hopelessly premature and futile, and for which they had not the slightest aptitude or stomach.

One of them, John Mitchel, was perhaps the most vitriolic writer of his generation (Dillon 1888). His inflammatory goads, taunts and exhortations so alarmed the British government that it rushed through a custom-made law which proved useful against Irish rebels until modern times – the Treason Felony Act 1848. This was intended to deal with offences which fell between treason and sedition, and transformed certain forms of sedition from a misdemeanour to a felony – entailing a much longer sentence and the confiscation of property (the last allowing the seizure of printing presses and publishing houses). No one in Parliament had the slightest doubt that the Bill was intended to deal with Mitchel and his immediate associates: the principle that a public law should not be brought in to deal with a private person was set aside. The legislative dimension of criminal justice has on occasion been as much distorted by governments seeking to deal with political offenders as have the procedural and penal dimensions. The doctrine of the separation of powers has suffered accordingly. Despite the passage of the Bill (crammed through to Royal Assent in the few days when some 300,000 and 500,000 Chartists were due to present their third and final monster petition to Parliament and revolution was feared), Mitchel zestfully continued to publish inflammatory articles, was duly rounded up, put before an undoubtedly packed jury, tried (though he eagerly proclaimed his guilt) and sentenced to 14 years' transportation. Further trials and sentences followed when other publishers provocatively followed in his footsteps. The leaders of the Irish Confederation willed themselves to think that in Ireland's fraught social and economic condition only a spark was needed to start a general conflagration: they also feared a pre-emptive round-up, since Habeas Corpus was suspended. In the French style a Directory was set up. This was simply more dangerous posing, since it apparently never met and its members immediately dispersed. There followed an interlude of dream-like choreography. Some went among the peasantry – a kind of revolutionary progress with banners – and eventually encountered and opened fire on a police column. After this hopeless and meaningless engagement in a cabbage-plot the leaders drifted apart, were arrested and put on trial. Four were found guilty of treason and sentenced to the usual aggravated death penalty – to be drawn on a hurdle to a place of execution, hanged until dead, bodies quartered and disposed of as Her Majesty might direct. The government promptly commuted these atavistic sentences to transportation for life.

There ensued a bizarre legal battle. It was argued that treason committed in Ireland was a category of offence *sui generis*, certainly not a misdemeanour but neither was it a felony, subject by commutation to transportation. O'Brien and his co-convicts hoped to remain imprisoned in Ireland, or even to avoid penalty altogether, since the government would not execute them. To clear up doubts, and despite murmurs in the Commons about retroactive legislation, an Act was passed – the Transportation for Treason (Ireland) Act 1849 – and O'Brien and his colleagues were dispatched to Van Diemen's Land. Another constitutional principle had been breached.

Gentlemen convicts

There was immediate government acknowledgement of the exceptional nature of these offenders. Their offences were acknowledged to be political and no attempt was made to degrade them to the status of common criminals: almost as importantly, all were acknowledged to be gentlemen. These two considerations interlocked, since a gentleman who committed a criminal offence of selfish gain or immorality – fraud, murder, theft, rape – was deemed to have forfeited his status: his act had sullied and repudiated it and transmuted him into the baser sort. In the transportation rolls there are many such gentlemen turned into convicts, and dealt with accordingly (though they frequently secured more congenial employment than labouring in the penal colony). But through a type of penal theology O'Brien and his associates were accorded a seemingly impossible status – truly gentlemen yet truly convicts. Fighting their legal battle to avoid transportation, the Young Irelanders had received exceptionally lenient treatment in Dublin's Newgate and Richmond prisons. Both were run by local officials and supervised by personages sympathetic to or affected by nationalist sentiment. Each man in the Young Ireland leadership, therefore, was allocated a room with virtually unrestricted contact with the outside world. They brought in pictures, books and carpets and made themselves wholly comfortable. As leader, and social superior, O'Brien had two rooms, and the chief officer's wife cooked for him the supplies sent in daily by his family.

Instructions were issued that all the men were to be transported as gentlemen, separated from other convicts and wearing their own clothes, and not offered any indignity. Mitchel was given a 'very handsome' cabin, furnished with couches, chairs and a table. Subject only to the restriction that he be escorted while on deck, he did as he wished. He was thus placed in a position superior to any ship's officer, except the captain. Mitchel was first conveyed to the convict station at

Bermuda where he also enjoyed superior accommodation, although he had the hardship of being the only prisoner in his class. For reasons of security (a possible Irish-American rescue) and health he was removed after eight months and told he would be sent to the Cape Colony, where he would be given conditional liberty. In the event, the Cape colonists refused to allow any convicts to land (an important event in imperial history) and after some months at moorings Mitchel went to Van Diemen's Land – joining his later-sentenced companions who had arrived some months previously (Mitchel n.d.). All had been treated with great liberality. Their descriptions of the voyages (some of which survive in well-kept journals) come close to tropical versions of the Grand Tour. Some subsequently found it expedient to manufacture suffering, but the exercise was half-hearted and lacking in conviction.

Honour

On arrival at Hobart Town, the men were given tickets of leave, and, bound by their parole, were free to live as they wished in their several police districts. Some took to farming, one to medicine, two to tutoring, another to running a newspaper; others had sufficient funds not to work, and spent their time riding, walking and writing. One was successful in courting and marrying a local girl. There was a sizeable free society in Van Diemen's Land and the men were hospitably received in respectable and well-to-do households. They had absolutely nothing to do with the ordinary Irish or English convicts.

The question of escape arose, and the related difficulty of honour. The first man to go, Terence Bellew McManus, fled on 15 January 1851. He had been briefly imprisoned as a punishment for leaving his assigned district. On his release he did not reinstate his parole and escaped to San Francisco, where he received an effusive welcome from the Irish community, which in the wake of the Irish famines was seething with anti-British feeling. Another of the group resigned his parole by giving 24 hours' notice to the district magistrate, evading arrest, and also reached the US. Two of his colleagues, John Mitchel and John Martin, investigated his escape, considered it to be dishonourable, and wrote and asked him to return. O'Donohoe had three times been imprisoned in the colony for various offences, and considered that these repeated punishments freed him of the obligations of his parole. He too reached San Francisco.

By now the Irish '48ers in America had accumulated substantial funds, some of which had been intended for revolution in Ireland. They had established a Directory, and it sent an emissary to Van Diemen's Land to arrange O'Brien's escape. Having served four years in the Colony, and in hope of a pardon, O'Brien decided not to go. John Mitchel took his place. Etiquette had to be observed: Mitchel had, after all, set himself up as an adjudicator in these matters. Accompanied by his Irish-American rescuer he presented himself to the magistrate, withdrew his parole and, with a certain amount of menace, mounted a fast horse and rode off. He made a successful departure from the island after some weeks in hiding and followed the now well-worn course to San Francisco and thence to New York.

O'Brien, Martin and O'Doherty were given conditional pardons not long after Mitchel had reached New York. Their honourable conduct in not escaping (notice the different views of honour) was cited by Home Secretary Palmerston in granting the pardons. At first debarred from entering the UK, full pardons were granted at the end of the Crimean War and Martin and O'Brien returned to Ireland.

Class will tell

In a postscript to the Young Ireland insurrection (if that is what it can be called) there was in September 1849 an abortive attack on a police barracks; several of the attackers were captured. These were not gentlemen and were transported to Van Diemen's Land as ordinary convicts: three for 14 years and four for seven years each. All went through the normal convict stages – confinement in a penal station while at labour in a convict gang, then passholders, tickets-of-leave and finally conditional pardons. Much the same happened to a party of Irish Confederation sympathisers in England, five of whom were transported for life. One was a kind of gentleman – an art student – and he was granted a ticket-of-leave on his arrival in the colony. He set up a business, his fiancée followed him from Ireland and on receipt of his full pardon continued to live in what was now called Tasmania (Davis 1991). There is no record of contact between the Young Ireland leadership and their belated followers, though all were in Van Diemen's Land at the same time. Liberty certainly, but little equality and fraternity.

There is a curiosity here. The leaders and inciters of the movement were treated less harshly than their followers. That class indulgence was the issue is clear beyond a doubt. Apart from their followers, O'Brien and the others were in Van Diemen's Land at the same time as three Chartists – John Frost, William Jones and Zephania Williams. These men had been convicts for several years. Theirs was the same offence as O'Brien's. Their treason was an armed attack on Newport, South Wales, in November 1839. Although they received some indulgence in being allowed to wear their own clothes and being put to clerical tasks in the penal establishment rather than manual labour, they received none of the wider advantages given to the Young Irelanders. Frost had to wait for 13 years for his ticket-of-leave and (with Jones and Williams) received his conditional pardon at the same time as Smith and O'Brien only because the disparity in the treatment of the two groups had become so embarrassingly obvious. Earlier appeals for tickets-of-leave and conditional pardons were rejected.

The Dynamitards

In 1867 Alfred Nobel patented dynamite. In this and related nitroglycerine-based explosives exiled Irish revolutionaries in the United States saw the end of the British Empire. Almost 100 times more powerful than gunpowder, and when absorbed into an inert substance (such as certain earths), dynamite was easily moved and safe to handle. It could be easily concealed, exploded remotely and – a critical consideration – could be manufactured from readily available materials. The Irish, of course, were not the only revolutionists to see the possibilities of dynamite and similar explosives, and the March 1881 assassination of Czar Alexander II by Nihilists was the start of a decade or so of dynamite scares in Europe. Nihilists and anarchists apparently lurked everywhere.

This is not the place to provide an account of the dynamite campaign in England and Scotland – although it was a true terrorist venture – the indiscriminate use of explosions to bring terror to the populace at large and therefore pressure on the government. Bombs were placed in the London Underground, in left-luggage offices at mainline stations, at gasworks, at public buildings and at barracks. Two groups were involved. One was directed by Jeremiah O'Donovan Rossa, imprisoned in 1865 for his part in the Fenian conspiracy, in 1871 given release by Gladstone on condition of expatriation and since then an exile in New York. The other was the Clan na Gael (still in existence) which emerged from the faction-fighting among Irish-American revolutionaries in the late 1860s, and which acted as fundraiser and paymaster for Irish revolutionaries. Rossa advertised for money and for men. If Irish-Americans would give him both, he promised to hurl the 'fires of hell' at England. Clan na Gael was more circumspect but was in exactly the same business. At one point the two cooperated.

Bombs could not easily be smuggled into the United Kingdom but could be made from ingredients easily available from chemist shops, paint shops and chemical suppliers. (In New York Rossa sponsored and advertised dynamite classes ($30 the full course) and published a detailed 25¢ pamphlet on its manufacture.) Rossa and the Clan had decided that no bombers would be taken from Fenian and other ranks in

Ireland or Britain, since those must be supposed to be penetrated and compromised by the government. This was only half a smart decision, since the police did not have a long thread to follow when men of Irish-American appearance, dress and speech began to buy up quantities of sulphuric and nitric acid and glycerine. That, luck and some carelessness meant that by 1883 ten Dynamitards were serving life sentences, mainly at Chatham convict prison; there they would remain until the release on medical grounds of four in 1896, and the remaining six in 1898. A few obvious dupes in Scotland received shorter sentences.

The story of the imprisonment of these men can be summarised. They were subjected to the full rigours of a convict system intended to repress crime and crush the malefactor, and minutely designed and carefully operated to do so. Coarse and barely sufficient food, hard and exhausting labour, no recreation or stimulation and long hours in a cold, bleak and carefully comfortless cell were wrapped in a sequestration penetrated only by tenuous and infrequent contacts with the outside world. Hope itself was extinguished. On reception all had been told that this had to be endured for at least twenty years before the government would even begin to consider release. With the bleakest of expectations, kept apart from each other yet forced to mix with the criminals they despised, and whose company, language and conduct they regarded as part of their deliberate degradation by the government, these dynamite prisoners were forced upon their own resources, which several simply did not have.

For the greater part of their confinement, the Dynamitards were forced to face the fact that they had been forgotten or rejected by their fellow countrymen. Despite it all, some endured and resumed political activity on release. Thomas Clarke became the driving force behind the 1916 Rising in Dublin, but even he admitted to the severity of his ordeal. Several of his comrades became insane, or successfully pretended it, and were released on that ground. One, Patrick Daly, recovered sufficiently to become one of the senior revolutionaries in Ireland, and to undertake extensive lecture tours in Britain and America. But penal servitude prematurely aged the men, left ineradicable psychological scars and was physically crushing.

Here we have a very different story to that of the Young Irelanders. Why? Class was not an issue. With one or two exceptions these were working men. None had influence or connections in conventional political circles. And whereas Young Ireland had emphasised honour to a point that Don Quixote would have found excessive, these were thoroughly modern terrorists. And terrorism was completely rejected, even by old-style Fenianism which regarded it as unlikely to rouse the nation, besmirching of national honour and therefore wicked as well as futile. A section of Fenianism had joined the wider nationalist movement and had moved firmly into constitutional channels. Re-energised and disciplined, this coalition was winning concessions and victories, and saw its future in eventual independence towards which Home Rule was the first step. Rural dissatisfaction had been substantially reduced by the land reforms which began in the 1870s, and though it rose again in the Land War of the 1880s, success diminished it once more. A relatively secure and prosperous proprietary peasantry became established. Many religious grievances had been settled. The Dynamitards were Americans or Irish exiles and had conceived and waged their campaign without reference to the Irish in Ireland or the consequences for the now large Irish communities in England and Scotland. They were not only physically isolated from that wider community on whose behalf they claimed to act: they were also politically and morally detached.

Why then from the early 1890s did constitutional politicians such as John Redmond, leader of the Parnellite and minority section of the now split Irish Parliamentary Party, begin to seek clemency for the Dynamitards? Redmond and his colleagues needed to assert their own nationalist credentials and to outflank any prospect of reviving extremism, as well as their clericalist rivals in parliamentary nationalism (Ryan 1945: 173–5). It was widely agreed, they insisted, that past disorder in Ireland had been the outcome of British misrule. Gladstone had appeared to embrace that argument when he secured the Fenian amnesty in 1869–71. There was almost – but not quite – a statement that the wickedness of the Dynamitards was a measure of the past injustice to Ireland. To the British government they put the argument that in peaceful and settled times it was best not to leave any sense of grievance – close the book and move on.

It is not only in romantic literature and opera that suffering can transform the most degraded; extreme hardship had transformed the Dynamitards' moral standing in the Irish political scene. Widely reviled when convicted, their torment and the harshness of their convict experience enabled them to be cast as victims rather than be remembered for their callous disregard for life and property. Despite claims that they had been treated with exceptional severity, a close reading of their files shows that their hardship and suffering arose simply from being treated as ordinary convicts. The campaign to free them started on health grounds, and when the men were released their state – widely reported in the British, Irish and American press – the passage of time and the security of Ireland itself overshadowed their culpability. From being objects of execration they became objects of pity – their crimes largely forgotten and the government portrayed as pitiless, even criminal.

The Irish Republican Army

The years 1916–22 were full of incident in Ireland and England, as the Anglo-Irish war developed to its full paramilitary, terrorist and counter-terrorist climax. By the concluding months civil authority had completely broken down in large sections of the countryside and many towns. Raids, killings, ambushes, robberies, arson and explosions filled the daily newspapers. To counter IRA terror and guerilla activities, criminal law and procedure were substantially set aside – first by various forms of martial law, and then by unofficial killings and retaliation by Crown forces, and finally by such official measures as hostage-taking, carrying hostages prominently in military convoys and collective reprisals. Elements in the hastily recruited Black and Tans and Auxiliaries were out of control, and their outrages were tolerated, denied and justified (and possibly encouraged) by ministers. This crescendo of violence, with associated lying and hypocrisy on both sides, soured Anglo-Irish relations for a good half-century and more.

Against this background of lawlessness in Ireland, large numbers of internees, remands and convicted prisoners were transferred to England: Irish prisons simply could not cope. The Home Office, already scarred by earlier experiences of Irish political prisoners, did whatever bureaucrats could do to resist the transfers: keep them in Ireland or let the War Office look after them. Cabinet decided otherwise.

Hunger strikes

The Irish political prisoners had been hunger-striking for some years – sometimes with great success. The threat of hunger-striking ensured political status and various privileges for internees, some remands and some convicted prisoners, but battles were fought over who qualified for this category, and there were several advances and retreats. Where granted, political status conferred an extremely liberal regime – free mixing with one's fellow politicals ('association'), separation from ordinary criminals, exemption from a reception bath, haircutting and shaving, and from work. Smoking was allowed, as was one's own clothing, outside food, a moderate allowance of alcohol, books and newspapers at the prisoner's own expense. This amounted to little more than the inconvenience of civil detention: as few restrictions as were compatible with imprisonment.

Sinn Féin (by this time the political arm of the IRA) had come to see imprisonment as a political and training opportunity. It had constructed a sophisticated support organisation (itself a useful assessment, filtering and recruitment device) which raised funds, organised visits and comforts, and agitated. This organisation was deft in its use of the hunger strikes to gather support in Ireland and in Irish communities in Britain, the United States and Australia. Waverers could be won to the Sinn Féin camp, while supporters were reinforced in their beliefs. Irish nationalists whose path was political rather than physical force were caught up in the protests and petitions. Some of this was an anxiety not to be outflanked by Sinn Féiners, some a general nationalist anger combined with sympathy for a countryman apparently starving to death in an English or Irish prison cell. By the end of the Anglo-Irish war virtually all those in ordinary prisons (as distinct from some 200 in convict prisons, serving sentences of penal servitude) enjoyed political status: all pretence that a crime is a crime is a crime had been dropped.

The line for the British government was drawn not in terms of the conditions but the fact of confinement. This was tested in the summer and autumn of 1920 by the hunger strike of Terence MacSwiney, Lord Mayor and IRA Commander of Cork. Arrested in possession of a police signal which had been intercepted and deciphered, MacSwiney was sentenced to two years' hard labour by a District Court Martial. 'I have decided I shall be free alive or dead in a month as I shall take no food for the period of my sentence,' MacSwiney told the court. Transferred to England he refused food for 74 days and died in Brixton prison on 25 October 1920.

MacSwiney's demand was not for an amelioration of prison conditions (which with some reluctance the government had been and would be forced to concede), but for his freedom. Having been tried by a properly constituted court on the clearest of evidence (which he did not contest), had MacSwiney been released the administration of justice in Ireland would inevitably have collapsed. So the government reasoned, and this conclusion was probably correct. The spectacle of a brave if misguided man starving to death attracted worldwide attention, incensed Irish Catholics at home and abroad and caused fissures in English opinion well beyond the usual liberal and progressive circles. MacSwiney's death was self-wrought, but this fact was swamped in a torrent of anti-British feeling. No other Irish prisoner tried to win liberty through hunger strike after MacSwiney, and after another and much less noticed death at Cork prison other strikes then being staged petered out. The cost of this victory (if so it could be called) for British policy and support in Ireland was enormous and the political damage was irreversible. A prisoner had won an important battle in the continuing war.

Security and control

By this time Irish society was polarised, and the vast bulk of Irish Roman Catholics actively or passively supported the rebels, as did sections of the Irish communities in Britain, the US and Australia. Prisoners' treatment was closely scrutinised, and effective and efficient means were used to bring their complaints, real, exaggerated or fabricated, to public notice and international attention. The Irish administration at Dublin Castle sought whatever political advantage it could by haphazardly allowing political status. The Prison Commissioners in England tried to control the Irish political prisoners by keeping them in small groups and distributing them around the country. This was not always possible. But in whatever numbers these Irish prisoners were an administrative nightmare. Any attempt to impose criminal discipline on them brought an outcry from the outside, and defiance inside. Confrontation was sought and wise officials evaded it whenever possible. The hunger strike was an ever-present fear.

The security facilities at English prisons were fairly minimal – ordinary criminals were generally a docile lot and rarely attempted escape. They had nowhere to go and every hand was against them in what was an essentially law-abiding and authority-respecting society. With the Irish politicals almost the exact opposite was true: their comrades in the organisation aided escapes and sympathisers secreted and repatriated them. With its staff depleted by the war and its establishments shrinking because of the decline in criminality, the English prison service had neither the resources nor the energy to cope. A number of spectacular escapes were only part of the story. Several prisons were placed under special watch because armed attacks were expected from outside. A major riot at Dartmoor came close to taking over that prison, raising the possibility of loss of life as well as major damage to property, the reputation of the British government, and the morale of its armed forces. In the files there is certainly a sense that officialdom had been strained beyond its resources. Governors of prisons were left to get on with things as best they could – in essence temporising and negotiating – but on at least one occasion borrowing a machine-gun from the army. The IRA in England had shown that it could mobilise thousands of people outside a prison for several days on end; disorder, violence and international attention followed. Imprisonment continued to exist – but only just. Contingency plans of all kinds existed to use the highly unwilling army. Had the Anglo-Irish Truce not been signed in July 1921 it is hard to see how breakdown in the prisons could have been avoided.

In the months of the negotiations which took place after the Truce and before the signing of the Treaty, the Irish political prisoners understandably became more restive and the officials more intimidated, not least by the politics of any action they might take, or not take. Within hours of the Treaty being signed on 6 December 1921 all internees were released. Convicted prisoners had to wait for a month until the Dáil – split 57–64 – ratified the Treaty. The same Under-Secretary at Dublin Castle who had issued internment and deportation orders for the British government now under the authority of the Irish Provisional Government issued a list of those to be released – 534 serving long sentences of penal servitude and imprisonment: some very serious offences up to and including murder. Legal processes had now become so marginal that only a letter was needed to effect the releases, but even that was overlooked and later had to be demanded for the record.

What lessons?

There are many curiosities and ironies here. There were, for example, in the same prisons as the Irish rebels conscientious objectors who were treated considerably worse than the Irish: their offence was refusing to fight for the Empire, not fighting against it. Their support in the wider community, however, was both small and marginal and rarely effective. Secure in their privileged confinement, the Irish sometimes passed them newspapers, food and comforts. Having its activists in English prisons was an inconvenience but also undoubtedly was a major boost for Irish republicanism. Yet what was government to do? The most basic objectives of criminal justice are the protection of the state through the suppression of disorder, and the reduction of crime. The problem for government in dealing with conscionable offenders – especially those with a substantial following – is that conventional policies can produce results opposite to those being sought: having passed through a type of political sound-barrier government needs a very different set of controls. Using the familiar levers, disorder can be increased unexpectedly and alarmingly within the community and penal institutions. The political or other cause which the government intends to suppress can be reinforced and its appeal magnified. Inaction is unthinkable, since that would be an abdication of government, yet action within the conventions of a liberal democracy can rebound. No democratic government has resolved this conundrum.

More broadly, what we see here are the limits of criminal justice in response to what Winston Churchill once told his wife was the prime rule of politics: necessity. Under pressure of numbers, violence, international relations and inadequate resources, criminal law and the penal process have been and will be simply set aside. This has sometimes happened under circumstances where few would argue that the government has chosen the lesser evil. This leaves us in a curious moral position with those conscionable offenders whose strength and ability to inflict injury on the national interest fall short of the law of necessity. Are the bombs of animal rights' militants more wicked than those of Irish paramilitaries? Surely only force, support and political necessity dictate policy, and is that kind of discrimination not what government is for? But having accepted this, what price the language of justice? What then are the principles of justice which we should seek to apply to the conscionable offender? What is political crime? Does it exist only when it fails, for prospering, who calls it crime? And in societies more segmented, and as politics become more professional and inaccessible, how are we to deal with those who take criminal actions to further their cause? Is the tyranny of the majority wholly defensible – and if not, what alternatives can democracy and law offer?

'A fine long list of questions,' I can hear Sir Leon say, 'but do you have any answers?'

Bibliography

Most of the essay derives from research on archives, special collections and contemporary journals and publications which I conducted for my forthcoming book *Irish Political Prisoners 1848–1922: theatres of war*. This will be published by Routledge in mid-2002, and contains an extensive bibliography and guide to sources. I have, however, included some references here to direct the reader who may wish to explore specific topics.

Statutes

Treason Felony Act 1848: 11&12 Vict., c.12.
Transportation for Treason (Ireland) Act 1849: 12 & 13 Vict., c.27.
Prison Act 1877: 40 & 41 Vict., c.21.

Books and essays

Costello, F.J. (1995) *Enduring the Most: The Life and Death of Terence MacSwiney*. Dingle: Brandon Book Publishers.
Davis, R. (1991) 'Young Ireland Prisoners in Van Diemen's Land' (unpublished). Tasmania Historical Research Association, *Papers and Proceedings*, 38, 3 and 4.
Davis, R. (1987) *The Young Ireland Movement*. Dublin: Gill and Macmillan.
Dillon, W. (1888) *Life of John Mitchel*, 2 vols. London: Kegan Paul, Trench & Co.

Duffy, C.G. (1883) *Four Years of Irish History, 1845-49.* London and Paris: Cassell, Petter, Galpin & Co.

Holdsworth, W.S. (1903–72) *A History of English Law.* London: Methuen.

McConville, S. (1981) *A History of English Prison Administration.* London and Boston: Routledge & Kegan Paul.

McConville, S. (1995) *English Local Prisons 1860–1900: Next Only to Death.* London and New York: Routledge.

McEvoy, K. (2001) *Paramilitary Imprisonment in Northern Ireland: Resistance, Management and Release.* Oxford: Oxford University Press.

Mitchel, John (n.d.) *Jail Journal or, Five Years in British Prisons.* London: R. & T. Washbourne.

O'Malley, P. (1990) *Biting at the Grave: The Irish Hunger Strikes and the Politics of Despair.* Boston, MA: Beacon Press, 1990.

Radzinowicz, L. (1948–86) *A History of English Criminal Law and Its Administration from 1750,* 5 vols; vol. 5 with Roger Hood. London: Stevens & Sons.

Radzinowicz, L. (1999) *Adventures in Criminology.* London and New York: Routledge.

Radzinowicz, L. and Hood, R. (1979) 'The Status of the Political Prisoner in England: The Struggle for Recognition', *Virginia Law Review,* 65 (8), 1421–81.

Royal Commission on Capital Punishment, 1949–53, Parliamentary Papers 1952–3, Cmnd. 8932, VII, 677.

Ryan, M.F. (1945) *Fenian Memories.* Dublin: M.H. Gill & Son.

Chapter 4

The English police: a unique development?

Clive Emsley

When Sir Leon Radzinowicz began his monumental *History of English Criminal Law* during the 1940s the history of the English police was not a subject that generated much academic interest. Even by the time that Volume 4, *Grappling for Control,* appeared in 1968 with roughly half of its focus on the spread of modern, bureaucratic policing in Victorian England, there was little else of much weight on the subject. The history of the development of the English police remained largely the preserve of ex-policemen or enthusiasts for the police like the former Indian Army officer, tea and rubber planter, Charles Reith (1938, 1940, 1943, 1948, 1952, 1956; and see Hejellemo 1977). There was a naivety about Reith's Whiggish view of the superior English system compounded by a woeful ignorance of police developments on continental Europe and in North America. Radzinowicz's acute critical faculties ensured that he avoided Reith's naivety; moreover, rather than assertion, he provided interesting comparative material on police development, mainly from France. However, he also possessed a Whiggish perspective. Radzinowicz agreed with Macaulay that 'the history of England is the history of progress' and he saw this as being 'as true of the criminal law … as of the other social institutions of which it is a part' (Radzinowicz 1948: ix). The aim of what follows is twofold: first to assess how far Radzinowicz's view of English police development holds up when the context is expanded beyond the confines of the history of the law as has happened with the research of the last decade or so; and second to assess the extent to which that development was peculiarly English.

Policing in England

The research that went into *A History of English Criminal Law* is formidable and the book remains a mine of information and explication on legal developments and procedures. Volume 1, for example, contains a hundred pages on eighteenth-century capital statutes that constitute an indispensable starting point for any work on the Bloody Code (Radzinowicz 1948: 611–98). Similarly Radzinowicz's discussion of the rewards and Tyburn Tickets that underpinned entrepreneurial detective policing remains unsurpassed and is essential reading for anyone exploring how offenders were pursued and prosecuted during the eighteenth century (Radzinowicz 1956a: Part I). However, any historian subscribing to the idea of history as progress is inclined to assume that significant and lasting change has been for the better, that reformers urging such change were right, and that change came about because of the recognition of the validity of the reformers' arguments as put forward in various books and pamphlets. This is not the place to embark on a discussion of how individuals read and interpret books and other reading matter. Nevertheless, it is worth remarking how difficult it is to make assessments of this sort for the past, as, for example, has been shown by recent debates on the 'reading revolution' in early modern Germany and the cultural and Enlightenment origins of the French Revolution (Engelsing 1974; Wittmann 1991; Chartier 1990; Darnton 1996). Part of the problem has been that historians, and perhaps especially those who see a progressive pattern to history, have too often assumed that the assessments of reformers were accurate, that 'sensible' people read and essentially understood them as such, and that, in general terms, ideas lead to action as a simple cause and effect without much recognition of the wider cultural, economic, political and social contexts in which the reformers' texts were read. The traditional interpretation has it that there were serious problems in the policing system of eighteenth-century England, that the reformers perceived these problems and highlighted them in various publications, and that politicians read these publications, were ultimately convinced and acted.

Henry Fielding, Sir John Fielding and Patrick Colquhoun have become a veritable holy trinity of eighteenth- and early nineteenth-century police reformers in the eyes of the Whig historians. Henry Fielding published a series of pamphlets and jury charges on the subjects of crime and police reform and, together with his half brother, Sir John, 'the blind beak', he significantly developed the Police Office in Bow Street, notably with its thief-takers, the celebrated 'Runners', and its publicity machine circulating details of suspects and things stolen.

Colquhoun acted as a stipendiary magistrate following the creation of six new Police Officers under the Middlesex Justices Act of 1792. He was instrumental in the creation of the Thames River Police. But he is probably best known for his *Treatise on the Police of the Metropolis* which first appeared in 1795 and ran through seven English editions in ten years. Radzinowicz was not the first to identify this holy trinity of police reformers, yet the depth of his research and the authority and power of his writing gave a new academic weight to this interpretation. More recently, however, historians have come to recognise the importance of other individuals and other agencies in developing the policing system of eighteenth- and early nineteenth-century London. Moreover, while little Whiggish history of early policing developments ventures outside the metropolis, it is clear that there were also important developments in the policing of the provinces of Hanoverian England.

The prevention and detection of crime, the maintenance of public order and the preservation of the state and status quo are all tasks that can fall under the rubric of modern policing. The Fieldings argued strongly for the former, but were critical of the intrusive nature of political policing in France that might be said to be essential for the preservation of the state (Radzinowicz 1956b: 6–7). And with regard to the maintenance of public order in times of crisis, it is unlikely that their proposed reforms would ever have led to a police system sufficient to confront a large number of determined rioters. The Fieldings' work with regard to policing, in particular the Bow Street thief-takers and Sir John's ambitious Grand Preventive Plan to develop his and his brother's system of information distribution (Styles 1983), focused essentially on the detection of crime. The short-lived horse patrol on the main thoroughfares during 1763–4 might have constituted a significant preventive measure, but it was terminated through lack of funds. Radzinowicz's treatment of the short life of this patrol is indicative of how the Whiggish perception coloured his interpretation. Radzinowicz wrote of the 'apathy indeed hostility of government' towards this measure which left Sir John feeling bitterly disappointed (Radzinowicz 1956b: 60–2). Sir John may indeed have felt bitterly disappointed, but whether the government can be criticised for apathy and hostility is a moot point. Historians have the luxury of being able to focus on single issues; so too do reformers. Politicians, however, are compelled to juggle many issues at the same time. George Grenville's government was never particularly stable. Grenville was not greatly liked by George III. He took over as first minister in April 1763 following the resignation of George's favourite the Earl of Bute, but his government had to reorganise with the death of the Earl of Egremont in August. Perhaps the most surprising thing is that Grenville ever offered to fund the horse patrol in October of that year. In the early months of the following year he was embroiled in the debate over the legality of General Warrants; at the same time he sought to cement his popularity by rigorous financial economy. In the latter regard he was helped by the conclusion of the Seven Years' War which enabled a significant reduction in taxation. Even a relatively small sum from the Treasury to finance a horse patrol for London would have been ammunition for his opponents. Radzinowicz noted the suggestion to Fielding from Charles Jenkinson, the Secretary of the Treasury, that the county of Middlesex should pay for such a patrol. To Radzinowicz, this was the central government forsaking its responsibilities. Yet Jenkinson's suggestion was in keeping with the overall system of government of eighteenth-century England where policing remained essentially a matter for local administration. Moreover, the creation of new offices funded by central government was increasingly viewed with suspicion as providing new opportunities for government patronage and influence.

There were significant improvements in forms of preventive policing in London during the eighteenth century that had little to do with the Fieldings, and everything to do with local government, sometimes with the encouragement of central government. The work of Elaine Reynolds has been important in reassessing these improvements, particularly the development in the night watches of the metropolis. Radzinowicz complained that 'the Legislature made no serious attempt to remedy' the shortcomings of the Westminster Police in the mid-eighteenth century, and implied criticism of the Westminster Constables Act of 1756 for leaving the night watches under parish control (Radzinowicz 1956b: 79–80). Blaming 'the Legislature' is easy and misses the point that much eighteenth-century legislation tended to be introduced not by governments but by individual members as private bills. The situation with respect to law and order in the metropolis was changing, and governments began to take more and more interest from the mid-century, yet this did not mean direct involvement and still less did it mean financial commitment. The Westminster Watch Act of 1774 was prepared and steered through Parliament, not by a minister, but by Sir Charles Whitworth, MP for Minehead. Whitworth was a government supporter and chaired parliamentary enquiries into the state of police in Westminster, but it was he who had to negotiate with the powerful London vestries and take cognisance of their suggestions before piloting the bill through the Commons (Reynolds 1998: 51–7). Radzinowicz described the 1774 Act as limited but 'useful and if properly administered, [it] might have resulted in some improvement'

(Radzinowicz 1956b: 81). Yet the criticism that he notes of the Act comes from a reforming committee of 1812 with its own agenda. Reynolds's work, drawing heavily on vestry minutes, shows Westminster vestries working together with each other to obtain and implement the Act and then setting their watching systems on an increasingly professional and hierarchical footing. Furthermore, she stresses that '[w]hile police authority [in London] did remain divided among several local bodies and officials, decentralization was not necessarily synonymous with defectiveness' (Reynolds 1998: 57). Reynolds is an American; the point might be made that American police forces are decentralised to this day, and it is not necessarily their decentralised nature that gives rise to concerns about their defects.

John Beattie's new study of crime and policing in the square mile of the City of London from the mid-seventeenth to the mid-eighteenth century describes similar developments. The City's commercial and financial elite jealously guarded their municipal independence; they used the legislature as and when it suited them. By the beginning of the eighteenth century the authorities within the City had recognised their need for a paid, regular watch and they sponsored legislation in Parliament to this end. Among the most significant Acts was that of 1737 which imposed a uniformity of watching across the City's wards and authorised the collection of a rate to fund the system. Evidence from the Old Bailey Sessions Papers reveals some of the watchmen to have been active and courageous in their pursuit of offenders. Over the same period there were also significant developments in the system of parish constables deployed through the City. The number of householders who served as constables in person declined over the century. They were replaced by hired men who, increasingly, appear to have taken the position on a regular basis as their living, or at least one component of it. The burdens of the constable increased, but the City authorities recognised this and offered financial inducements for extra work such as the apprehension of rogues and vagabonds, and the policing of crowds at public ceremonies and public punishments (Beattie 2001).

There were other policing improvements in the provinces of Hanoverian England and these were developed with little reference to the urgings of the Fieldings. County benches appear to have been sympathetic to some of Sir John's plans, but his proposal to reorganise the high constables of counties into crime fighters met with a cool response. The idea, formed in the context and with the priorities of London, was not thought to have much relevance for the counties and would have necessitated a major reorganisation of the role of high constable, a position generally filled by gentlemen of some substance.

Fielding's proposal was something that very few local magistrates were prepared to countenance (Styles 1983: 147–9). The high constable was a man of substance, but not so the petty constable. For a variety of reasons in the provinces, as in the City of London, the social status of these parish servants appears to have declined during the eighteenth century. At the same time their burdens, few of which involved criminal offenders, increased. Yet men could increasingly be found serving as constables with a degree of permanence and, it must be supposed, a degree of competence, or why else would they have been permitted to retain the position? In Essex semi-permanent constables and watchmen were active in detective policing on the border of the metropolis from at least the early 1780s. Contrary to the criticisms voiced by police reformers and echoed by Whig police historians, in other parishes of Essex and elsewhere, although they were not often proactive in cases of theft and in terms of wealth they occupied the bottom rung of the parish hierarchy, the constables were invariably 'literate, physically active and ex-perienced men' (King 2000: 65–79). Evidence for the City of York reveals similarly competent constables, and here the Common Informer, the functionary charged by the corporation with the supervision of the economic regulations of the city, increasingly acquired more general policing functions. In the middle of the century he was supervising other parish constables, particularly with reference to street lighting and the control of drunks and vagrants. Thomas Robson, the Informer from 1776 to 1796, began to adopt a thief-taking role; this was continued and developed by his successors, Joseph Pardoe and his sons (Haywood 1996; see also Williams 1999: 176–7). A complete picture of policing in eighteenth-century England requires more research, yet it is clear that the situation was not static, nor was the overall picture one of an archaic system in serious decline.

Throughout the eighteenth century crime rates, as reflected in the numbers of individuals indicted at assizes and quarter sessions, and concerns about crime appear to have fluctuated with war and peace and with dearth and plenty. The precise relationships, however, are not easy for the historian to unravel. The decision of victims to prosecute would seem to have had a more pronounced impact on indictment statistics than the level of crime, and it is not simply the case that dearth prompted more people to steal and that war removed a significant number of potential offenders – young men – from the country as soldiers and sailors. Nor was the same effect always felt. There seems to have been a general concern that peace, and the demobilisation of thousands of servicemen brutalised by war, would lead to an upsurge of crime (King 2000: 153–68). Such concerns appear to have been somewhat muted in the aftermath of the Seven Years' War when Grenville's government decided not to continue the Bow Street Horse Patrol, especially in comparison with the aftermath of the American War of Independence when the threat of an increase in crime was compounded by fears generated as a result of the suspension of transportation. In 1782–83, as demobilisation began in the wake of defeat in America, the government urged magistrates to be zealous in prosecuting offenders, it promoted new legislation toughening punishment and the control of suspect individuals, and it is from this time that it agreed to fund foot patrols working out of Bow Street along the main highways in and out of the metropolis.[1] Ten years later Britain was at war again. This war, qualitatively and quantitatively different from its eighteenth-century predecessors and intensified by a sharp ideological element, provided the backdrop to the career as a magistrate and to the writings of Patrick Colquhoun.

Radzinowicz believed that the government was wrong to appoint Richard Ford as Chief Magistrate at Bow Street in 1800 on the death of Sir William Addington. Ford, he insisted, was 'a man of far inferior ability' to Colquhoun. He concluded that Ford was selected either because it was the usual practice to appoint a justice already attached to the office or because Colquhoun would have been too controversial since he was committed to a fundamental reform that would have reduced Bow Street's pre-eminence in the hierarchy of Police Offices in London (Radzinowicz 1956b: 229). At this distance it is difficult to assess the respective abilities of Colquhoun and Ford. The former wrote about policing London and, through the creation of the Thames River Police, contributed to significant reform. However, Ford had been chief magistrate at Bow Street in all but name since 1794. He had played a key role in the government's assault on radicalism during the 1790s, liaising closely with the Home Office and assisting with the examinations for treason and sedition both there and before the Privy Council. Ford was no simple placeman but an able, hard-working and highly regarded government agent who had been entrusted with delicate tasks, notably the kind of political investigations which the Fieldings had criticised in the French context but which Pitt's government believed was necessitated by the ideological element of the French Revolutionary War and by the growth of British popular radicalism (Hone 1982: 69–70; Sparrow 1999: 17 and 177–8).[2] Colquhoun's celebrated *Treatise on the Police of the Metropolis* may have been published at least in part because of his failure to gain the attention that he thought that he deserved from the Home Office; and he spared no expense in presenting free copies to individuals whom he considered to be influential (Paley 1989: 98). A glance at Colquhoun's voluminous letters, written as they were in his tiny script, might suggest that busy administrators greeted their arrival in the post with resignation rather than any enthusiasm. Towards the end of 1799 Colquhoun drafted a police bill for London but, as Radzinowicz himself noted, 'there is no collateral evidence that the Home Secretary had actually requested [him] to draft this bill' (Radzinowicz 1956b: 309). The draft bill, together with three related bills also penned by Colquhoun, arrived when Pitt's government was seeking to engineer a union with Ireland in the wake of the 1798 rebellion, when a defeated British army was being evacuated from Europe and when the novel and controversial tax on incomes, established to meet the escalating costs of the war, was in its first year of implementation. Finding the money to implement a thorough-going reform of London's police and appeasing the vested interests within the metropolis who would have resented losing control of their police were unlikely to have a high priority on the government's agenda given the circumstances. Colquhoun's appointment to Bow Street in 1800 would have committed the government to a programme of police reform in London that may have appeared necessary in the eyes of Colquhoun himself and those of subsequent Whig historians, but more general demands for such reform were not apparent. The brief Peace of Amiens remained a hope rather than a promise in 1800 when Ford took over at Bow Street. The concerns about the thousands of soldiers and sailors demobilised from the French Wars and the ensuing parliamentary enquiries into the Police of the Metropolis were still more than a decade away.

Police reform in Hanoverian England stemmed significantly from local experiment, not simply from reformers highlighting abuses and problems and putting pressure on the centre, at the centre. That was how things were done in the Hanoverian state. During the Revolutionary and Napoleonic Wars military recruitment and the campaigns against popular radicalism were encouraged by central government but were left in the hands of the local administrative elite, notably the county magistrates. The system creaked. The men who carried out various local government duties found themselves very hard pressed at times; indeed, one or two appear to have refused to take out their *dedimus* and be sworn in as a justice because of these pressures.[3] Leading county worthies occasionally expressed concerns about the lack of magistrates in a locality. Rotation offices were established in busy but unincorporated urban centres such as Birmingham and Manchester, where county magistrates visited on a regular basis to resolve problems and deal with minor offences. But there always remained a reluctance to appoint men as magistrates who were felt to have insufficient social standing. The Home Office was not always informed promptly of serious public order problems and used a variety of agents to conduct delicate investigations; not the least among these were its new London stipendiaries, though it is worth noting that Colquhoun appears never to have been requested to undertake such an investigation (Emsley 1979). In the end, the system could be said to have worked; food riots, Luddism and radicalism were contained, and the war was won. But any enthusiastic reformer with plans for a centralised policing system was running against the tide, especially given the enormous costs of the wars. Minor changes and minor developments such as the revival of the Bow Street Horse Patrol in 1805 were possible. But neither Parliament nor the propertied classes who paid the bulk of the taxes and the poor rates were keen to see government finding areas of new expenditure. Indeed the French wars witnessed increasing demands for cheap government and for what was described as 'economical reform'. The costly Hanoverian war machine defeated Napoleon, but its hour of triumph ultimately led to it being dismantled precisely because of its cost (Harling and Mandler 1993).

Nevertheless, within 15 years of the end of the Napoleonic Wars a significant new and expensive step in policing was taken with the creation of the Metropolitan Police of London. This was a police institution very different from the reforms proposed by the Fieldings and Colquhoun, and very different from any other local institution in Hanoverian England. It was uniformed and hierarchical, and much closer to a military organisation than the reformers ever envisaged or than subsequent Whig historians have allowed. Moreover, it did not depend upon the London magistracy and thus on men like the Fieldings and Colquhoun; its police authority was not a traditional local official, or officials, but the Home Secretary himself.

Radzinowicz wrote of London, after the Napoleonic Wars, as primarily dependent on 'the antiquated system of night watchmen' with each parish separated from its neighbours. Where there was protection 'it was the result of individual initiative or of voluntary association, usually embarked upon as a response to some atrocity and disappearing as the memory had faded' (Radzinowicz 1968: 158). This is the traditional image portrayed by police reformers and by historians such as Reith and, subsequently, T.A. Critchley (1978) and David Ascoli (1979). Yet, as Elaine Reynolds has shown, there were significant improvements during the eighteenth century and if the system was 'antiquated', it was so in the sense of being old rather than being unreformed and decrepit. Many of the men who patrolled as watchmen in early nineteenth-century London were not the broken-down, incompetent 'Charlies' described in the traditional histories. After 1815 almost all of the recruits to St James's, Piccadilly, were ex-soldiers or ex-sailors who provided testimonials written by their former officers. In 1828 St Marylebone had 260 professional watchmen all of whom had been sworn in as constables (Reynolds 1998: 118 and 121). The wealthier parishes were better able to provide for policing than their less well-off neighbours. The enormous expense of the wars widened the gap and the growing demands of poor relief in the first years of peace did nothing to decrease it. At the same time, local government administration began to face the same fiscal criticisms as central government; critics wanted greater accountability and an end to corruption, jobbery and privilege. 'At the point when parochial opposition to Peel's Police bill could have been most effective,' Reynolds argues, 'some key parishes which could have mounted an effective opposition were hamstrung. They were too busy defending themselves against charges of corruption and exclusivity' (Reynolds 1998: 144).

Modern historians, particularly social historians who have been the group most interested in the history of crime and policing over the last twenty or thirty years, tend to emphasise the impact of social forces and pressures in preference to the importance of great men in bringing about change. But it is impossible to deny Robert Peel the principal role in the creation of the Metropolitan Police. Peel had become Home Secretary for the first time in 1822, determined to reform both the criminal law and policing. The assumption of the Whig historians is that he was motivated by a progressive, enlightened humanitarianism with respect to the former and convinced by the sort of arguments put forward by the Fieldings and Colquhoun with regard to the latter. It is possible that Peel was an enlightened humanitarian, though V.A.C. Gatrell has recently argued persuasively that Peel's reform of the criminal code can be seen to have been driven primarily by his political conservatism; it was a reform to preserve the institution (Gatrell 1994). By the same token, it is possible that Peel had been convinced by tracts on police reform, but Ruth Paley has suggested that the formulative experience for his London police reform was his service as Chief Secretary for Ireland, which is scarcely mentioned in the Whig accounts (Paley 1989: 124–5; Palmer 1988).

Peel received due acknowledgement and congratulation from Radzinowicz for penal and police reforms, but he was also criticised for being unfair to the memory of Colquhoun (Radzinowicz 1956b: 230–1). And if Colquhoun is Radzinowicz's passed-over hero of London police reform, then Edwin Chadwick is his similarly passed-over hero of provincial police reform, and the two were linked to each other by Jeremy Bentham – a third and much greater mind, who never saw his penal and policing reforms adopted by government. Chadwick was one of the three members of the Royal Commission that investigated the need for a rural constabulary between 1836 and 1839. As with the trinity of the Fielding brothers and Colquhoun, the Whig history of English policing had long singled out Chadwick as a founding father whose ideas might have been followed more rigorously, and again the force of Radzinowicz's research and writing underpinned this interpretation. Radzinowicz summarised the conclusions of the Royal Commission's Report and appeared broadly to accept them (Radzinowicz 1968: 227–32). He believed that the Whig government which had passed the Great Reform Act of 1832 had reservations about police reform and that Chadwick's efforts on the Commission were 'foredoomed to failure'. The forces of inertia were too strong, and there were also problems with confronting the power of local autonomy, the refusal to face up to the financial cost of policing, and the continuing concern that any moves towards centralisation by central government posed a threat to the liberty of the subject. It was, according to Radzinowicz, only the force of Chartist disorder that finally shifted the forces of inertia (Radzinowicz 1968: 215–21 and 232). The most recent research on policing during the 1820s and 1830s and on the Royal Commission, however, suggests that significant modifications are needed to this interpretation.

The work of David Philips and Robert Storch (Philips and Storch 1994, 1999) shows the Whig government of the 1830s to have been contemplating some form of provincial police reform even while struggling with the reform bill. The initial plan of 1832 was a measure with strong centralising tendencies and was never put before Parliament, but Lord John Russell, the Home Secretary, was under pressure from several sources for police reform before Chadwick began urging a Royal Commission on him. Chadwick, according to Philips and Storch, was keen to get his ideas introduced before anyone else, but as the Commission embarked on its deliberations Russell cautioned him to ensure that the proposals were politically realistic:

> There is one thing always to be kept in mind. We are endeavouring to improve our institutions. I think they have been lax, careless, wasteful, injudicious to an extreme; but the country governed itself, & was blind to its own faults. We are busy in introducing system, method, science, economy, regularity & discipline. But we must beware not to lose the co-operation of the country – they will not bear a Prussian Minister, to regulate domestic affairs – so that

some faults must be indulged for the sake of carrying improvement in the mass.

(Quoted in Philips and Storch 1999: 120)

Regardless of the warning, the Royal Commission in April 1839 published a proposal for a centralised policing system for rural areas. The following month it looked as if Peel would become Prime Minister and, but for the young Queen Victoria's insistence on keeping her Whig ladies-in-waiting, he would have done. A government more reluctant over police reform might have let the matter drop in spite of the Chartist disorders that summer, but the Whigs pressed ahead with reforms in three major urban areas – Birmingham, Bolton and Manchester – and also with the first County Police Act. And if such reform did not follow the Royal Commission's plan, neither Chadwick nor the Whig historians can seriously protest that he had not been urged to think in terms of what was practical in the given circumstances.

In addition to demonstrating the Whig government's commitment to police reform, Philips and Storch have amassed considerable evidence to show that the rulers of the counties were themselves experimenting with different forms of policing during the 1820s and 1830s. Significantly, much of this evidence is to be found in the papers of the Royal Commission. Chadwick prepared questionnaires for the rulers of the counties so as to assemble information on the state of the police in the provinces that could be used as evidence for the Commission's report. But, as with the case which he had prepared a few years earlier on the Poor Law, Chadwick appears to have known his favoured solution before he conducted his research. The questions that he posed were often loaded; moreover, he tended to use only that evidence which suited him. He ignored information that showed magistrates working, admittedly with varying degrees of success, to improve provincial policing through the existing systems of local government. There is also at least one clear instance of his editing and rewriting evidence to sharpen an argument (Philips and Storch 1999: 124).[4] The material collected by the Commission provides an important insight into provincial policing before the police, and an insight rather different from that presented in the report that Chadwick wrote. Too many historians have been too quick to accept the conclusions of the Royal Commission, and too ready to assume that it approached the question of rural policing with an open mind. None of this is to suggest that the policing of rural England was in good shape before the enabling legislation of 1839 and 1840, but rather that local government was not complacent and that local police structures were neither all static nor all moribund.

Comparative perspectives

The County and Borough Police Act of 1856 cemented a structure of police administration which had begun to emerge over the previous half century and that was to continue without major change until the 1960s. The Home Secretary was the police authority of the Metropolitan Police. The police of an incorporated borough were responsible to a watch committee appointed by the elected town council. A county police force was responsible to a police committee of magistrates established by the local bench, and after 1888 to a standing joint committee composed of an equal number of magistrates and elected county councillors. There was no central control of the provincial police, but the 1856 Act promised a Treasury grant of 25 per cent towards clothing and pay for efficient police forces and established the inspectorate whose annual reports would assess such efficiency. When in 1874 this grant was increased to 50 per cent, any vestiges of reluctance to conform and to seek the grant evaporated. But how far were such developments and structures unique?

The eighteenth-century Enlightenment fostered ideas about how the use of reason might engender progress, in the sense of greater happiness, prosperity and security within society. These ideas influenced Europe's rulers who, after the upheavals of the French Revolution and the Napoleonic Wars, generally ruled over much larger states. The old rural order was disintegrating, and with it the local seigneur's management of his locality. It was increasingly accepted that rational, centralised bureaucracies could do something about vagrancy and disorder, could and should establish and maintain new thresholds of public behaviour and ensure the moral management of those, essentially the poorer classes, who were perceived as requiring such management. Within this broad intellectual framework each European state was unique, with its own traditions, its own evolving pattern of government and its own individual rulers. Police institutions, organised in bureaucratic, hierarchical structures and concerned with crime prevention, order maintenance and a degree of moral management, were established across Europe in the late eighteenth and early nineteenth centuries. The basic forms were often the same, though there were distinct national variations. For a variety of reasons, both contemporary and subsequent historians tended to put the greatest stress on the differences in origin, form and development.

Eighteenth-century Englishmen from all social classes appear to have been more or less agreed that they possessed freedoms and liberties that set them apart from the inhabitants of Continental Europe. Continental

Europeans were seen as subject to authoritarian princes, arbitrary laws and popery. In general, those travellers who observed and wrote about European policing structures – most notably those of France – while recognising some advantages, considered that the political intrusiveness of the *lieutenant général de police de Paris* and the military nature of the *maréchaussée* that patrolled the main roads in the provinces could not be tolerated in the land of liberty. Radzinowicz provided a detailed account of the 'menacing features' of French policing that so disturbed English opinion (Radzinowicz 1956b: 539–74). However, there were also times when he accepted the accounts of these commentators uncritically as, for example, when he cited Colquhoun's revelations of the 'terrifying efficiency' of the Paris police, yet admitted that Colquhoun's account was erroneous at least in so far as it gave the wrong man as *lieutenant général* in the story (Radzinowicz 1956b: 250). In reporting European views of the English, Radzinowicz was more critical: French accounts, 'though often brilliant, are not free from prejudice' (Radzinowicz 1948: 700). But Radzinowicz's assessment of foreign observers' criticisms of the English system of criminal justice only implicitly picked up the perception of most thinkers on the other side of the Channel in the decades before the French Revolution that the English notion of 'freedom', with its political factions and aggressive commercialism, was no model for them (Maza 1997: 221). What worried people in France about the *maréchaussée* at the outset of the Revolution was not its military nature but its lack of numbers and the judicial role of its senior officers who acted as both policemen and judges. And in subsequent decades what often appears particularly to have fostered dislike of the Gendarmerie, the successor to the *maréchaussée*, was its role in enforcing conscription, not the fact that the men themselves were soldiers (Emsley 1999b: 33–5, 39, 71–3 and 111). On the question of policing it appears that eighteenth- and early nineteenth-century English and French observers regarded each other's systems with mutual ignorance and incomprehension, commonly fitting what they saw into their own prejudices and aspirations. Yet, in some very broad respects, developments in the two countries during this period shared similarities.

Other states of Continental Europe followed the French model in creating military gendarmeries, and while no such force was established in England, the government at Westminster established a gendarmerie-type institution in Ireland and sanctioned the creation of others elsewhere in its imperial possessions. But once these military policemen are removed from the equation, capital city and provincial police look rather similar in their administrative structures. The Metropolitan Police of London were directly responsible to central government, as were the police of Paris; moreover, with the creation of the *sergents de ville* in 1829, the French also sought to develop a uniformed police who would appear more civilian to the public, and who were readily approachable. In 1791 it became a requirement that every town with a population in excess of 5,000 should have a *commissaire de police*. Under Napoleon appointments to the post were centralised; the choice was made in the Ministry of the Interior from a shortlist of three prepared by the local prefect. However, the number of officers serving the *commissaire* of a particular town depended entirely on what the municipal government was prepared to recruit and pay for. A succession of disorders in Lyons led to the creation of a police system directed by the Prefect of the Rhône in 1854, but outside the capital this was to be the only French civilian police force linked directly to the state during the nineteenth century. The *commissaires* provided a link with Paris, but there was no funding of local police from the treasury and no system of inspection as in England. In the countryside since 1795 every commune had been required to recruit and fund a *garde champêtre*, a field guard. The Gendarmerie was commonly scathing in assessments of these men, and various proposals were mooted to bring them directly under Gendarmerie control in the belief that this would improve their effectiveness. Proposals were suggested to reform the *gardes* during the July Monarchy, but Legitimists and Liberals in parliament could not agree on the best way ahead and reform had to await the early years of the Second Empire. Napoleon III required that all candidates for the position of *garde champêtre* should have served in the army; he gave his prefects the final say in who should be appointed and made the *gardes* subject to supervision by the nearest *commissaire*. But he also recognised a reluctance among the local elites to increase local taxes and to see the state encroach too far into the localities; thus the *gardes* remained under local authority and their pay remained frozen (Gaveau 2000).

A broad typology of police in nineteenth-century Europe suggests three principal kinds: state military, the gendarmeries; state civilian, principally the capital city forces under the direct control of central government; and municipal civilian, police recruited, paid and largely directed by the representatives of local government. Early nineteenth-century Prussia, for example, was a state with a long militaristic tradition. It relied upon military garrisons for dealing with serious popular disorder, and the *Städteordnung* of November 1808, which was part of the modernising process begun by reformers in the wake of military disaster, declared that policing was a Crown prerogative. Yet this declaration did not result in a centralised policing system. The police in Berlin were linked to central government, but *Sergeanten* and

Schutzmänner in the towns and the countryside remained dependent on the localities. And the Gendarmerie, created by the reformers in 1812, remained tiny and thinly spread for most of the century. England had no gendarmerie, but otherwise its structures of police organisation and administration were similar to those of France, Prussia and other Continental states (Emsley 1999a). There is a problem that structural comparisons might tend to overemphasise similarities. Nevertheless, the typology based on structures presents a picture very different from that of the Whig historians who portrayed little more than centralised and largely militarised police on continental Europe and non-centralised, civilian police in England. Nor were the scale and effectiveness of surveillance and intrusive, political policing as marked as the Whig historians would allow, and such policing was not confined to Continental Europe.

The revolutionary activity and outbreaks in France and in other parts of continental Europe during the nineteenth century reveal why European governments considered political policing and surveillance necessary. Paradoxically these outbreaks also, in themselves, gave the lie to the effectiveness of such policing. Nineteenth-century Whigs, Liberals, Radicals and Tories at Westminster liked to boast that their political structure was more stable than that of Continental powers, and events appeared to bear them out. A corollary was that they were above political policing and surveillance. Such ideas were an extension of the 'freeborn Englishman' notions from the eighteenth century, and these notions had been reinforced by success in the wars against Revolutionary and Napoleonic France, and by perceptions of more sinister, all-pervasive forms of political police being developed under Joseph Fouché and of detective police following the model of Vidocq, the classic example of poacher turned gamekeeper. As noted earlier, the British government considered it necessary to develop a system of political policing during the Revolutionary and Napoleonic Wars. This involved some of the stipendiary magistrates in the metropolis, but its nerve centre was the Aliens' Office established within the Home Office. While the Aliens' Office fell into abeyance at the end of the wars, the use of spies and secret agents continued during the economic distress and political agitation of the postwar years. There was an insistence, apparently at the highest levels, that members of the new Metropolitan Police would not be employed in such categories, or in plain clothes. Nevertheless, serving senior police officers rapidly came to believe that plain clothes' policing was essential for the pursuit and apprehension of offenders, while political radicalism ensured that a degree of political policing and surveillance was maintained, occasionally leading to scandals as with the affair of Metropolitan Police Sergeant Popay in 1833 and the revelations concerning the opening of Joseph Mazzini's mail in 1844 (*Parliamentary Papers* 1833; Smith 1970). Probably in the quarter of a century following 1848 there was very little political investigation and surveillance carried out by policing agencies in England (Smith 1985: chapter 5; Porter 1987: chapter 1), and this was at the same time as the French were developing their system of special *commissaries*, especially the *commissaires spéciaux de surveillance des chemins de fer*, and that the police agencies of German states were developing closer cooperation particularly to check political subversion (Payne, 1966: 221–32; Jäger, 1999). The points to stress, however, are that political investigation and surveillance on Continental Europe was not all-pervading, effective and ever-present, that such policing, while limited, also existed in England, and that it could involve members of the New Police.

The traditional historians of English policing, among whom Radzinowicz must count as the most astute, can be criticised for accepting too readily the complaints of police reformers about the old police. Much of the recent research on the early development of the English police has stressed significant change before 1829, and also that there were continuities, not least in poor-quality men, long after that date. A uniformed, strictly disciplined, hierarchical institution of 3,000 men, directly responsible to central government and patrolling regular beats across virtually the whole of the metropolis, was a new experience for London, and also for England. Indeed, at that time no other capital city in Europe had a similar institution. The Prefect of Police in Paris had less than 100 *sergents de ville* in 1829, while the Gendarmerie Company in Paris did not come directly under his authority. The very gradual spread of 'new police' institutions across provincial England was also novel, though in the case of the towns and cities especially, the novelty of the policing requirements of the Municipal Corporations Act of 1835 and the creation of the watch committees might also be overstated. And taking a wider perspective, developments in policing during the late eighteenth and early nineteenth centuries were not unique to England or even the British Isles.

Radzinowicz might be criticised further for accepting English criticism of first the Bourbon and then the Napoleonic police. Governments tend to be rather more crafty, observing developments elsewhere and, when faced with problems at home, pragmatically reshaping and developing systems within their own national rhetoric but drawing on their broad observations. The Municipal Corporations Act imposed on English corporate towns and cities as much uniformity in policing matters as existed in similar towns in France and the German states. The

1856 Police Act, with its national inspectors reporting annually to Parliament and its Treasury grant for efficient forces, might even be argued to have imposed a greater centralisation than existed in France or Prussia. There were no systems for inspection in those states, and no provision for Treasury funding. By its Police Law of 1850 the conservative Prussian state, shaken by recent revolution, sought to appoint a senior police officer in each municipality. The municipalities objected. They protested, along lines that would not have been out of place in the English context, that they should not have to fund a police that they did not control. They took the state to court and won. The English might not have relished going down what they understood as a path mapped out by a Prussian minister, yet by the end of the nineteenth century they possessed a police system that, in some respects, was subject to a more centralised supervision than the civilian police in either Prussia or France.

In England since the middle of the nineteenth century there has been a drive towards bigger police forces and greater centralisation, always in the name of efficiency and, since the early twentieth century at least, also in the name of greater opportunities for police officers in terms of promotion and specialisation. Traditional histories of the police, including Radzinowicz's formidable work, have tended to follow this line of argument and to underpin it by accepting the eighteenth- and nineteenth-century police reformers' assumptions that a fragmented police system meant an inferior police. Moreover, they assumed that, historically, the more centralised states of Continental Europe had more centralised police systems. Perhaps some of their assumptions were correct, but perhaps too these assumptions need to be recognised for what they are, and subjected to some critical analysis.

Notes

1 Radzinowicz (1956b: 136 n 9) notes the Treasury paying a regular grant for this patrol to Sir Sampson Wright, Fieldings' successor at Bow Street, from August 1783.
2 Ford's role in the supervision of the London Corresponding Society can be seen, for example, from his letters in the Portland Papers held by the University of Nottingham: PwF 3928, 3931, 3933 and 3934, Ford to Portland 2 October and 10 and 23 December 1794, and 1 July 1795; and for his energy in coordinating the stipendiary magistrates in dealing with riots in London in the summer of 1795, PwF 3937, Ford to Portland 15 July 1795.
3 East Yorks Record Office, Grimston MSS, DDGR/43/21, William Hildyard to Thomas Grimston, 23 February 1801.

4 Appendices A and B of Philips and Storch (1999), based primarily on the Commission Papers in PRO HO 73.2–9, reveal the extent to which provincial magistrates favoured a paid police during the 1830s and list some 200 local policing schemes in operation 1836–39.

Bibliography

Ascoli, D. (1979) *The Queen's Peace: The Origins and Development of the Metropolitan Police*. London: Hamish Hamilton.

Beattie, J.M. (2001) *Policing and Punishment in London 1660–1750: Urban Crime and the Limits of Terror*. Oxford: Oxford University Press.

Chartier, R. (1990) *Les origines culturelles de la Révolution française*, Paris: Seuil.

Critchley, T.A. (1978) *A History of Police in England and Wales*, 2nd edn. London: Constable.

Darnton, R. (1996) *The Forbidden Best-Sellers of Pre-Revolutionary France*. London: HarperCollins.

Emsley, C. (1979) 'The Home Office and Its Sources of Information and Investigation, 1791–1801', *English Historical Review*, 94 (372), 532–61.

Emsley, C. (1999a) 'A Typology of Nineteenth-Century Police', *Crime, Histoire et Sociétés/Crime, History and Societies*, 3 (1), 29–44.

Emsley, C. (1999b) *Gendarmes and the State in Nineteenth-Century Europe*. Oxford: Oxford University Press.

Engelsing, R. (1974) *Der Bürger als Leser: Lesergeschichte in Deutschland 1500–1800*. Stuttgart: Metzler.

Gatrell, V.A.C. (1994) *The Hanging Tree: Execution and the English People 1770–1868*. Oxford: Oxford University Press.

Gaveau, F. (2000) 'De la Sûreté des Campagnes. Police Rurale et Demandes d'Ordre en France dans la Première Moitié du XIX Siècle', *Crime, Histoire et Sociétés/Crime, History and Societies*, 4 (2), 53–76.

Harling, P. and Mandler, P. (1993) 'From "Fiscal-Military" State to Laissez-faire State, 1760–1850', *Journal of British Studies*, 32, 44–70.

Haywood, L. (1996) 'Aspects of Policing in the City of York, 1722–1835'. Unpublished MA thesis, University of York.

Hejellemo, O. (1977) 'A Tribute to an Unusual Historian of Police: Charles Edward Williams Reith (1886–1964)', *Police College Magazine*, 14, 5–8.

Hone, J.A. (1982) *For the Cause of Truth: Radicalism in London 1796–1821*. Oxford: Clarendon Press.

Jäger, J. (1999) 'Die informelle Vernetzung politischer Polizei nach 1848', *Zeitschrift der Savigny-Stiftung für Rechtsgeschichte*, 116, 266–313.

King, P. (2000) *Crime, Justice and Discretion in England 1740–1820*. Oxford: Oxford University Press.

Maza, S. (1997) 'Luxury, Morality, and Social Change: Why There Was no Middle-Class Consciousness in Pre-Revolutionary France', *Journal of Modern History*, 69, 199–229.

Paley, R. (1989) ' "An Imperfect, Inadequate and Wretched System"? Policing London Before Peel', *Criminal Justice History*, 10, 95–130.

Palmer, S.H. (1988) *Police and Protest in England and Ireland 1780–1850*. Cambridge: Cambridge University Press.

Parliamentary Papers (1833) (627) XIII, *Report from the Select Committee on the Petition of Frederick Young and Others*.

Payne, H.C. (1966) *The Police State of Louis Napoleon Bonaparte 1851–1860*. Seattle, WA: University of Washington Press.

Philips, D. and Storch, R.D. (1994) 'Whigs and Coppers: The Grey Ministry's National Police Scheme, 1832', *Historical Research*, 67, 75–90.

Philips, D. and Storch, R.D. (1999) *Policing Provincial England 1829–1856*. London: Leicester University Press.

Porter, B. (1987) *The Origins of the Vigilant State: The London Metropolitan Police Special Branch before the First World War*. London: Weidenfeld & Nicolson.

Radzinowicz, L. (1948) *A History of English Criminal Law: Volume 1, The Movement for Reform*. London: Stevens & Sons.

Radzinowicz, L. (1956a) *A History of English Criminal Law: Volume 2, The Enforcement of the Law*. London: Stevens & Sons.

Radzinowicz, L. (1956b) *A History of English Criminal Law: Volume 3, The Reform of Police*. London: Stevens & Sons.

Radzinowicz, L. (1968) *A History of English Criminal Law: Volume 4, Grappling for Control*. London: Stevens & Sons.

Reith, C. (1938) *The Police Idea*. Oxford: Oxford University Press.

Reith, C. (1940) *Police Principles and the Problem of War*. Oxford: Oxford University Press.

Reith, C. (1943) *British Police and the Democratic Ideal*. Oxford: Oxford University Press.

Reith, C. (1948) *A Short History of Police*. Oxford: Oxford University Press.

Reith, C. (1952) *The Blind Eye of History*. London: Faber & Faber.

Reith, C. (1956) *A New Study of Police History*. London: Oliver & Boyd.

Reynolds, E.A. (1998) *Before the Bobbies: The Night Watch and Police Reform in Metropolitan London 1720–1830*. London: Macmillan.

Smith, F.B. (1970) 'British Post Office Espionage, 1844', *Historical Studies*, 14, 189–203.

Smith, P.T. (1985) *Policing Victorian London: Political Policing, Public Order, and the London Metropolitan Police*. Westport, CT: Greenwood Press.

Sparrow, E. (1999) *Secret Service: British Agents in France 1792–1815*. Woodbridge: Boydell Press.

Styles, J. (1983) 'Sir John Fielding and the Problem of Criminal Investigation in Eighteenth-Century England', *Transactions of the Royal Historical Society*, 5th Series, 33, 127–49.

Williams, C.A. (1999). 'Police and Crime in Sheffield, 1818–1874'. Unpublished PhD thesis: University of Sheffield.

Wittmann, R. (1991) *Geschichte des deutschen Buchhandels. Ein Überlick*. Munich: C.H. Beck.

Part 3
Prisons

Chapter 5

A 'liberal regime within a secure perimeter'?: dispersal prisons and penal practice in the late twentieth century

Alison Liebling

The manner in which the Prison Service of this country meets the challenge of containing long-term prisoners in conditions that combine security and humanity will have a lasting effect on the Service as a whole.

(Advisory Council on the Penal System 1968: 3)

Introduction

Prisoner: If I bang up at 5 o'clock dead on, will you unlock me first so I can get into the queue for the hairdresser?

Officer: OK – I'll unlock your side from the back tonight. No problem, mate.

Officer: If you go away now … you can have my *Daily Mail* at bang up!

Prisoner: You're on!

Senior Officer: Gary, next time you talk to me, breathe the other way. Get my drift?

Prisoner: Yes boss.

It was a Wednesday evening, approaching 5 o'clock, in 1995. Teatime 'bang-up' in a high-security dispersal prison. This was C wing – for lifers and long-termers. The wing was self-consciously slightly more liberal than the other wings in the prison in terms of its staff–prisoner relationships and its enforcement of some of the establishment's rules,

97

such as locking up prisoners who did not work. It was often compared to the regime at Long Lartin, which was still considered to be 'the true dispersal prison'.[1] C wing also prided itself on its careful selection of experienced and motivated staff, its constructive work with prisoners and its distinct 'enhanced' ethos. Its population of 86 included 18 high-risk category A prisoners, several IRA members and several well-known 'London gangsters'. The prisoner above, who was told to 'breathe the other way', had been drinking hooch. The Senior Officer who had chosen not to formally sanction the behaviour was demonstrating his awareness of the prisoner's indiscretion, and warning him not to push it too far. 'He's basically a good lad,' said the officer. They exchanged smiles and the prisoner looked apologetic. It was this type of 'leniency' (or 'accommodation' or 'corruption', depending on one's perspective) which characterised the 'true' dispersal prison during the 1980s and which came under serious scrutiny in the mid-1990s.[2]

> We made every mistake it was possible to make: lack of control, lack of direction, lack of structure … it was confrontational, demanding; we bred prima donna's … they'd walk past officers, senior officers, principal officers, assistant governors until they got to the top man. Now, the dynamics have been transformed. Power has gone back to the prison officer. We have convinced prisoners that we are back in control. We have had no escapes since 1995. You have a tight-knit team at the top, all very much committed to the same ideals.
>
> (Senior manager, PSHQ)

Telling the story of the English dispersal prison is a challenging task.[3] Their history is inextricably linked to the cyclical development of small units for difficult prisoners which support the dispersal structure (see Liebling 2001; Bottomley and Hay 1991). The author of this account is aware that there are others who are more familiar with the early stages, and that her own reading of history has become irrevocably coloured by the retreat from liberal regimes characteristic of the 1990s. In this sense, this paper does not claim to present the *definitive* history of the dispersal prison. It offers an analytic 'from the ground' account of recent and current understandings and sensibilities, as they relate to maximum-security custody in England and Wales. It is informed by official documentation, the literature and exposure to the recollections of key players in, and recipients of, the dispersal estate since its creation in 1968. I have tried to answer this question: would Radzinowicz have approved of the prison his report created?

The paper is based on two long-term research studies carried out in two dispersal prisons by the author and colleagues during 1995–7 and 1998–9, on incentives and earned privileges (IEP) and staff–prisoner relationships respectively (Liebling *et al* 1997; Liebling and Price 2001). It is supplemented by a review of the literature, including some landmark studies carried out by others; a collaborative project evaluating the new system of close supervision centres (Clare and Bottomley 2001); a more recent series of visits and informal interviews with staff and prisoners in several dispersal prisons and in Prison Service Headquarters, carried out during February and March of 2001; and an analysis of adjudications data for dispersal prisons for the period 1993–2000.

The idea of dispersing or absorbing the highest security prisoners among the general population of a number of prisons with very secure perimeters was adopted by the Labour government in 1968, following a recommendation made by a subcommittee of the Advisory Council on the Penal System chaired by Sir Leon Radzinowicz. The arguments which persuaded the subcommittee were largely negative: that the concentration option or 'fortress prison' preferred by Mountbatten would lead to a repressive, dangerous and 'last resort' environment.[4] Separating and concentrating the most dangerous prisoners – a notion which many prisoners, staff and others supported – would lead to an explosive environment. Despite the costs, the likely operational problems and the likely impact on those prisoners who were not Category A[5] but were housed in conditions of maximum security, the aspiration to accomplish a reasonable regime, variously characterised as 'open', 'liberal' and 'relaxed', was a serious and worthy one. Such openness would bring problems of control, but the proposed alternative – repression – would bring greater problems of order and legitimacy. Effective security at the perimeter, along with order and a viable quality of life within the regime, were dual but compatible aspirations.

This paper explores the origins, history and recent experiences of the dispersal system in England and Wales. What did Sir Leon envisage when he and his subcommittee outlined their vision of 'a liberal regime for the humane and constructive treatment of long-term prisoners'? What has the lived experience been like? How plausible was this 'ideal' (never an ideal, of course, but a least negative option) and what were the dangers? How do dispersals look today, and has current practice and ideology shifted away from, or come closer to, the original Radzinowicz prescription? What is the meaning of the principles mentioned above? How far can the late modern dispersal prison be described as providing or aspiring to 'a liberal regime within a secure perimeter'?[6]

I would characterise the history of dispersals as shown in Table 1.

Table 1 *Dispersal prison history*

Period	Phase
1968–1972: origins	Penological optimism, secure perimeters, apprehension and humanity
1972–1984	Losing control, and regaining it. The end of Rule 1
1984–1993	Negotiating order and reducing resistance
1994–1995	The escapes, and austerity; an end to Barlinnie, the CRC Units and trust
1995–1998	The recovery programme: security, security, security
1999–2001	The pursuit of a reconfigured legitimacy

They were established with humanitarian aspirations, although with all the operational difficulties of opening, or in this case converting, a prison. Attempts to deliver a liberal and constructive regime were fraught with difficulties. Dispersal prisons experienced more than a decade of sporadic but serious disorder and some tightening up as a result. The period following the Control Review Committee Report in 1984 was more peaceful, and staff–prisoner relationships were placed centre stage, but prisoners demanded escalating privileges. The escapes in 1994 and 1995, and a Home Secretary dedicated to 'decent but austere' conditions, transformed the dispersal prison. The original aspiration to achieve liberal regimes, as it turned out in practice, was regarded as almost foolish with this type of prisoner. Over the last two years, dispersal prisons have become strangely invisible, and apparently more ordered, as well as secure, for the first time in their history. No Governor is prepared to describe them as 'liberal', although interestingly, some prisoners do. The following section explores these developments in more detail.

The origins and early experiences of dispersal prisons

Sir,

In February 1967 your predecessor asked the Advisory Council on the Penal System to consider the regime for long-term prisoners detained in conditions of maximum-security, and to make recommendations ... During the course of its inquiry the Sub-committee [under the chairmanship of Professor Radzinowicz] became increasingly doubtful about the possibility of establishing a satisfactory regime within a fortress-type prison in which all maximum-security prisoners were concentrated. As a result, the Sub-committee concluded that the setting-up of a small prison for a restricted category of long sentence prisoners in conditions of near absolute security is not the right solution to what are admittedly very difficult problems, and it recommends that these prisoners should instead be dispersed among three or four larger prisons with strengthened perimeter security.

Your obedient Servant, Kenneth Younger.

The Radzinowicz Report was written in response to an inquiry by Lord Mountbatten into the escapes of Wilson and Biggs from Birmingham Prison and George Blake from Wormwood Scrubs in 1966. There was concern about the growing numbers of prisoners being received into custody who were serving very long sentences, partly as a result of the abolition of the death penalty.[7] There was also considerable unease with the regimes of the three Special Security Units at Durham, Leicester and Parkhurst prisons for the highest escape risk prisoners. Mountbatten had recommended a system of security categorisation, and in 1967 the then Prison Department drew up a first and provisional list of 138 male convicted prisoners who were considered to be Category A.[8] These prisoners were mainly fairly young, fairly violent and persistent in their criminal activities. A few had been sentenced under the Official Secrets Act and were considered more stable. A few others were less stable, and a few were serious sex offenders liable to attack by others. More than half had attempted to escape from prison or were suspected of making plans to escape. Twenty-four had assaulted prison officers. They varied in their levels of cooperativeness. Some were so effective in their trafficking and gangster activities that they could prejudice the life of the whole establishment:

> A considerable proportion of those now serving long determinate sentences, and a smaller proportion of those serving life sentences, are violent anti-social recidivist criminals. Some of these people can be as difficult to control inside prison as they are dangerous outside it, and the community must recognise the onerous task placed on the staff of the prisons in which such prisoners are contained. In addition, the increase in organised violent crime means that some criminal gangs may be able to command considerable resources that could be used to assist a member of the gang to escape.
>
> (ACPS 1968: 76)

Mountbatten had also recommended that high security risk prisoners should be concentrated in a single, 'fortress-style' prison on the Isle of Wight. This key proposal was overturned by the recommendation of the subcommittee that high security risk prisoners should instead be dispersed throughout a number of prisons, to offer such prisoners a more humane, open kind of regime. The Advisory Council acknowledged that 'the arguments are finely balanced'. They warned that a 'liberal regime of the kind which the sub-committee recommends' could not be introduced unless it were accompanied by 'an extremely high degree of perimeter security' (p. v). Members were divided as to whether this extreme degree of perimeter security might include the presence of armed guards, but despite a note of reservation signed by six Council members, this appeared as a recommendation in the report. Concern was expressed about the ill effects of a less liberal regime on staff and prisoners. Such a concentration of the most dangerous prisoners in one place would lead to negative labelling, a 'nothing to lose' ethos, a shortage of options for the difficult to place, a faith in the process of classification not justified in practice and the atmosphere of a single segregation unit. It might also lead to a negative reputation for the Prison Service abroad. Instead, a liberal regime within a secure perimeter would provide for the good governance of the prison and the interests of staff, and would encourage prisoners to lead a 'good and useful life'. This recommendation came with a call for an increase in the 'co-efficient of security in our closed prisons':

Our conclusions are that:
(i) there needs to be an increase in the co-efficient of security in our closed prisons, especially those in which long-term prisoners are contained;
(ii) given an adequate, well-led, alert and well-trained staff, the necessary general increase in security can be obtained by a very considerable strengthening of perimeter security;

And also that
(iii) within such perimeter security, and with adequate staff and buildings, it becomes possible to continue and develop a liberal regime for the humane and constructive treatment of long-term prisoners.

Without the necessary general increase in security the Prison Service will not, in our view, be able to make steady progress in the treatment of long-term prisoners, and will continue to be liable to crises of confidence, and the oscillations of public feeling, that have confused and disheartened staff in recent years.

(ACPS 1968: 76–7)

The necessary ingredients of this liberal and constructive regime were activity, a reasonable atmosphere and good facilities. The aim of such a regime was to change the attitudes and behaviour of prisoners, and to achieve this via the Governor and staff of the prison, armed with the new knowledges offered by sociology and psychiatry. A man in prison did not cease to be 'the father of his children' or a human being:

> If our society is concerned, as it is, and as it must be, with the worth of all individual men and women, and if it believes that in the last resort what men have in common is more important than their differences, then it cannot treat as less than human those men it finds necessary to send to prison. This means that the community must provide for the Prison Service the necessary resources to enable men to be contained for long periods in conditions that combine security with humanity.
>
> (*Ibid*: 77)

The principles of self-respect, choice, variety, movement and the earning of additional privileges through work and cooperative behaviour were essential to the organisation of a long-term prison. The report argued that there should be constructive relationships between prisoners and staff, and regular individualised reviews of progress.[9] The prisons were envisaged as having a population of about 400 prisoners each.

Close relationships, communication, flexibility and activity, together with individually tailored interventions, were more likely to produce change in the individual prisoner than antagonistic or inflexible regimes.[10] Prisoners should be able to have those personal possessions they so chose – books, a wireless, photographs, letters – subject only to the limitations of security and space. A prisoner should be able to 'paint his cell with a colour scheme of his own choice' (p. 35), provided he understood that occasional moves might be required in the interests of good order. Prisoners should be able to draw on private cash and have items sent in by visitors to make their stay more comfortable (within reasonable limits). Wing committees should be established to make decisions and offer proposals on relevant matters. Semi-skilled industrial work and education should be available. Newspapers and television should be easily accessible, and relationships with partners and the outside world should be actively encouraged. Visits should take place in comfortable chairs and in pleasant surroundings. Liberal discretion should be used to allow visits to last longer than the statutory minimum period and to take place more frequently. Experiments should be attempted with weekend visits and home leave. In keeping with the reservations about institutions generally, some concern was expressed about the effects of long-term sentences: in particular, the possible deterioration of already disturbed or damaged personalities.[11]

The Advisory Council assumed that a minority of disruptive or unstable prisoners would have to be contained in a separate segregation unit within a larger prison. This resource should be used 'intelligently' and the prisoners within it should be subject to regular review.

The requirements of security (that is, the prevention of escapes) and order (the prevention of disturbances) could be achieved only by providing satisfactory regimes in long-term prisons (ACPS 1968: 19). The humane regime envisaged was dependent on two essential prerequisites: an increased ratio of staff to prisoners over other prisons (to about one uniformed officer for three prisoners) and the establishment of separate segregation units.

Some variation between the regimes of these maximum-security prisons was expected and was to be encouraged, if only to experiment with solutions to the problems posed by long-term imprisonment. The subcommittee also expected, and supported the proposition, that most offenders labelled as psychopaths would be catered for in these prisons, which would themselves be supported by an improving medical service. A continuing programme of research should be carried out on the effects of different types of regimes on different types of prisoners, the effects of long-term imprisonment more generally, the effects on staff and changes in the administration of such prisons. Staff and prisoners should be fully involved in such research, so that its impact on the establishments could be made as valuable as possible. The report argued that the governors of such maximum-security prisoners should have plenty of experience and should show concern for and understanding of the complexities of human nature, without 'sentimentality'.

The 'essential elements' of the dispersal policy then were that difficult prisoners were 'absorbed' into the general population, and that the regime was liberal (see King and Elliott 1977: 325–6; and Radzinowicz 1999: 116, on his use of the 'infuriating concept' in criminal justice).[12] Both of these elements were linked to rehabilitative ideals (Sparks *et al* 1996: 104).

Four prisons were initially identified for use as dispersal prisons and their security levels were upgraded accordingly. Very quickly, others were identified, whose upgrading was more difficult to achieve. Long

Lartin and Albany, for example, had been Category C establishments, which probably influenced the type of regime established. King and Elliott describe this transformation in function as they were added to the estate, and the introduction of the new grade of senior officer, in their detailed study of Albany (King and Elliott 1977). After two major disturbances, at Albany and Parkhurst, the number was increased again, from six to a proposed nine (King and Elliott 1977: 302).[13] It was intended that no more than 15 per cent of each establishment's population would be Category A. They did not live up to expectations. Several major disturbances took place during the 1970s and 1980s (see Table 2). Two substantial reviews of dispersal prisons took place in 1973 following major disturbances at Gartree and Albany prisons (see Williams v Home Office 1981; and King and Morgan 1980: 74–5). These reviews introduced the ill-fated control units and the Circular Instruction 10/1974 (the arrangements for transferring prisoners temporarily from dispersal prisons into local prisons; see King and McDermott 1990; Sparks et al 1996; and note 13 below). There were increases in wing management staff (for example, the introduction of Assistant Governors on each wing). This first attempt at small units 'failed abysmally' (personal comment):

> The Prison Service solution was far too inflexible and the determined combination of penal pressure groups put so much pressure on Ministers that they were pleased to see the control units closed.
>
> (Senior manager, PSHQ)

As King and Morgan argue, the net effect of these measures was to heighten tension in the dispersal prisons (King and Morgan 1980: 75). Further major disturbances took place, most notably the 1976 Hull riot (Thomas and Pooley 1980) which was associated (alongside other disturbances during the 1970s) with the activities of PROP, a union representing the rights of prisoners, and some 'paying back' behaviour by prison staff. At least ten major disturbances had taken place in dispersal prisons by 1983. It was significant that these disturbances took place not 'in the crowded and highly disadvantaged conditions of local prisons, but in the comparatively relaxed and privileged regimes of the dispersal prison' (Ditchfield 1990: iii). There had been significant reductions in the quality of life for many prisoners as a result of the introduction of the dispersal policy and the early breakdowns in order. Why were they so 'susceptible to major breakdowns in control' (Home Office 1984: 7)? The explanations offered included the increased

Table 2 The original dispersal estate

Prison	Wakefield	Hull	Parkhurst	Wormwood Scrubs	Gartree	Albany	Long Lartin	Frankland
Time span	1969–date	1969–86	1969–95	1969–89	1970–92	1970–95	1973–date	1983–date
Capacity	585	318	306	288	315	238	420	318
% Category As	8%	10%	10%	3%	14%	13%	11%	14%
Major Disorder	–	1976	1969, 1979	1979	1972, 1978	1971, 1972, 1983	–	–

opportunities for trouble, rising expectations, decreasing incentives (for example, restrictions on the availability of parole) and the types of prisoners concerned. King and Elliott add to this list the rise of sophisticated cliques, the mixing of short-term with long-term prisoners, the growth of campaigning and the arrival from special wings elsewhere of prisoners who were no longer treated as special (King and Elliott 1977). According to King and Elliott, the spirit of the dispersal prison had left Albany by 1972. The only two dispersals not to have a major riot over this period were Long Lartin and Wakefield. Their apparently successful approach to control needed to be understood and developed elsewhere. It was the liberal model – enhancing choice, self-respect, responsibility, and good relationships – that seemed to work, particularly in Long Lartin.

The arguments for and against dispersal or concentration were rehearsed many times: in May 1973 following disturbances at Albany and Gartree (Home Office 1973; King and Elliott 1977), following the Hull riot in 1976 (Home Office 1977; Thomas and Pooley 1980), in the May Committee Report in 1979 (Home Office 1979; also King and Morgan 1980: chapter three), the CRC Report (Home Office 1984), after an escape from Gartree in 1987,[14] and most recently again in 1994–5 with the Supermax project (King 1999). Almost always, the balance of disadvantage was felt to lie with concentration. At every review, reference was made to the developing American experience, where variations on concentration and dispersal were attempted over time. The advantage of concentration, the American experience suggested, was a lower 'body count' (Bottoms and Light 1987: 20; Ward 1987; King 1991). Reduced disruption and violence could justify practices verging on the unacceptable (although, King has argued, more recent experience at Oak Park Heights in Minnesota suggests that the right architecture can assist in the accomplishment of control, security *and* legitimacy – see King 1991, 1999). Scotland operated a form of concentration at Peterhead before experimenting with an imaginative approach to small units in later years (Coyle 1991; Bottomley, Liebling and Sparks 1994). English officials and many penologists, meanwhile, preferred (even if marginally) this culturally and penologically more attractive route.[15]

'Looking the other way': negotiating order and some dilemmas in the late 1980s and early 1990s

In 1984, following a major disturbance at Albany, the Control Review Committee defended dispersal once again on the grounds that it solved two problems: the problem of security and the problem of control.[16] Some subversive prisoners who were not Category A were better handled in higher-security establishments. This did add, however, to the difficulties of order maintenance, as subversive prisoners had considerable freedom to manipulate staff and prisoners in the relatively open regimes they were in. King and Elliott powerfully argued this case in their account of the Albany disturbances:

> The Radzinowicz sub-committee, in its advocacy of the dispersal method for dealing with the 'most difficult and dangerous prisoners' rather than the concentration method, thought that the majority of such men 'would be absorbed into the general population'. Where they were not absorbed, the use of Rule 43, to remove disruptive and subversive prisoners to the segregation unit, would provide a safeguard for the continuance of the 'liberal and constructive regime' which the sub-committee wished to see. As we have shown, Albany did disperse its difficult and dangerous prisoners among the general population – a general population that was bewildering in its variety. And it did maintain a liberal regime based on the almost complete freedom of association from unlock in the morning until lock-up at night. So many problems ensued, however, that the heaviest reliance on the use of Rule 43 did not contain them. Indeed, it must be obvious that the measures that were eventually introduced in an attempt to solve the problems represented very severe inroads into, if not a complete reversal of, the two main elements in the dispersal policy: the principle of absorbing difficult prisoners, and the principle of maintaining a liberal regime.
>
> (King and Elliott 1977: 325)

The CRC famously argued that a structure of incentives should be in place so that bad behaviour was not rewarded. Two of the many tensions of dispersal regimes were: the conflation of security and control problems, which were sometimes but not always related (see King 1999); and the conflict between good provision, in the interests of self-respect, good order and even reducing the urgency to escape, and the interests of the rest of the prison population. Dispersal prisons had better conditions and facilities than most other establishments. Personal autonomy was high – and the prisoners arguably enjoyed more freedom the 'deeper' they were in. Prisoners elsewhere in the system justifiably felt that difficult and high-security prisoners were being rewarded for bad behaviour. The CRC Report recommended the improvement of the structures of the dispersal system to 'send the right signals' to prisoners, and a new system of small special units with 'varying degrees of structure' for especially difficult prisoners. These units offered limited respite to a turbulent and difficult-to-manage dispersal estate (see Pearson 1987; Bottomley, 1994; Walmsley, 1991). The report emphasised the importance of staff–prisoner relationships for order maintenance, arguing that:

> At the end of the day, nothing else that we can say will be as important as the general proposition that relations between staff and prisoners are at the heart of the whole prison system and that control and security flow from getting that relationship right. Prisons cannot be run by coercion: they depend on staff having a firm, confident and humane approach that enables them to maintain close contact with prisoners without abrasive confrontation.
>
> (Home Office, 1984: para 16)

CRC also recommended the development of a research programme, steered by a Research and Advisory Group.[17]

The early history of dispersal prisons is characterised by variation between regimes and considerable autonomy. They were also characterised by close but sometimes conflictual staff–prisoner relationships and some fear. There were areas, in the early days, where staff were 'out of control', and arguably staff and prisoners were more inclined to take collective action than seems to be the case today (Rutherford 1984; Home Office 1979). Following the CRC Report in particular, the form of order achieved in dispersals can be characterised as a partly negotiation or exchange model, with Long Lartin at the extreme end of this model. It is significant that no major disturbance is recorded in the official literature after 1984.[18] The preferred regimes represented a working out in practice of Jenkins' dictum that 'you may have to lose some control in order to gain control' (see Bottoms and Light 1987, p. 15). The CRC Report had recommended some major changes in structures and incentives. But few of these changes materialised. The negotiation model resulted in gains in power and privileges for prisoners, and some advantages for staff, including the threat of transfer. A growing number of prisoners convicted of terrorist offences became significant players in the bid for power and autonomy. Other dispersal prisoners too were articulate rational maximisers, who were prepared to take a long-term view of their circumstances and had the organisational skills needed to make strategic inroads into the conditions of their confinement.

There were some concerns about the balance of power in these prisons as they evolved. Prisoners made demands on uncomfortable staff. On the other hand, many prisoners were 'drawn' into a kind of conformity, and many approved of the humane approach to their confinement. The special units, designed to take out the most disruptive prisoners, were largely conflict-free, and were regarded by some as an imaginative attempt to break the cycle of violence,[19] but by others as indulgent. They were prone to 'siltage' – prisoners wishing to stay, rather than work progressively back to the mainstream – and 'slippage' – a liberal drift from their original purpose and a reluctance or inability to accommodate the most disruptive prisoners (Liebling 2001). Internal accountability was sought with prisoners, but was less straightforward in relation to staff, many of whom were ambivalent about this type of imprisonment (see Fitzgerald 1987; Thomas and Pooley 1980; but also Liebling 2001). Officers were both under-using and over-using their power in different locations, and were, in places, out of their depth:[20]

A dispersal is either a cons' prison or a screws' prison. What you really want – prisoners too – is the balance. We used to be on D wing – in 90/91. That was the best wing – the lads ran it. The prison was new then. There was a big staff meeting – the staff were told to be more polite to us! They really got told by management to be liberal. It was a much more liberal regime then. D wing was run as a dispersal wing [is supposed to be run ...]. Lads were doing long, heavy sentences, it had lifers, who were spread all around the prison then, so the screws were nervous. You had a lot of 'nothing to lose' prisoners all over the place. We had all these dark corners, inmates would stick together over issues. All that.

(Prisoner)

A lot of the problems on this wing are caused by the fact that inmates have been here too long – they get very cliquey, have a real strength amongst them. They should be moving them through the system. A lot of the staff don't want to work here – they are frightened. The regime is too relaxed, the prisoners have been given too much for too long. Now's the time to take it back off them.

(Officer)

The decision to attempt a liberal regime within a secure perimeter was in many ways a brave one. Unlocking prisoners for large portions of the day and encouraging freedom and responsibility brought problems

(Sykes 1958: Sparks *et al* 1996; Pearson, personal comment) and did make relationships a key form of 'quiet power' (Liebling and Price 2001): 'People think relationships are the easy bit. In truth it's the most difficult' (Pearson, personal comment). Anxieties about the drifting and open-style dispersal regime sometimes expressed at regular meetings of the Dispersal Prisons Working Group[21] were tempered by much greater anxieties about the likely reaction if boundaries were redrawn. There were well-grounded fears that these sorts of changes, if attempted, would provoke major disorder (as they had in the past; see for example King and Elliott 1977; Thomas and Pooley 1980):

> So we ran the system knowing there was some collusion, and with relatively weak perimeters by today's standards. Our key task was to run quiet prisons that did not have major disorder.
>
> (Senior manager, PSHQ)

> I found a lot of stress here, and a lot of sick. But when I spoke to a GV there was one guy who I held in very high regard as a PO, and during the interview, this excellent ex-PO [I had to push him – 'stop bullshitting me'], he almost cried. He said, 'you've no idea, it's absolutely dreadful', he said 'I don't sleep at night when I am duty Governor the next day'. I said 'why is that?' It was the prisoner thing, everything was too prisoner oriented. Now … as you know … I am very much in favour of positive regimes but this was too much. Prisoners were doing what they wanted; they were abusing staff and nothing was happening. So I had to draw a line in the sand with the prisoners.
>
> (Senior manager)

The redrawing of boundaries did lead to disturbances, although they were contained. In that sense, what happened next 'made it possible' to redraw the boundaries in a dramatic and unprecedented way.

Mountbatten's revenge: the escapes from Whitemoor and Parkhust (1994–5)

Two remarkable sets of escapes from Whitemoor prison's Special Security Unit and from Parkhurst, both dispersal prisons, brought to light a serious breakdown in the balance of power in maximum-security establishments. The concessions given to prisoners in Whitemoor's SSU were 'unacceptable'. Prisoners had intimidated staff to the extent that they were shopping for prisoners, instructions were not complied with, levels of property held by prisoners were 'incredible' and searching procedures were resisted. An officer interviewed as part of the Woodcock Inquiry expressed surprise that a prisoner could actually shoot one of them during the course of the escape.[22] The escape from Parkhurst was similarly linked to under-enforcement of security procedures, influential prisoners having 'runners' who did their cleaning for them and so much access to private cash that paid work in prison was unnecessary. Security was not confined to the perimeter after all, but consisted of daily practices and interactions. The 'good' staff–prisoner relationships developed were not 'right' relationships (cf. Home Office 1984). 'Good' could mean 'we never see an officer on a wing' (Liebling 2000). Words like 'appeasement', 'conditioning', 'corruption' and 'laxity' became widespread currency in the English penal vocabulary. This section of the paper tells this story in some detail.

> It is the duty of those who are concerned with devising the regime
> of the prison to recognise the onerous burden that this places on the
> prison officers who are in charge of dangerous men.
>
> (ACPS 1968: 12)

The context in which the transformation of the dispersal estate took place was unique. There had been a series of major disturbances in mainly local prisons in 1990. The Woolf Report which followed had, unusually, departed from popular 'toxic mix' theories of breakdowns in order and suggested instead that prisoners had legitimate grievances about the manner of their treatment (Home Office 1991). At about this time (1991), Whitemoor prison, the newest of the dispersals, was opened. Arguably the Radzinowicz Report had always concerned itself with order. Mountbatten had been primarily concerned with security.[23] In the interests of order, now a major concern, and with the assumption that security was almost guaranteed by a modern secure perimeter, Whitemoor was operated with a strong message that prisoners should be treated in a way that generated compliance, where possible by consent. In 1994, the Prison Service almost re-experienced the humiliation of the Biggs, Blake and other escapes which had led to the Mountbatten Inquiry of 1966.

These escapes, and the Woodcock and Learmont reports which followed (Home Office 1994 and 1995 respectively), were a 'gift' to those seeking to rein drifting prisons in, and to many Governors:

They compelled the Service to bring about long overdue change within a time scale that would have been impossible otherwise.

(Senior manager)

But the reports and their recommendations constituted a genuine threat to those prisoners who were used to maximising freedom in conditions of captivity:

Woodcock and Learmont made it possible. Even prisoners saw the legitimacy of it. Michael Howard had nearly lost his job; Derek Lewis lost his. This was not us being capricious. Fighting us in that context was not a good idea. Looking back, the escapes were a gift.

(Senior manager, PSHQ)

The first of these inquiries, the Woodcock Report, was published in December 1994 (Home Office 1994) after six high-security prisoners, five of whom were convicted of terrorist offences, escaped from Whitemoor's Special Security Unit on 9 September 1994. An officer was injured in the escape, by a shot from one of the two pistols held by the escapees. An inquiry was set up, led by Sir John Woodcock and a team of mainly police detectives. The 'withering' report exposed serious weaknesses in the establishment's security procedures, unacceptable levels of concessions given to prisoners by intimidated staff, and a lack of management by senior staff at the establishment and area manager levels. The large amounts of property permitted in prisoners' cells made searching impossible. Public expense telephone calls were given too readily and written instructions were not complied with.

At the time, the SSU[24] housed ten of the highest risk prisoners in the system, all rated as Category A (exceptional risk), that is those who are considered to 'pose a danger to the public, the police or the security of the state'. The regime in the unit allowed for a high degree of recreation and movement internally, as the unit was believed to be escape-proof. During a search after the escape, a pound of Semtex was found, with fuses and detonators, concealed in the false bottom of a prisoner's paint tin. The word 'appeasement' was used to describe regime conditions in the unit.

Among the recommendations made by the report were the volumetric control of prisoners' possessions, more frequent searching of cells, the limiting of private cash, the ending of shopping trips by staff and more stringent security arrangements relating to visits to high security prisoners. 'Poor custom and practice' was to be brought into line with policy: 'It could be said that what the Prison Service needs to do most of all is to comply with its own written instructions' (Home Office 1994: 84).

Following the publication of the report, the Home Secretary announced that all of the report's recommendations had been accepted.[25] He also announced the appointment of General Sir John Learmont, a former quartermaster-general for the army, to conduct a comprehensive, independent review of security throughout the Prison Service.[26]

Whitemoor had not been built as a dispersal prison but had originally been intended to be a Category B training prison. The decision to change the designation of the prison and to add an SSU had had adverse consequences (for example, insufficient office space for staff, and officers' shifting expectations at the prison). Supervision and observation in the SSU were minimal: staff did not want to 'rock the boat'; levels of property in possession were high (running to 82 boxes and a bicycle for one prisoner) and details were poorly recorded. Searches were 'cursory' and were strongly resisted by prisoners: '... it took the police carrying out the criminal enquiry four days to search and log just one inmate's property all of which was physically located within the SSU and available to all the prisoners' (Home Office 1994: 30).

The physical congestion of the SSU might have been orchestrated. Staff were 'conditioned' by prisoners and visitors.[27] The problem of excessive property plagued all dispersal prisons at that time. 'Rubdown' searching of visitors was a sensitive issue resulting in considerable conflict (and apparent attempts by civil servants to debate the issue with prisoners over 17 months and to slide it away from the attention of ministers, pp. 38–40).[28] Visitors came often and were very familiar to staff; prisoners made it clear that they did not like staff walking about during visits. The concessions allowed produced a sense of resignation among the staff. Security in relation to visits was 'unbelievably lax' due to conditioning, familiarity and intimidation: '... the effect on staff morale and overall control had been to further shift the balance of power towards the inmates' (p. 64).

Staff were inexperienced. The privileges allowed had drifted beyond humane treatment to become major concessions. Officers went shopping for prisoners (which some officers found demeaning),[29] levels of private cash were very high[30] (a prisoner's annual entitlement was £115 plus £75 hobbies allowance), and too many private telephone calls (which had been extended after Woolf) were made. Staff had been 'conditioned' into decreased vigilance. One lesson was that close staff–prisoner interaction required careful supervision and management.

There was an overall feeling that prisoners had 'won the battle'; the regime in the unit was constantly challenged and shaped as a result. The regime of non-confrontation was driven by excessive fear of riot and insufficient fear of escape.

The response to the report was divided. The government accepted all of its 64 recommendations. Others felt the report was wholly inappropriate. A review by Roy King, argued that:

> In 30 years of observing and researching the prison system I cannot recall a report less deserving of serious attention but more dire in its largely unnecessary consequences than Sir John Woodcock's 'The Escape from Whitemoor Prison' ... From the point of view of the future of the Prison Service, the fall out is immense: It is not just unwarrantably damaging careers, it is squandering resources, setting back overdue reforms, storing up control problems, and no doubt, further dividing an already beleaguered Prisons Board.
>
> (King 1995: 63–7)

The major changes taking place in the Prison Service since the mid 1980s – Fresh Start, agency status, privatisation, management reorganisations and the reforms introduced following Woolf – had not been taken into account at all by the report, and yet constituted an essential context in which the escapes occurred. Accusations of a deliberate policy of appeasement of IRA prisoners were not seriously explored:

> It quickly becomes clear, from the way the scrabble playing officers are exposed in the opening paragraphs of Woodcock's Report, that this is going to be an inquisition in which any serious appreciation of the mundane dynamics of prison life and how they might realistically be managed are going to be subordinated to the provision of glib judgements and superficial soundbites. He appears to have started from the proposition that some things, which no doubt would puzzle many outsiders and outrage others, were self-evidently wrong ... net curtains ... staff shopping for prisoners ... the number of personal possessions allowed ... he proceeds to represent these ... as the kind of rotten core of the Prison Service in which 'a disaster (was) waiting to happen'.
>
> (*Ibid*: 64).

As it happens escapes from prisons were declining, not increasing, at the time. As with Mountbatten, it was the qualitative, not quantitative, nature of the escapes which demanded an instant reaction. Some fine-tuning might have been required, but 'there was no serious case for a high profile public inquiry' (King 1995: 65):

> Either an internal review or an Inspectorate review would have produced a better informed analysis and a better considered set of recommendations ... One is left with the inevitable conclusion that the public inquiry into Whitemoor and the choice of a policeman to head it owed more to political than operational needs.
>
> (*Ibid*: 65)

One of King's assumptions, which has proved correct in part, is that the peace process in Northern Ireland would lead to the end of IRA prisoners and the end of the need for dispersal prisons to deal with them. It is the case that the departure of Irish paramilitary prisoners has dramatically changed the dynamics of dispersal prisons. It has not, however, resulted in their demise.

The Prison Service was seen by its critics during this time as following something of a fortress route: physical changes to security at Whitemoor alone cost £5 million. Cuts to other parts of prison budgets were necessary in order to pay for these security upgradings. Specialist searching teams (Dedicated Search Teams) were deployed in many establishments. Fifty additional staff were required to do this job at Whitemoor. Woodcock himself may not have intended his report to have such major and generally applicable consequences for the Service – if the existing rules had been enough, why was there a need for these extra provisions? It was not the first time that the Prison Service had overreacted to a report on prison security. But was this an overreaction?

> The implementation of the Woodcock recommendations, coming on top of Michael Howard's preference for austere regimes and the clampdown on home leave, must have been deeply disturbing to those members of the Prisons Board who remained committed to the Woolf agenda. To prison Governors and staff, who had been struggling to come to terms with the complexities of sentence planning and prisoner compacts, and where the first tender shoots of programmes concerned with offending behaviour were just beginning to show through, fears will have been aroused that the new emphasis on security with its attendant changes in staff–prisoner relations, will simply store up control problems for the future. Certainly Lord Justice Woolf himself views what he has called 'knee-jerk' responses as undermining the delicate balance

which he sought to promote between security, control and justice and he has publicly said so.

(Ibid: 66)

King was right about changes to staff–prisoner relationships, as we shall see below. There was a second major escape, from another dispersal prison, only months later. The three escapees had been able to make tools (such as wire cutters), the constituent parts of a ladder and had managed to acquire a gun with blank ammunition. They had made a key that opened all the gates between the sports area where they had started and the outer wall. The key had been tested several times before the escape, and the three prisoners had been able to store much of their equipment in a workshop designed for purposeful training.[31] Once outside the prison, the prisoners were able to hire a taxi. They were wearing their own clothes, and they had had enough money on them to make a start. However, their plans to leave the island were unsuccessful, and they were eventually recaptured five days later. The amount of undetected preparation made by the three prisoners was a particular matter of concern.

Some of the items used in the escape were thought to have been brought in by visitors during visits. Rubdown searches were not always carried out, and staff were often too busy fetching prisoners or searching to supervise the visits room adequately. Prisoners suspected of receiving goods from visitors could be placed on 'closed visits' – but these were rarely imposed. The concept of 'family visits' had been introduced at Parkhurst following the Woolf Report. This allowed Category A and B prisoners with young children to meet their families in a more normal environment, monthly. These visits were held in the sports hall and lasted all day. Eight prisoners at a time could qualify for this privilege. According to Learmont, a number of high security prisoners soon dominated the family visits' scheme and began to resist security procedures at these and other visits. The rationale for the scheme was enhanced family contact, but Learmont concluded that the system was abused by those prisoners who were most capable of taking advantage of lax security. He argued that the concept had been successful in other lower security prisons, but was not appropriate for dispersal prisons. The practice was subsequently stopped in all dispersal prisons.

On the wings, staff were reluctant to carry out rubdown searches and cell searches to avoid confrontation with prisoners. Guidelines for property allowed in prisoners' cells were not followed. Building work was holding up new security arrangements. Prisoners were able to enter wing offices and could be intrusive and intimidating. Overall, Learmont described an 'aura of inefficiency' over security matters. The regime was too 'open'.[32] Parkhurst was typical of other dispersal prisons in offering what it saw as an open regime. Learmont described it as the opposite of the Control Review Committee ideal: it was easier to allow prisoners 'to do what they want to keep order' (Home Office 1995: 53).

The Learmont Report acknowledged that maintaining stability in a prison for long-term prisoners, some of whom pose serious difficulties to staff and management, requires a complex set of negotiations between staff and prisoners over the minutiae of prison life. But at Parkhurst, the resolution of this process fell too heavily in the favour of a number of the most challenging prisoners. Organised prisoners managed to influence the allocation of prisoners to wings: '... the power they held enabled them to condition staff to allow them to live a life of comparative freedom' (p. 54).

One wing in particular had 11 cleaners who did very little of their own cleaning and yet received a bonus pay from staff; runners did their work and other tasks for them. The word *appeasement* was again used to describe this line of least resistance taken with prisoners. Poor leadership or management of staff on the wings was compounding this problem. Prisoners had more or less unlimited access to private cash, so that if they did not work, they could still afford to buy goods in prison, provided their families could send money in. According to the report: 'It is revealing that, when twenty High Risk prisoners were transferred from the prison after the escape, the total private cash balance held on behalf of inmates fell from around £20,500 to £6,200' (Home Office 1995: 58), and 'Phone cards were purchased by prisoners up to £40 per week, and were often used as trade, to buy drugs and to gamble' (*ibid*: 57).

An unwillingness to confront prisoners on these issues was found among staff. Prisoners in some areas of the prison were opting out of regime activities and managing to exist largely unsupervised by staff, who were reluctant to enforce a rule allowing them to lock up prisoners who did not go to work during the day.

A Governor interviewed by Learmont commented on the Statement of Purpose:

A major difficulty is ambiguity. Governors have bought into the humane approach identified by Woolf and others but are now confused by the switch to a more austere approach. There are two strong but different philosophies shown in the Statement of Purpose. The purpose of the Service is not to pursue two different aims but to achieve balance.

(Home Office 1995: 81)

Learmont made a suggestion for a slightly revised Statement of Purpose, which was rejected. But the next period, 1995–2000, was to witness dramatic physical and operational changes to the dispersal system. Phone cards were taken out, the amount of property allowed was drastically reduced and controlled, prisoners' privileges were reduced and had to be earned, and massive security changes occurred. The concept of security was transformed. It was no longer about the perimeter, but was made up of thousands of daily practices inside the prison. The perimeter wall was only one small part of a secure prison. Procedures and practices mattered too: 'Security is only as good as your weak link on the landing … You depend on your residential areas being watertight' (senior officer). As one senior manager put it: 'we were fighting over the right to enter and search a prisoner's cell. This was new territory'. Residential areas had to become 'watertight'.

The post-Woodcock and Learmont Reports era brought about major transformation. Considerable criticism was made of these developments, their extreme nature and the apparent reversal of the Woolf agenda, so clearly laid out only a few years before. Terms like 'appeasement' and 'conditioning' changed the language and tone of prison life, bringing about a more vigilant, risk-averse culture and a more closely monitored performance agenda.

Reconfiguring the dispersal prison 1995–2000

How do I see my role as area manager for dispersals? Control, and support. If staff can feel confident about saying to prisoners, if you don't go to work, you will be locked up, then staff and prisoners will be more secure, and safer. We do have murders: Long Lartin was rather 'murder-prone'. Long Lartin has used IEP to turn itself around from a fairly laissez-faire culture to somewhere where staff are in control. Area managers have to be on wings. If they sit in the Governor's office, they get told it's all OK. Headquarters want us to know what our prisoners are doing, to understand our prisons, to know about the subculture. We need to be able to advance into it with a good map. We need better quality intelligence. We need well selected, properly trained, well-supported staff, who are equipped for the job – establishments will be increasingly difficult to run.

(Phil Wheatley 1995, 'Dispersal Prisons: Present and Future', speech to the Dispersal Boards of Visitors Conference)[33]

In 1995, the dispersal prisons were brought together under a single Director. This was established as a Prisons Board post, which gave it huge symbolic as well as material significance. This development created a channel of communication between the establishments and between each prison and their operationally highly experienced line manager. This move has been very important in shaping policy and practice subsequently. Phil Wheatley became Director of Dispersal Prisons in December 1995, under the then new Director General, Richard Tilt.[34] The previous Director General, Derek Lewis, had been sacked in a dramatic show-down between himself and the then Home Secretary, Michael Howard, over who should be blamed for the escapes (Lewis 1996). The Wheatley reign lasted from 1995 to 1999.[35] It was during this period that most of the clawing back was achieved. These years brought about increasing consistency between establishments and considerable reining in of the 'outliers'. A spotlight was placed over the dispersal estate, as each establishment prepared to renegotiate and strengthen its power base. This involved prison staff in a major change of style – about which they had serious misgivings. Even Governor grades were anxious that the pace was too fast and the turnaround too dramatic:

> All this is a great idea, it's been something we have been wanting for years, but it's not been properly thought through. All we have done is put a structure to what existed already and tighten up on a few things. A lot of it is knee-jerk, like the [removal of] cooking oil. All dispersals but Long Lartin have said 'don't do it', and they've been ignored ... Hopefully, there'll be a riot in week three and they'll stop it.
>
> (Senior manager)

> When I came here we had 90 sick; adjudications took all day, they were so complicated. Prisoners were rude, aggressive, anti staff, staff locked themselves in offices; they were afraid, and so we've gone about ... improving things to the extent we've staff who want to come to work, where our assaults are against the national trend, which is up, our assaults are *down*, violence against prisoners is down, staff sick: we have days when we have nil casual sick, like today when we have nil adjudications and when we have [them] it's what I call mickey mouse stuff ... that I could reduce even further by getting wing managers to take more of an interest ...
>
> (Senior manager)

Several new policies were introduced during this period:[36] the volumetric control of prisoners' property; a system of incentives and earned privileges; the removal of phone cards; the ending of the handing-in of property by prisoners' families; a new mandatory drugs testing programme; and dramatically increased internal and perimeter security, including the use of dedicated search teams, named 'burglars' by prisoners. The new Director of Dispersals had a clear task to achieve:

> I did make sure that everyone volumetrically controlled their establishments. This was an outward and visible sign that 'things had changed'. It was very dramatic. As we went through the process, some colleagues said privately they thought I was 'mad'. That shows what a change this was. We didn't fudge it. Prisoners had had things in their cells for years, and we went in to take them away. One of the most dramatic transformations in the way we run prisons over this period is that now if we introduce a policy, we implement it. If we accept recommendations, we introduce them. And we police it now, and monitor our own success.
>
> (Senior manager, PSHQ)

A colleague and I witnessed this process of emptying prisoners' cells of prized property: two pillows became one; two chairs became one; two cupboards became one; the accumulation of clothes disappeared and were stored in reception, then were sent out on visits. When the volumetric control boxes first physically appeared, prisoners threw them onto landings. The boxes came back. Prisoners held meetings, formed committees in the exercise yard, consulted their ringleaders – this was too much. Governors held the line. Staff and prisoners together emptied hundreds of cells, almost overnight. It was our most dramatic prisons research experience to date (see Liebling 1999).

Implementing incentives and earned privileges and volumetric control in a dispersal prison: a case study

In Full Sutton, the first purpose-built dispersal, where we were carrying out research at the time, prisoners on C Wing had pushed staff as far back as they could go: there were (unbeknown to the Governor) shopping trips, prisoners could use curtains to reduce visibility into their cells, staff were exceptionally polite and they were deliberately quiet when they opened cell doors ('they don't rattle your cage'). The prisoners were a powerful group with expectations of negotiation rights. They had been in the wing for a long time and had arguably formed a clique. It was known that there were problems of drug use, violence and intimidation on the wing. Prisoners had access to large amounts of private spends, for example they could spend up to £40 a week on phone cards. They cooked in groups, and were able to experience high degrees of status and agency. Staff were mixed in their view of the regime:

> A lot of the staff don't want to work here – they are frightened. The regime is too relaxed, the prisoners have been given too much for too long. Now's the time to take it back off them.
>
> (Officer)

> We did need to tighten up – it was intimidating, prisoners ganged up on us. It was terrible.
>
> (Officer)

> C wing was briefed to have a differential regime; it was more liberal. We found out by mistake that staff were going shopping. There was real slippage, the wing was lacking in procedural methods. The prisoners see their regime as being tightened up and of course, they blame me. I am pulling it back. If staff don't like confrontation, they give in. I am having to do it myself – it is hard work. They need an organised, structured person on top of them. We built an animal on C wing, putting the lifers together.
>
> (Senior manager)

Such a mixture of consideration and 'appeasement' was a 'monster',[37] but staff were nervous about the extreme nature of the transition ahead and the rapidity with which all these changes had to be introduced. In one week, volumetric control was introduced and the use of fat was withdrawn following a serious assault on an officer at Whitemoor. A suicide went undiscovered overnight because prisoners had persuaded staff that they should be allowed to cover up the spy holes which looked into their cells. Phone cards were removed and prisoners had to come to terms with an identification number system instead, which restricted the opportunity to use phone cards as trade. This forced them to be dependent on earnings made in the prison. They would have to work. The staff held regular meetings with the prisoners and explained again and again that these changes had to happen. Ringleaders were transferred out. Individual prisoners lost their chances of recategorisation, or parole, through protest:

When I first came, prisoners would not talk to an officer grade at all – staff were just passing things on to us. Staff were afraid of prisoners – they had gone through a lot. Staff were just coming to me. They were not working off their own initiative. Basic procedures were not followed – applications, for example.

(Senior manager)

The clawing back process was tense and difficult. Staff were nervous. We became nervous:

[Fieldwork notes]. Attended the morning meeting. Staff gave boxes out last night. They are trying to introduce volumetric control on D and F Wings first. They went into D wing. F wing threw them back on the netting (organised). 'We have identified one or two who are stirring/inciting (one of them has a lot of property). Be aware of this today – it may not go as smooth as anticipated …' A prisoner is anxious that volumetric control will have implications for his cockateil (the instruction only mentions budgies). There is lots of property in bundles outside windows and doors. The boxes are big (bigger than Woodcock recommended).

Prisoners were angry, and protested that these changes were intended for Special Security Units, not ordinary dispersal locations. They participated in group discussions with us, but they were angry and impatient:

[Fieldwork notes] They don't let each other into the conversation. They are all individuals; wanting our attention individually. Two collared Grant and I, one on each – the others couldn't get a look in. We can't talk in a group. It is intimidating. The other prisoners are tired of hearing the same one or two voices …

Morning meeting. Discuss F Wing; it's gone OK, there was not much stuff off them … We expected to find the boxes out on the netting again this morning – and we didn't. It's all gone OK in the end. 'I think we have won. They have accepted'. It is not as bad as inmates thought. 'We used all our own staff. It went quite well, except for one inmate, and we were expecting that'. The Governor asks if the staff are comfortable with what they are taking away? Especially in relation to items used for passing the time. The average volume of property prisoners have is one and a half boxes.

The prisoners were confused by a sudden implementation of rules and procedures that had been ignored for years. They were angry at what they saw as a change of understandings, and were often, at this tense stage, the victims of formal disciplinary procedures, where behaviour which had been overlooked was repeated (such as blocking observation panels and drawing 'modesty curtains' across their doors). The prisoners expected a certain 'lenience'. 'It come out of the blue – *that's* what I didn't like'. We could see why prisoners felt frustrated. They were paying a price for previous under-enforcement. New procedures were explained, but they were experienced as petty and restrictive – and as a change in the terms of imprisonment. Prisoners were losing time, losing their 'recats' (chances of recategorisation) and getting transfers – and this was 'trouble-free implementation':

'There are a lot worse things coming in' … I said to him, 'We are expecting you to be able to "take it like a man", the things that are coming at you. How can we trust you in a Cat C if you are so easily led?' [To me …] 'He was one of those who sat out. I do feel we are trying to do too much, too soon … If I have to fight with prisoners to keep my job, then I will – but we are pushing them into a corner'.

(Senior officer)

Senior managers began to ask, 'why did we give them curtains to begin with?' Some prisoners felt coerced by other prisoners – a reaction was being 'orchestrated' by one powerful individual:

One individual is leading the reaction – we will get rid of him, and he knows that. He is on the committee. The other prisoners are frightened of him … The frightened ones have to choose, do they go with the staff or with the prisoners – it is sometimes finely balanced. He doesn't want to go, so we have got him. We have said, we will not have one leading the rest of them. He wants Gartree, and we are arranging that for him. We have told him, if he doesn't watch it, he will go north. The stakes are very high. We could lose the prison. You know you have got a job to do, at the end of the day, we have to do as we are told too.

(Officer)

But there was powerful collective feeling.

Since Manchester, we went so far the other way, we gave them too much, now we are reversing – they will scream. Time out of cell, pay, phones and phone cards, all at once. With volumetric control – we have been feeding them information for months. It went smoothly. I thought it would be *much* worse. They expected it to be worse … Most could get what they had into the boxes. We had our inventories in place … that is unusual in a dispersal. First to get these things is always F wing [a small, semi-segregated wing] – they feel picked on. The prisoners are saying, 'You wouldn't have gone into C wing and done this'.

(Senior manager)

From our point of view, we quite like the fact that what happened (the boxes thrown out on landings) did happen – that has taken the fire out, because the others know it has been accepted, despite some resistance, and that in the end, it was not as bad as they expected. We are listening to them – but no one is really listening to us. We didn't agree with the 'shopping' policy. Staff do believe that these are the right policies, but feel that they are coming in too soon. We don't want confrontation. We want them to be responsible and to earn everything they get – they are looking for an easy option in life, they just take, take, take. This is a culture shock for them. It's got to be done.

(Officer)

Staff are subject to what I call the coastline effect – they have been worn down over time by constant nagging by prisoners. The prisoners target the weak links. They think it's easier to say yes than no – but it's not.

(Senior manager)

This era was experienced by prisoners, and witnessed by many, including ourselves, as deeply punitive. There was something profoundly unpleasant and depriving about having things taken away. Staff were very reluctant to do it. The necessity was recognised by many, but the accomplishment of this new form of penal order – almost overnight – was excruciating. The new boundaries were fiercely contested, but perhaps for the first time, there were no concessions: 'I agreed to bring the curtain down at night, but I still thought we could use it for getting undressed. Obviously not' (Prisoner).

The simultaneous introduction of a scheme whereby prisoners had to earn what were in effect a reduced set of privileges by 'good behaviour', also caused major clashes. There was a particular problem with the cleaners. They were the trusted, powerful men on the wing. The problem

125

was, they didn't fulfil the criteria for the enhanced (more privileged) regime. They were not engaging in constructive activities, addressing their offending behaviour or signing their compacts. Staff did not distribute jobs according to those sorts of criteria. Staff negotiated with managers that they would explain the criteria to their cleaners and give them a month to do something about their behaviour. The staff thought this was fairer than simply applying new rules:

> Dispersals are potentially difficult at any time. There was a time (here, a few years ago) when prisoners ignored staff and staff ignored Governor's instructions; staff locked themselves in offices. We made the rules clear to staff and prisoners; made sure that processes were fair and seen to be objective. We gave staff confidence. We had had enormous levels of sick, assaults, etc. We tackled that. We made managers manage. We certainly com-municated with staff ... We made sure staff did their job. It is a different world now; it's a pleasure to walk around the landings. Prisoners know that we are serious. We have communicated with prisoners, and that is why we are implementing all these policies more slowly.
>
> (Senior manager)

These changes did cause disturbances, which happened in a sur-prisingly clear way, in almost a direct relationship to the closeness or distance of relationships between staff and prisoners (Liebling 1999, 2000). Here was the key dilemma: the CRC were right – staff–prisoner relationships were at the heart of everything, but some clearer thinking was urgently needed about what constituted 'right' or 'good' relation-ships. There were significant losses over this period in prisoners' perceptions of relationships, staff and regime fairness, progress in prison, and clarity and consistency of treatment. The losses were experienced throughout the prison estate (see Table 3).

A look at institutional data for Full Sutton (Table 4) illustrates the nature of the changes taking place: fewer assaults and injuries, higher levels of 'policing' and lots of complaints. The power base of staff was shifting significantly. I have argued elsewhere that the period 1995–6 brought about a major shift in the power bases on which staff could draw, so that they had less exchange power available, but more coercive power available (Hepburn 1985; see also Liebling 2000).

Many prisoners did recognise the necessity of this change and many gained a higher degree of safety and a calmer life. However, they also found the changes traumatic and threatening, and resented the new

Table 3 *Overview of outcome effects of policy changes in five prisons 1995–1996*

	Local	Training	Dispersal	Young offender	Women's open	All cases
Behaviour	↓	↑				
Order		↑↑	↑		↓	
Relations with staff	(↓)			↓	↓↓	↓
Staff fairness	↓	↓	↓	↓	↓	↓
Regime fairness[38]	↓	(↓)	↓	↓	↓	↓
Woolf dimension[39]	↓	(−)	↓	↓	↓	↓
Making progress	↓	↓	(↓)	↓(↓)	↓	↓
Participation	↓	↓		↓		↓

Source: Incentives and Earned Privileges Research (Liebling *et al* 1997).

Table 4 *Selected primary institutional indices (adjusted to annual rates per 100 prisoners) of behaviour and control change, Full Sutton, 1995–1996*

	Full Sutton 1995	Change	Full Sutton 1996
Population	550		546
Total assaults	13.3	↓	7.9
Head injuries	11.3	↓	5.9
Adjudications	201.5		228.2
Control and restraint	10.9		12.5
Reportable incidents	31.3		32.6
Security information reports	205.8	↑	489.4
Requests and complaints	105.5	↑	193.4

intrusions into their autonomy. Perhaps the culmination of this period was the 'showdown' between the Service and a number of prisoners over the introduction of the new system of close supervision centres during 1998.[40] This was a contested step – and arguably the Prison Service were persuaded to retreat a little. The self-consciously restrictive, punitive and heavy-end CSC system has been revised during 2001 to reintroduce a degree of flexibility and legitimacy to the treatment of difficult and dangerous prisoners:

Radzinowicz was not sentimental about prisoners. He said we would have to have segregation units, which looked like they were separate. That was the thing we never really managed to do. That was to do with the taking over of existing prisons, the unhappy reliance on Rule 43, and so on. He was right when he said we would have to recognise that an open regime could be manipulated by some to the detriment of others and we would have to cater for them. We are now doing something of what Radzinowicz said would be necessary. We are doing it for the whole system rather than for individual establishments, which means we are probably doing more than he envisaged. But its success does seem to depend on getting this bit in place.

(Senior manager, PSHQ)

Entering the twenty-first century: penal practice and prospects for the high security estate

You can say no to prisoners now, in the knowledge that you'll be backed. Staff have days off now. It's more professional. You're more accountable now. There's no racism, no brutality. We use the control we've got more carefully. There is much more structure: a prisoner who wants to behave will get rewarded. We are using more power, but, if you like, more legitimately. There's a clearer process.

(Senior manager, PSHQ)

Is this a liberal regime within a secure perimeter? I'd say it's a *controlled* regime within a secure perimeter. I don't like the word 'liberal' ... I wouldn't say we are governing prisons with the prisoners' *consent*, but with their *approval*, if you can see what I mean. They are *informed*, rather than *consulted*. We are not taking them for mugs, but we're not allowing them to run the place.

(Senior manager, PSHQ)

There are lots of reasons why we are enjoying what we are enjoying ... I guess it's all a cycle. There are lots of young staff now who have never experienced dispersals when they are terrible; they have only experienced control. We thought it was our job to take all that nonsense. Maybe these wouldn't stand for it. There is no solidarity, no esprit de corps any more – the prisoners reflect young men in society ... They want their drugs, their TVs and they are selfish. They are not a team. Then the older guys want an easier life – there is a respect for them amongst the younger lads, and they have a stake in control. Their agenda is to keep the place quiet. The difference is dramatic. Now, when Governor grades walk on the wings, they just chat, you don't get buttonholed.

(Senior manager, PSHQ)

The return to power by the Prison Service was largely achieved during the late 1990s, albeit with a heavy price paid by prisoners. The mood was tense, and some dramatic deepening of the prison experience took place (see Liebling 1999; also King and McDermott 1995 on the 'depth' and 'weight' of imprisonment, after Downes 1988). It is possible that the 'dehumanising moment' of 1995–7 was linked to the mood of a failing Conservative government in decline. Whatever the cause, ministers were furious about the excessive privileges enjoyed by high security prisoners at some dispersals. The atmosphere of the years to follow was frenetic (personal comment 2000).

Since about 1998, it appears that the roller-coaster of legitimacy (Sparks 1994a) may have turned upwards. It is a revised form of legitimacy in which order and control are primary.[41] Perhaps surprisingly, these dimensions now seem to be valued instead of resisted by many prisoners. It seems that to view these kinds of developments in prisons as cyclical is to miss the changes in understanding and in external conditions which change the terms of the debate. There have been moves towards greater transparency, fairness in *process* and in levels of safety, although fair processes, like relationships, are being deployed to oil the wheels of a much more powerful system. It was to be another few years before the close supervision centres emerged from their early hostilities (see King 1999; Clare and Bottomley 2001).[42] Senior managers in Prison Service Headquarters feel that it has been precisely this most contested step – getting the segregation or exclusion bit 'right', or making it effective on their terms – that has enabled the dispersals to reach a kind of stability.[43] The social structure of the prison has been deliberately disrupted, but the fragmentation and disorganisation involved has reduced rather than multiplied gang activities and violence (see Wacquant 2001). There are more 'horizontal cleavages' among prisoners, and a less marked 'vertical cleavage' between prisoners and staff today, to use Wacquant's language. But if there is more of an 'iron fist' in the prison today, it may surely have some claim to legitimacy if it has reduced the rule of razor blades and powerful inmate leaders. It is possible that the system as it stands today is closer to the Radzinowicz blueprint than at any time during its turbulent history:[44]

It is liberal. You can cook your own food, it's quite relaxed, it's not a strong POA prison, the environment is good, the staff know me, they know my interests. Security is over the top. But yes, they let you have your birds, and your guitars ... one lad's got a violin.

(Prisoner)

This is despite an unplanned, creeping concentration. There are now fewer establishments (there are five, where Radzinowicz envisaged three or four), but the concentration of Category A prisoners is much higher than he would have expected at around 30 per cent (see Table 5).[45] This minimises some of the disadvantages (such as too many prisoners held in conditions exceeding their security requirements), but arguably increases the need for a more controlled internal environment. The increased control achieved applies to staff as well as to prisoners. Perhaps it has taken twenty rather turbulent years to learn how to operate a dispersal system. Rereading King and Elliott's *Albany* in the light of modern practices, it is striking how lock-down searches now seem to flow relatively smoothly, compared to the three-day, un-expected, misunderstood and heavy-handed exercise described by King and Elliott in 1972 (1977: 295–7). Still, the vulnerability to extreme fluctuations seems to be in the air.

The last major incident to take place in a dispersal prison, apart from a number of hostage incidents and some individual instances of serious

Table 5 *Selected figures on the current dispersal estate*[46]

Prison	Wakefield	Long Lartin	Frankland	Full Sutton	Whitemoor
Opened	1966 (1594)	1960	1983	1987	1991
Capacity	585	522	559	596	534
% Category As	15%	19%	25%	34%	34%
% Basic	1%	6%	1%	2%	1%
% Standard	44%	53%	43%	54%	42%
% Enhanced	55%	41%	56%	44%	57%
% VPs	100%[47]	–	66%	54%	39%
Complaints to ombudsman (annual)	65	107	72	124	72
Positive assaults adjudications	1.4%	4.8%	4.1%	4.9%	10.4%
% of positive drug tests	0.06%	10.9%	7.0%	5.3%	14.3%

violence, was at Full Sutton during 1995. Those working in headquarters describe a sort of unprecedented 'peace' in the maximum-security estate ('it's probably as good as I have seen it in my career'). This apparent stability (see Figures 1–7, below) has been achieved by a major shift in the balance of power and a more controlled approach to establishments and to individual prisoners.[48] There have also been some significant shifts in the nature of the population, with a much higher proportion of vulnerable prisoners. Prisoners feel 'less in charge of their world'. But they describe dispersal prisons as 'no longer frightening places'. There are drug problems – and still there are individual instances of violence. But as one prisoner put it, 'there is no mad social life ... it is a very controlled environment'. For the first time, there are offending behaviour programmes. There is sentence planning, a comprehensive assessment system, and an attempt to offer constructive interventions:

> The overarching purpose of dispersal prisons [is] ... to protect the public from our most high risk and serious offenders and this could not be done simply by delivering security and control.
>
> (Senior manager, PSHQ)

Since Woodcock the major change in Dispersals has been effective sentence management and realistic, focused Offending Behaviour

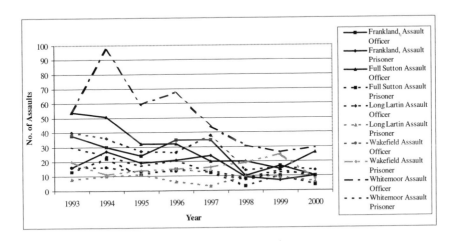

Figure 1   *Assaults in dispersals, 1993–2000*

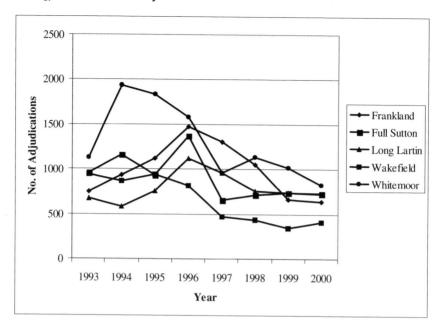

Figure 2   *All adjudications in dispersals, 1993–2000*

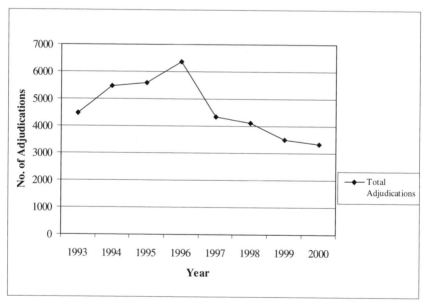

Figure 3   *Total adjudications (dispersal prisons), 1993–2000*

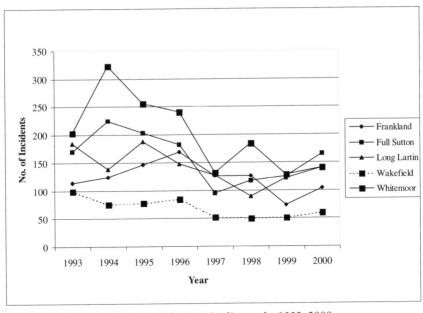

Figure 4   *Threats and abusive behaviour in dispersals, 1993–2000*

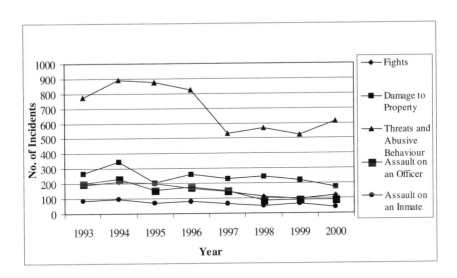

Figure 5   *Fights, damage to property, threats, abusive behaviour, assaults on officers and inmates in all five dispersals prisons, 1993–2000*

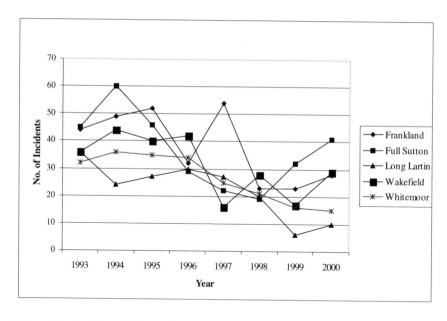

Figure 6   *Number of fights in dispersals, 1993–2000*

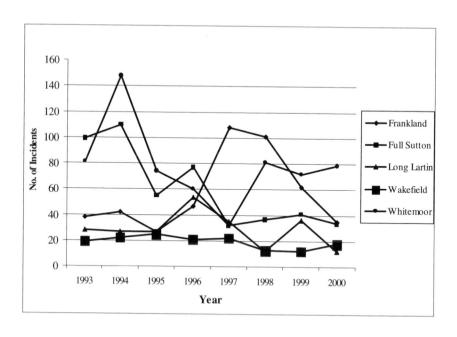

Figure 7   *Incidents involving damage to property in dispersals, 1993–2000*

Programmes. Instead of containment and avoidance of disorder at almost any price ... we have now supplemented greater control with a method and a means to progress prisoners through dispersals. It is worth co-operating now. Before, you were stuck in dispersal so [you had to] be demanding and disruptive to control your environment. You had nothing to lose.

(Senior manager)

It is still 'the deep end', and the problem of negative labelling identified by King and Elliott is widespread:

You're at the bottom of the ladder and the top of the ladder, if you know what I mean. You're the worst, so this holds you up. You don't progress. It's high status, in the bad sense. You are generalised. But you've got a nice cell, good association, great work, good staff. It's humane in that I don't feel threatened. It's a clean and safe environment. But it's a very negative place. There are not a lot of positive vibes. You don't get good news in these places. People get bad news – and that has ramifications for all of us. This is not 'alright'. Do you know what I mean?

(Prisoner)

Movement is restricted, and rubdown searches routinely take place as prisoners go from the wing to other locations. As these previously contested practices take place, and further changes are introduced, prisoners acquiesce. When they felt more powerful, they would resist and protest, individually and collectively:

That's the thing we have tackled. We have changed their expectations about what they can get away with before we will react. We have moved more towards 'the Albany model', if you like, but a more legitimate version. We are clearer about what we allow ... What's changed is the subculture doesn't run loose so that we are just dealing with the excesses. It doesn't take off like it did.

(Senior manager, PSHQ)

Since the 1990s, the social order of the prison has broken down. There are no 'No. 1 prisoners' any more. The population is less organised, there are no inmate leaders. The 'what' is no longer negotiated – only the 'how'. The influence of drugs cannot be overestimated, but it is also a change in the population. We have

135

Control and Restraint, and we have 'feminised' establishments [with the introduction of women officers]. Sentences have changed beyond recognition. Decency is a less risky word.

(Senior manager)

There are still tensions, but they are individualised. The tensions are to do with restrictions on movement and the need for self-control,[49] and at this deep end of custody, the need for a personal strategy for down-grading. It is a 'situational-plus' model of social control, with a certain amount of self-governance added.[50] There are, as described by Sparks, Bottoms and Hay in Albany, fewer developed tensions between individuals (Sparks et al 1996). Those disputes that do arise seem linked to the drugs trade. Wings are physically subdivided into spurs, so there is less scope for a developed economy. Prisoners have fewer goods and resources, and they have televisions in cells:

> Prisoners accept it when we have a lockdown. It used to generate loads of mess and rubbish in the exercise yard. Staff seem better able to deal with incidents and problems – they are happier to talk to prisoners.
>
> (Senior officer)

Segregation units are not full, and in some cases have been reduced in size. Special security units have not been filled following the release of Irish prisoners under the peace process. On the other hand, trouble is actively prevented: intelligence is used to identify and remove individual 'problem prisoners'. The processes are more carefully controlled: 'We get the right few, and we gather evidence. We no longer transfer out the whole gang' (Senior officer).

More *formal* power is used, but it is deployed in a more rule-governed way.[51] As one officer said:

> This is not a supermax. There is a level of humanity. We have a duty of care and that involves some flexibility. We have good relationships. The atmosphere is better, calmer, there is less friction. I enjoy working here. We have a good rapport. I like coming in here and having a good chat with them about the football.
>
> (Senior officer)

Staff feel increasingly accountable – the number of complaints by prisoners is very high (Ombudsman 2000; and Table 4). Increasing access to several avenues of external review is widely used. Staff are reluctant to put themselves at risk, so resort to unofficial violence is rare, and the use of official violence is 'literally the last resort'.

Moves are afoot to make dispersal prisons places where offending can be addressed.[52] They are aspiring to be something more than 'human warehouses' (Cohen 1974), where progress is impossible until prisoners move on. Prisoners are asking for more courses – they want to have their risk reduced, so they can get off Category A, and start to see light at the end of the tunnel. They are doing imprisonment on the terms of those in power. Where there is resistance (and there is less) it takes the form of 'gleaning'; censoriousness (see Mathiesen 1965) is targeted at the establishment for not providing more tackling offending behaviour opportunities. The CRC recommendation about 'sending the right signals' has been brought into operation. The engagement of prisoners in their own incarceration provides a defence against the otherwise unimaginable psychological consequences of non-acquiescence.

The question for the new dispersal model is whether the new mode of compliance accomplished is too coercive, too closely linked to power, so that prisoners have acquiesced in rather than 'approved' the modern regime. Arguably, the Prison Service should never have sought *consent* from those it holds in custody, but it is conceivably appropriate to seek some form of moral approval by the majority to the form (if not the length) of imprisonment delivered. The quotient of external social control has undoubtedly increased – and following losses in legitimacy during the transition, there now seems to be acquiescence. Will this transition be sustained?

> [Only by] … progression planning to ensure that senior managers of the right 'type' are in post; and those managers must supervise and support main grade staff to avoid a return to collusive appeasement. The estate has changed. [We now have] standards, a discrete Directorate, and focused management teams [who are] less likely to return to the sentimental liberal regimes. Slippage today is more likely to come from staff complacency or avoidance of confrontation.
>
> (Senior manager)

So is the modern dispersal prison a form of imprisonment that can be delivered humanely and fairly? Those who knew Radzinowicz well tell me he would have had no problem with discipline and control. These notions are not necessarily in conflict with his strong commitment to humanitarian principles. A certain amount of power has positive as well as negative consequences. Perhaps open regimes do not make 'good sociological sense' (Young 1987: 112) after all, particularly without the right architecture, management and staffing arrangements (see King 1991). It is interesting that recent abuses of power by prison staff have come to light in local prisons and young offender institutions and not in dispersals, where staff are very careful with the power they hold and are tightly managed by those above them and those below them, who know what their entitlements are. Some of the staff in Whitemoor (and elsewhere) were anxious that the collective memory of major disorder is fading, and that the accomplishments of security and order are already dangerously taken for granted (personal comment 2001). Control cannot be held at the highest levels for long. Already there are signs that negotiations and compromises are creeping back in. Is this for reasons of humanity or pragmatism? Perhaps Sykes is right after all and there are sociological limits to total systems of power (Young 1987; Sykes 1958).

Reflections on the liberal penal project (and its demise)

The history of the dispersal estate is in part a story of good intentions. Radzinowicz recognised how easily concentration leads to inhumanity. But it is also a story of pragmatism, short-termism, compromise and sometimes injustice. It is a tale of the complexity of the prison world, and the fragility of liberal and humanitarian ideals, when they are practised in sensitive, volatile penal environments:

> No one in their right mind would have wanted what we had then. It was control by fear. Now we have gone through a recovery programme, we are in a position to deliver a positive regime which seeks to allow prisoners some control over their day-to-day activities, in a constructive setting, but one in which the real risks associated with their population are recognised.
>
> (Senior manager)

> You can't be 'Mr Big' in a dispersal prison now and enjoy it. We have delivered safety and consistency, which is better for the less high profile prisoner. There has been a redistribution to the otherwise more powerless prisoners. This offers them protection.
>
> (Senior manager, PSHQ)

In many ways, the story told is the story of a dramatic transformation in the terms of imprisonment, away from one, perhaps implicit, model of legitimacy towards another.[53] The liberal model has always attracted its critics: under the guise of rehabilitation, psychiatric control, indeterminate sentences, treatment ideologies join the other custodians 'in the jostle for power in the prison world' (Cohen 1974: 410). The word liberal cannot be used by those working in dispersal prisons: its resonance goes too deep. Yet it is possible that a liberal regime, in the 'due process' sense of the term (von Hirsch 1976), is being more effectively delivered than at previous stages in recent history. As Peter Young argues, a lack of clarity about the use of important concepts like control and order, and by implication concepts like liberal and humane, leaves the prison world vulnerable to multiple interpretations (Young 1987: 99; and see Sparks and Liebling, forthcoming). The early history of dispersal prisons illustrates the significance of his argument. A failure to specify the meaning of the term 'liberalism' has resulted in its being held accountable for what now looks like arbitrary and unaccountable power.[54]

If we return to the Radzinowicz Report, the two key parts of his plan not now in place are, first, the variation between the regimes of these maximum-security prisons (there is much more deliberate control from the centre and greater uniformity between them); and second, prisoners are not entitled to home leaves or generous visits. This is in line with the CRC recommendation that prisoners should have incentives to get out of dispersals to lower-security prisons, where visit entitlements are more generous. It is the case that offenders labelled as psychopaths are being catered for in dispersals, in the new 'Dangerous Personality Disordered' Units, recently opened at Whitemoor and soon to open at Frankland. Perhaps most marked is the choice of Governors for dispersal prisons. They are experienced and accomplished. They are also, in ways that some may regret, but others will welcome, without 'sentimentality'.

It seems that, for now, the Prison Service has won the control and security war.[55] Can a prison still be a symbol of government power since the introduction of agency status? It seems almost as though dispersal prisons represent a determined demonstration by the Prison Service *to* the government that the Service can embody the kind of power to discipline and challenge that the modern Labour government demands of it.[56] There are lessons here about the role of the prison, the centrality of its political and expressive functions, as well as a reminder about its sociological complexity. There are questions to be asked about the increasing quantity, depth and weight of imprisonment, and the apparent lack of, or *invisibility* of, resistance to the increasing amount of power wielded. In short, if Radzinowicz were here today, I suspect he would approve of the current dispersal prison system.[57] The paradox of the modern managerialist, 'characterless' age is its exposure (and in places repair) of the flaws of the so-called golden age that preceded it (Sennett 1998; Faulkner 2001). Effectiveness, safety, accountability and decency are reasonable penological goals to pursue, if necessary, with vigour. A deeper 'confusion' (Faulkner 2001) may lie in the broader civic and political sphere, where so many of the darker contours of penal life, management and sensibility are shaped.

Acknowledgements

The final version of this paper benefited greatly from the insightful and constructive comments of Roy King, David Shaw, Richard Sparks and Phil Wheatley, and also from helpful discussions following a seminar presentation organised by the High Security Directorate in December 2001. I would also like to thank Ian Blakeman, Tony Bottoms, John Goulds, Uma Moorthy, Mike Shannon, Claire Sweeney and Mike Webster for assistance with the preparation of this paper, and staff and prisoners at HMP Whitemoor, for continued access and interest. I am especially grateful to Helen Griffiths for her most efficient help with the presentation of data, proofreading and references. Finally, thanks are also due to David Gant, John Staples, Ivor Woods and others at Full Sutton, and especially Grant Muir, for memorable fieldwork days.

Notes

1 Staff at Long Lartin often referred to their establishment as the 'last Radzinowicz prison' during the late 1980s (Sparks *et al* 1996: 105). Fewer staff currently employed at new dispersal prisons have such a clear sense of the Radzinowicz name.
2 Not all dispersal prisons were the same, of course, and some (for example, Wakefield and Albany) had more restricted or paternalistic regimes (see Sparks *et al* 1996). Some commentators never saw the introduction of dispersal prisons as a liberalising move (e.g. Cohen and Taylor 1972; King and Morgan 1980).
3 Helpful accounts of key stages can be found in King and Elliott (1977), Bottoms and Light (1987), Home Office (1979), King and Morgan (1980), Home Office (1984), Thomas and Pooley (1980), King and McDermott (1995), Sparks *et al* (1996). The related stories of special units can be found in Bottomley and Hay (1991), Bottomley (1994), Liebling (2001), Walmsley (1991) and Bottomley, Jepson *et al* (1994b).
4 See Home Office (1966) and Price (2000) for a detailed account of Mountbatten's review of security.

5 Those prisoners requiring the highest degree of security, 'whose escape would be highly dangerous to the public or the police or the security of the state, no matter how unlikely the escape might be' (Prison Service Order 0900: 6; also Home Office 1966 and Price 2000: chapter 2).

6 The term 'liberal' is problematic, as I shall discuss later. For a more detailed account of a recent retreat from liberalism in criminal and social justice, see Faulkner (2001: 44 and 102–3), King (1999) and Stenson and Sullivan (2001).

7 There were 878 male adult prisoners (3.6 per cent of the total prison population of adult males) serving sentences of ten years and over in 1967.

8 There were 138 Category A prisoners in 1967. There are now 970.

9 The Radzinowicz Report was quite particular in its recommendations for staff, showing some sensitivity to the difficulty of the task envisaged: staff should have the opportunity to discuss difficulties and frustrations, what is going well on their wings and what is not. They should 'try to reach a better understanding of the causes of friction and of the behaviour of difficult prisoners' (p. 34), with the assistance of specialists. The subcommittee envisaged staff engaging in either security or 'treatment' roles in rotation, but being trained to take up either role. Training should be increased and staff ratios should be such as to allow officers to attend courses that are on offer (p. 74). Prison officers should 'be able to attend university courses, such as the short courses now held in criminology', and they should be able to see related work done elsewhere and abroad. 'A social club with good recreation facilities is needed' (p. 75). Communications within the establishment must be good – as prisoners could quickly exploit divisions between staff groups.

10 The report alluded to some research which showed that the social structure of a maximum-security prison is distinctive, with norms and values separating the prisoners from the staff and containing the sanctions of ostracism and violence for non-conformity with the prisoner culture. This culture was in part a reaction to the effects of imprisonment and might be amenable to influence by the formal organisation of the prison.

11 The state of knowledge about the effects of long prison sentences was insufficient, but enough was known to persuade the subcommittee that long-term prisoners should be exposed to a wide variety of stimuli, they should make as many decisions for themselves as possible, and they should not become dependent and institutionalised (p. 59). Regular reviews and moves between establishments should take place. Breaks without work, and breaks involving additional visits and other earnable privileges, should be possible in alternative establishments.

12 Radzinowicz argued that the concept of 'liberalism' is rightly associated in the criminal law and criminal justice system with the fundamental concepts of fairness, legality and the rule of law (Radzinowicz 1999: 116). Its meaning and application *in the penal context* has never been clearly articulated.

13 In addition, a strategy for 'cooling off' disruptive individuals in selected

cells in local prisons was introduced (CI 10/1974). This system, known as 'the ghost train' by those who witnessed or experienced it, remains in use today, albeit under revised procedures. A Dispersal Prisons Steering Group was established in 1977, giving a slightly greater level of oversight by Prison Department Headquarters. In reality, 'the group functioned so that each dispersal governor defended his own policy and resisted harmonization' (personal comment). This became a Working Party on Control in Dispersals in 1979, and was reconstituted with different membership and new terms of reference as the Control Review Committee in 1983.

14 After the Gartree escape, a decision was taken to retain and remodel the dispersal estate, reducing its overall size to six and distinguishing between those that could take high risk and standard Category A prisoners.

15 With the exception of King and Morgan, and the Prison Officers' Association (see King and Morgan 1980: chapter 3). Serious consideration was given to the building of one or two 'supermax' prisons following the Learmont Report (Home Office 1995). A project team did suggest that such an establishment was feasible, especially if paid for by taking one or two dispersals out of commission, but the newly formed Labour government abandoned the plan in the light of massive expenditure on the existing dispersals, the peace process and relative stability in the dispersal estate (see King 1999).

16 Andrew Rutherford noted that the CRC Report was 'put together by several of the most liberal senior officials in the prison department and there can be little doubt that it is one of the most sensible and sensitive documents to have emerged from the Home Office in recent years' (Rutherford 1987: 63). The Committee of eleven included Tony Langdon (Chairman), Arthur de Frisching, Ian Dunbar, Tony Pearson and Jim Perriss.

17 The research programme developed by the Research and Advisory Group (set up in response to the CRC Report; Home Office 1987), included a literature review on control in prison (Ditchfield 1990); the identification of control-problem prisoners (Home Office 1987: Annex C; Williams and Longley 1987); a number of studies of 'special units' (Walmsley 1991; Bottomley, Jepson et al 1994); a study of special security units (Walmsley 1989); and a study of 'control problems and the long-term prisoner' (Sparks et al 1996).

18 There have been some 'contained' disturbances, including one at Albany in 1985 (Sparks et al. 1996) and at Full Sutton in 1995.

19 Parkhurst C Wing, briefly, and Barlinnie for much longer, were two notable examples of this self-conscious aim (Sparks 1994b; Boyle 1977).

20 Two contrasting dispersal prison regimes, one more social, and one more situational, are described in detail in the study by Sparks, Bottoms and Hay, in Prisons and the Problem of Order (1996). Albany, with its apparently restrictive but good 'service delivery' regime, had a degree of legitimacy because it was predictable. Long Lartin, on the other hand, had high legitimacy in the eyes of many, but was regarded as capricious and less safe.

In these contrasting regimes, both had close staff–prisoner relationships (see also Coyle 1987).

21 Then chaired by Head of Custody Group.

22 One ex-IRA prisoner commented on the success of the strategy adopted by the IRA prisoners in Whitemoor for this reason (personal comment).

23 One of King's criticisms of the dispersals policy has been the conflation of problems of security with problems of control. He argues that concentration may be more appropriate for prisoners requiring high degrees of security than for prisoners who pose control problems. The categories do, of course, overlap. Troublesome prisoners are often 'upgraded' to ensure closer management, or they are allocated to a dispersal as Category B prisoners, who might be 'better suited' to a more secure regime (see King and McDermott 1990; Bottoms and Light 1987; Price 2000; Padfield and Liebling 2000: 41–2).

24 Special Security Units are small, physically separate units designed to house prisoners who are Exceptional Risk Category A. These prisoners do not pose a control problem, but are considered capable of orchestrating an escape (Walmsley 1989).

25 Despite some rigorous critique of the report and its recommendations. See e.g. the comments by King quoted at pp 115–117 above.

26 Sir David Yardley, a former local government ombudsman, was asked to determine whether disciplinary proceedings should be instigated against any member of the Prison Service. Some of those involved in the inquiry felt that the terms of reference should have included broader questions of context, such as the changes underway in the Service, population pressures, the need to strike a balance between care and control, and the management problems relating to difficult prisoners. These were all issues which absorbed time and produced distraction from the core security tasks. However, the inquiry did not consider these broader questions.

27 This pattern is familiar to those who have worked in the Maze prison in Northern Ireland, where such tactics were routinely employed by IRA prisoners.

28 Woodcock describes how the changing of clothes on visits became a ritual for 'looking one's best' and felt the officers involved had almost forgotten the security origins of such a procedure (Home Office 1994: 42).

29 One example of non-satisfaction was when an inmate threw a bag of new potatoes at the officers because the potatoes were too small. 'A great commotion had ensued which resulted in a supervisor ordering a second visit to the shops to obtain a larger variety' (Home Office 1994: 66).

30 'It has the potential to be a source of power to the holder. This power can exist both in relation to other inmates and in their ability to subvert staff' (ibid: 66).

31 All areas of the prison were covered by CCTV, but the control room in which the cameras are viewed was at the time staffed by inexperienced and largely untrained officers. Parkhurst provided opportunities for prisoners to work

in a laundry, tailor's shop, charity shop or welder's workshop or to carry out cleaning duties. Prisoners were allocated to jobs, as in most prisons, by a Labour Board. The prisoner's history was supposed to be taken into account when allocating to jobs. The main facility for manufacturing the escape items was the Vocational Training Course welding workshop, staffed by an instructor. A prison officer would be present in the area to supervise, normally from an observation box, but the officers would often use this time to write reports. Prison officers were not trained in metalwork for this job and so would not know whether what prisoners were doing was legitimate. One of the escapees was a qualified sheet-metal worker. In January 1994 he was assessed by the workshop instructor as being suitable to work in the welding workshop to work for his National Vocational Qualification certificate in welding. He was seen as competent enough to be left to work without supervision or interference. He became one of the highest-paid prisoners in the shop. This part of the escape plan story led Learmont to call for a review of all work and training available to prisoners in dispersal prisons.

32 The Control Review Committee Report, published in 1984, had defined the nature of an appropriately open regime as follows: 'By an "open regime", we certainly do not mean one that allows prisoners to decide what to do from day to day, but one that offers a range of constructive activities, the opportunity of association, and supervision by staff who have the time and training to take a personal interest in each inmate as an individual' (Home Office 1984: 5).

33 This was the first such conference and recognition of the important role played by Board members (at least potentially) in the prevention of and satisfactory response to major incidents.

34 He had previously been Head of Custody Group, and (briefly) Area Manager for London North. He had worked at Hull prison from 1971, one year into its life as a dispersal prison.

35 Phil Wheatley was promoted to Deputy Director in 1999. Brodie Clark (previously Governor of Whitemoor during its shift-to-power era) took over as Director of the Dispersal estate. Brodie Clark was promoted in 2000 to Head of Security, and was succeeded by Peter Atherton (also a former Governor of a dispersal prison). All three of the Directors of the Dispersal estate were very experienced and exceptionally well regarded operational men. Commentators have observed that the Wheatley/Clark regime was not the 'natural' successor to the Langdon/Dunbar era, and their ascension represented a major departure from a previous 'liberal humanitarian' ethos. Some might now argue that the tighter grip exerted from above has delivered a better quality of life for staff and prisoners in dispersal prisons (see final section of chapter).

36 These policies did not all coincide as dramatically in other dispersals as they did in Full Sutton. The personal identification system, for example, was introduced much later in other dispersals, although the introduction of IEP

and the greater emphasis on searching did reduce the accumulation of phone cards.

37 In fact, there seemed to be a conflation of some perfectly defensible practices (for example, staff being polite and quiet, the ability of prisoners to cook in groups) with some abuses (staff feeling demeaned). This detailed unpicking of the defensible from the indefensible – the deep structures of penological practice – requires considerable and constant attention (see Liebling and Price 2001; Bottoms 1998).

38 This dimension (five items) included a question on whether prisoners felt they were being 'looked after with humanity'. About half of those interviewed thought they were 'a little' (Liebling *et al* 1997).

39 The 'Woolf Dimension' consisted of a series of questions relating to consistency and clarity of treatment ('how clear are staff in telling you the rules?'; 'how consistently do staff interpret the rules?'; 'are you given reasons for decisions?'; 'how good is the speed of response to requests and applications?'; and so on).

40 These centres replaced the CRC Special Units and the Continuous Assessment Scheme, and were based on a graduated progression from very restricted conditions to more general conditions involving activities and intervention. They did not require the consent of those selected; and the basic, segregation and standard regimes were seriously resisted by the first intake of prisoners (see Clare and Bottomley 2001; HMCIP 2000). Segregation, according to Messinger the *logic* of control, may be proving to be the coercive core on which the newly controlled regime of the maximum-security long-term prison rests. The 'Chinese box' effect (Cohen 1974) of segregation within segregation certainly appeared to be the direction the Service was taking during the latter years of the century (see Clare and Bottomley 2001).

41 This question of what a legitimate penal regime might be is a significant and complex issue (see Sparks *et al* 1996). Different ideals are pursued at different points in history, and competing visions of 'justice', 'order', 'security' and so on can make diverse claims for legitimacy.

42 The first three years of the operation of the new close supervision centres were regarded by many as deploying a 'cruel and excessive' form of penal discipline (see HMCIP 2000; and on use of this term, Tonry 2001 and Jacobs 2001). They did seem to be 'peculiar institutions', with internal contradictions, which generated resistance and opposition (Wacquant 2001: 99).

43 There are other reasons for this increased stability, which include a much higher proportion of sex offenders in dispersal prisons. Sex offenders are generally regarded as more compliant (see Sparks *et al* 1996).

44 Although some of those who have recently retired see themselves, in the light of the changing mood, as the disappointed and 'unreconstructed product of the failed post-war liberal consensus' (personal comment).

45 Technically, a handful of other local prisons now also belong in the renamed

High Security Estate, like Belmarsh and Woodhill, because they offer maximum-security accommodation.

46 Source: Dispersals Directorate; Ombudsman's Office.

47 Strictly speaking, Wakefield does not house prisoners who are accommodated separately for their own protection, as all are sex offenders or vulnerable prisoners.

48 Figures 1 to 7 show an overall decline in levels of 'disorder', but a relatively small decline from the pre-1994 levels.

49 The need to keep control of one's self is described as very distressing and may, of course, have long-term damaging effects (see Gallo and Ruggiero 1991; Liebling 1999; Karim 2001).

50 See Bottoms *et al* (1990). By 'situational-plus', I mean a basically situational approach (more physical constraint) supplemented by meaningful incentives and other mechanisms to encourage 'self-governance' (see Garland 1997).

51 Knowledge (about the central significance of legitimacy, and the role of process) has been turned into power (more formal and by-the-book processes). The question is whether the use (and abuse) of *informal* power increases or decreases with the use of more formal power (see Hepburn 1985; Liebling 2000; and Liebling and Crewe, in progress).

52 Arguably the modern approach to tackling offending behaviour is a new model, involving less conflict between 'custody' and 'courses'. See further, Liebling and Price (2001).

53 A 'liberal justice' model, towards a 'decency' model, where decency incorporates safety (including public protection), accountability, standards and 'best value' (see further, Liebling, in preparation).

54 Richard Sparks has observed that Long Lartin was never 'liberal' in the true sense of the term. There was a lot of arbitrary power (see Sparks *et al* 1996). The historic shift may not be (simply) 'from less power to more'. Wakefield was not liberal either, but can be regarded as more restrictive and paternalistic (Sparks, personal comment): 'Radzinowicz may have introduced some confusion by using the term in the first place. Hence when it came to "talking back", the term liberal became the shorthand for everything that was to be rejected (adding further confusion)'. (Sparks, personal comment; see also Faulkner 2001).

55 The question, as Hugh Klare asked in his 1968 article in *New Society*, is, 'are we sure we are fighting the right war?' (see also Faulkner 2001: 126–7 on the return of the language of war in criminal justice).

56 Wacquant usefully reminds us that the 'new penal discipline' is justified by, and pursued in order to, provide support for neoliberalism outside. Garland, more broadly, argues that penality is a 'set of signifying practices' that 'help produce subjectivities, forms of authority and social relations' at large. (Wacquant 2001; Garland 1991).

57 What I do know, from my one serious conversation with him, is that he would approve of Home Office funding to research it!

References

ACPS (Advisory Council on the Penal System) (1968) *The Regime for Long-Term Prisoners in Conditions of Maximum Security (The Radzinowicz Report)*. London: HMSO.

Bottomley, K. (1994) *CRC Special Units: A General Assessment*. Report to the Home Office. Hull: University of Hull.

Bottomley, K. and Hay, W. (1991) *Special Units for Difficult Prisoners*. University of Hull: Centre for Criminology and Criminal Justice.

Bottomley, K., Jepson, N., Elliot, K. and Coid, J. (1994) *Managing Difficult Prisoners: The Lincoln and Hull Special Units*. London: HMSO.

Bottomley, K., Liebling, A. and Sparks, R. (1994) *An Evaluation of Barlinnie and Shotts Units*, Scottish Prison Service Occasional Paper No. 7. Edinburgh: Scottish Prison Service.

Bottoms, A.E. (1998) 'Five Puzzles in von Hirsch's Theory of Punishment', in A. Ashworth and M. Wasik (eds), *Fundamentals of Sentencing Theory: Essays in Honour of Andrew von Hirsch*. Oxford: Clarendon Press, pp. 53–100.

Bottoms, A.E. and Light, R. (eds) (1987) *Problems of Long-Term Imprisonment*. Aldershot: Gower.

Bottoms, A.E., Hay, W. and Sparks, R. (1990) 'Situational and Social Approaches to the Prevention of Disorder in Long-Term Prisons', *Prison Journal*, LXX, 83–95.

Boyle, J. (1977) *A Sense of Freedom*. London: Routledge.

Clare, E. and Bottomley, K. (assisted by Grounds, A., Hammond, C., Liebling, A. and Taylor, C.) (2001) *An Evaluation of Close Supervision Centres*, Home Office Research Study 219. London: Home Office.

Cohen, S. (1974) 'Human Warehouses: the Future of Our Prisons', *New Society*, 30 (632), 407–11.

Cohen, S. and Taylor, L. (1972) *Psychological Survival: the Experience of Long-Term Imprisonment*. Harmondsworth: Penguin.

Coyle, A. (1987) 'The Scottish Experience with Small Units', in A.E. Bottoms and R. Light (eds), *Problems of Long-Term Imprisonment*. Aldershot: Gower.

Coyle, A. (1991) *Inside: Rethinking Scotland's Prisons*. Edinburgh: Scottish Child.

Ditchfield, J. (1990) *Control in Prisons*. London: HMSO.

Downes, D. (1988) *Contrasts in Tolerance: Post-War Penal Policy in the Netherlands and England and Wales*. Oxford: Clarendon Press.

Faulkner, D. (2001) *Crime, State and Citizen: A Field Full of Folk*. Winchester: Waterside Press.

Fitzgerald, M. (1987) 'The Telephone Rings: Long-Term Imprisonment', in A.E. Bottoms and R. Light (eds), *Problems of Long-Term Imprisonment*. Aldershot: Gower.

Gallo, E. and Ruggiero, V. (1991) 'The Immaterial Prison: Custody as a Factory for the Manufacture of Handicaps', *International Journal for the Sociology of Law*, 19, 273–91.

Garland, D. (1991) Personal communication.

Garland, D. (1997) '"Governmentality" and the Problem of Crime: Foucalt, Criminology, Sociology', *Theoretical Criminology*, 1, 173–214.

Hepburn, J.R. (1985) 'The Exercise of Power in Coercive Organisations: a Study of Prison Guards', *Criminology*, 23 (1), 145–64.

HMCIP (2000) *Inspection of Close Supervision Centres, August – September 1999*. London: Home Office.

Home Office (1966) *Report of the Inquiry into Prison Escapes and Security (Mountbatten Report)*, Cmnd 3175. London: HMSO.

Home Office (1973) *Report of the Working Party on Dispersal and Control (Cox Report)*. Unpublished.

Home Office (1977) *Report of an Inquiry by the Chief Inspector of the Prison Service into the Cause and Circumstance of the Events at HM Prison Hull during the Period 31st August to 3rd September, 1976* (The Fowler Report). London: HMSO.

Home Office (1979) *Committee of Inquiry into the United Kingdom Prison Service – The May Inquiry*, Cmnd 7673. London: HMSO.

Home Office (1984) *Managing the Long-Term Prison System: The Report of the Control Review Committee*. London: Home Office.

Home Office (1987) *Special Units for Long-Term Prisoners: A Report of the Research and Advisory Group on the Long-Term Prison System*. London: Home Office.

Home Office (1991) *Prison Disturbances 1990 (The Woolf Report)*. London: HMSO.

Home Office (1994) *Report of the Enquiry into the Escape of Six Prisoners from the Special Security Unit at Whitemoor Prison (The Woodcock Report)*. London: HMSO.

Home Office (1995) *Review of Prison Service Security in England and Wales and the Escape from Parkhurst Prison on Tuesday 3rd January 1995 (The Learmont Report)*. London: HMSO.

Jacobs, J. (2001) 'Facts, Values and Prison Policies', *Punishment and Society: The International Journal of Penology*, 3 (1): 183–8.

Karim, N. (2001) *Post-traumatic Stress and the Psychological Effects of Long-Term Imprisonment*. Unpublished PhD thesis, University of Cambridge.

King, R. (1991) 'Maximum Security Custody in Britain and the USA: a Study of Gartree and Oak Park Heights', *British Journal of Criminology*, 31 (2), 126–52.

King, R. (1995) 'Woodcock and After', *Prison Service Journal*, 102, 63–7.

King, R. (1999) 'The Rise and Rise of Supermax: an American Solution in Search of a Problem?', *Punishment and Society: The International Journal of Penology*, 1 (2), 163–86.

King, R. and Elliott, K. (1977) *Albany: Birth of a Prison – End of an Era*. London: Routledge & Kegan Paul.

King, R. and McDermott, K. (1990) 'My Geranium is Subversive: Notes on the Management of Trouble in Prisons', *British Journal of Sociology*, 41 (4), 445–71.

King, R. and McDermott, K. (1995) *The State of Our Prisons*. Oxford: Clarendon Press.

King, R. and Morgan, R. (1980) *The Future of the Prison System*. Farnborough: Gower.

Klare, H. (1968) 'Prisoners in Maximum Security', *New Society*, 11 (288), 494–5.

Lewis, D. (1996) *Hidden Agendas: Politics, Law and Disorder*. London: Hamish Hamilton.

Liebling, A. (1999) 'Doing Research in Prison: Breaking the Silence', *Theoretical Criminology*, 3 (2), 147–173.

Liebling, A. (2000) 'Prison Officers, Policing and the Use of Discretion', *Theoretical Criminology*, 4 (3), 333–57.

Liebling, A. (2001) 'Policy and Practice in the Management of Disruptive Prisoners: Incentives and Earned Privileges, the Spurr Report and Close Supervision Centres', in E. Clare, and A.K. Bottomley (assisted by A. Grounds, C. Hammond, A. Liebling and C. Taylor), *An Evaluation of Close Supervision Centres*. Home Office Research Study 219. London: Home Office, pp. 115–64.

Liebling, A. with Arnold, H. (in preparation) *Measuring the Prison: An Adventure in Values.*

Liebling, A. and Crewe, B. (in progress) *The New Society of Captives: Masculinity and Modern Penal Culture.*

Liebling, A., Muir, G., Rose, G. and Bottoms, A.E. (1997) *An Evaluation of Incentives and Earned Privileges: Final Report to the Prison Service*. London: Prison Service.

Liebling, A. and Price, D. (2001) *The Prison Officer*. Leyhill: Prison Service and Waterside Press.

Mathiesen, T. (1965) *The Defences of the Weak: A Sociological Study of a Norwegian Correctional Institution*. London: Tavistock.

Ombudsman (2000) *Annual Report 1999–2000: Independent Investigation of Prisoners' Complaints*. London: HMSO.

Padfield, N. and Liebling, A., with Arnold, H. (2000) *An Exploration of Decision-Making at Discretionary Lifer Panels*. London: Home Office.

Pearson, T. (1987) 'Prison Service Order 0900', *Categorisation and Allocation*. London: Prison Service Circular Instruction (10) 1974.

Price, D. (2000) *Security Categorisation in the English Prison System*. Unpublished PhD thesis, University of Cambridge.

Radzinowicz, L. (1999) *Adventures in Criminology*. London: Routledge.

Rutherford, A. (1984) *Prisons and the Process of Justice*. Oxford: Oxford University Press.

Rutherford, A. (1987) 'The Control Review Committee Report – Discussant', in A.E. Bottoms and R. Light (eds), *Problems of Long-Term Imprisonment*. Aldershot: Gower.

Sennett, R. (1998) *The Corrosion of Character: The Personal Consequences of Work in the New Capitalism*. London: W. W. Norton.

Sparks, R. (1994a) 'Can Prisons Be Legitimate? Penal Politics, Privatization, and the Timeliness of an Old Idea', in R.D. King and M. Maguire (eds), *British Journal of Criminology, Prisons in Context*, 34 (Special Issue), 14–28.

Sparks, R. (1994b) 'Barlinnie Special Unit', in *An Evaluation of Barlinnie and Shotts Units*, Scottish Prison Service Occasional Paper No 7. Edinburgh: Scottish Prison Service.

Sparks, R., Bottoms, A.E. and Hay, W. (1996) *Prisons and the Problem of Order.* Oxford: Clarendon Press.

Sparks, R. and Liebling, A. (in preparation) *The Meaning of Humanity in the Penal Context.*

Stenson, K. and Sullivan, R.R. (2001) *Crime, Risk and Justice.* Cullompton: Willan Publishing.

Sykes, G. (1958) *The Society of Captives.* Princeton, NJ: Princeton University Press.

Thomas, J.E. and Pooley, R. (1980) *The Exploding Prison: Prison Riots and the Case of Hull.* London: Junction.

Tonry, M. (2001) 'Unthought Thoughts: the Influence of Changing Sensibilities on Penal Policies', *Punishment and Society: The International Journal of Penology*, 3 (1), 167–82.

von Hirsch, A. (1976) *Doing Justice, the Choice of Punishments: Report of the Committee for the Study of Incarceration.* New York: Hill & Wang.

Wacquant, L. (2001) 'Deadly Symbiosis: When Ghetto and Prison Meet and Merge', *Punishment and Society: The International Journal of Penology*, 3 (1), 95–134.

Walmsley, R. (1989) *Special Security Units.* London: Home Office.

Walmsley, R. (ed.) (1991) *Managing Difficult Prisoners: the Parkhurst Special Unit*, Home Office Research Study 122. London: HMSO.

Ward, D. (1987) 'Control Strategies for Problem Prisoners in American Penal Systems', in A.E. Bottoms and R. Light (eds), *Problems of Long-Term Imprisonment.* Aldershot: Gower.

Wheatley, P. (1995) 'Dispersal Prisons: Present and Future', Speech to the Dispersal Boards of Visitors Conference. HMP Full Sutton.

Williams v *Home Office* [1981] 1 All ER 1211–48.

Williams, M. and Longley, D. (1987) 'Identifying Control Problem Prisoners in Long-Term Dispersal Prisons', in A.E. Bottoms and R. Light (eds), *Problems of Long-Term Imprisonment.* Aldershot: Gower.

Young, P. (1987) 'The Concept of Social Control and Its Relevance to the Prisons Debate', in A.E. Bottoms and R. Light (eds), *Problems of Long-Term Imprisonment.* Aldershot: Gower.

Part 4
Research and Policy

Chapter 6

Criminology and penal policy: the vital role of empirical research

Roger Hood

Sir Leon's vision

Over sixty years ago, in 1940 to be precise, and roughly two years after he had settled in Cambridge at the age of 32, Leon Radzinowicz and his friend and supporter, the noted criminal lawyer J.W. Cecil Turner, published in the *Cambridge Law Journal* an article entitled 'The Language of Criminal Science' (Radzinowicz and Turner 1940a). Its purpose (along with their Introduction to the first volume of *English Studies in Criminal Science*, published in the same year (Radzinowicz and Turner 1940b: 9–12)) was to define the subject matter of criminology and to draw a distinction, as well as the connections, between it and the subject matter of criminal policy and criminal law: all three being elements of what they called 'criminal science'. The essence of their position, indeed vision for criminology, was summed up as follows:

> The study of criminal science has been until recently very neglected in England. On the practical side, however, in the general treatment of crime and criminals this country has made noteworthy progress, especially in the past half-century. This illustrates the national characteristic of recognising practical needs before theoretical principles are developed, or even appreciated. A scientific body of principle must however be ultimately established, and it has at last come to be realised that the problem of crime cannot be understood and solved merely by acting on philanthropic impulse, or a desire for progress. Crime must be studied scientifically in the light of tested facts, practical achievements, controlled experiments, and

comparative investigations. Like all other sciences, criminal science must advance by method and system ... It has first of all to explain the origins of crime; this involves intensive biological and social investigations ... including the personality of the delinquent and the conditions of society in which he is placed and acts; the influences of social conditions on the machinery of criminal justice; the origins, functions, and evolution of criminal law and punishment, all of which are the product of various social needs and attitudes. We have called this part of criminal science 'criminology'. Secondly, it has to ascertain on the basis of these investigations how best to fight against crime. We have called this part of criminal science 'criminal policy' ... which has as its immediate aim the study and systematisation of all measures to be taken against crime in the sphere of prevention, of legislation, and of punitive treatment, and its ultimate aim the coordination of the whole into the organised system of state activity.

(a composite of Radzinowicz and Turner 1940a: 19 and 25 and Radzinowicz and Turner 1940b: 9–10).

One must bear in mind that he was writing over sixty years ago and that since that time a greater understanding has developed of the problems of generating and interpreting 'knowledge' about crime. Consequently, certain modes of expression and concepts may now appear somewhat naive or over-simplified. Nevertheless, there can be no doubt that, at that time, Radzinowicz, like so many others, viewed criminology as a discipline that could provide a 'rational improvement' in the whole system for dealing with crime and criminals. Indeed, the section of R.A. Butler's White Paper of 1959, *Penal Practice in a Changing Society* (Home Office 1959: paras 17, 24) which looked forward to 'a fundamental re-examination of penal methods, based on studies of the causes of crime ... supported by a reliable assessment of the results achieved by existing methods' proclaimed 'that in this field research is as essential as in the fields of science and technology'. It was 'a faithful summary' of the memorandum Leon Radzinowicz had prepared in support of the establishment of an Institute of Criminology (Butler 1974: 7; Radzinowicz 1999: 193). Nevertheless, it is important to recognise that Radzinowicz was fully aware that the search for some general causes of crime, as if crime was a concrete, unitary phenomenon, was not only misconceived but also futile. 'The most that can be done', he wrote, 'is to throw light on the combination of circumstances associated with crime. And even then it must be recognised that these very factors and circumstances can also be associated with other forms of social maladjustment, or indeed with behaviour accepted as normal' (Radzinowicz 1961: 175–6; 1988: 92–6; 1999: 441–9).

Radzinowicz was no social engineer. He certainly did not view criminology solely as a scientific methodology to provide information to policy makers: 'the connection between criminological research and penal reforms should not be too dogmatically insisted upon' (Radzinowicz 1999: 451). Indeed, the application of criminological knowledge could be dangerous if it ignored wider social and political values: the control of crime was not the only consideration. He had seen the dangers when the positivism that had excited him as a student of Enrico Ferri became distorted and abused by fascist regimes in the 1930s. A system that achieved crime control through social repression at the expense of social justice was anathema to him. Rather, he championed a liberal and humane policy for combating crime. Yet, he many times expressed the view that if criminology were to cut itself off from considerations of criminal policy and social improvement it would become an arid, indeed useless discipline. 'After all', he wrote at the end of his life, 'criminology was perceived by its promoters not only as an academic discipline but also as a rich and evolving body of empirical knowledge and ideals which could become of some use in the practical business of enforcing the criminal law'. Conversely, he abhorred 'the imposition of political ideology on criminological premises and conclusions' which he regarded 'as the deadly threat to a balanced and fertile development of the discipline' (Radzinowicz 1999: 456).

Leon Radzinowicz also believed that criminologists should have a realistic perception of the limitations of their ability to explain such a complex socio-legal and behavioural category as crime. He counselled them to 'avoid crusading zeal, dogmatic beliefs and narrow expertise' (1961: 178). He would have agreed wholeheartedly with Garland and Sparks's (2000: 190) assertion that 'the social significance of crime and its control is so pervasive, so complex, and so contentious that no scientific discipline can ever dictate the ways in which these matters will be understood or addressed'. There is nothing peculiar to criminology about that, of course. The same could be said of other social issues such as health and environmental policies, as we are witnessing, for example, in relation to the role accorded to scientific evidence and advice in the debates about the regulation of food production and disease control.

Towards the end of his life, Sir Leon became more sceptical about the likelihood that criminological research would produce knowledge of a kind that would be able 'to reduce criminality or influence its shape or its trends'. He thought that what criminology could do best was to:

... help us better to understand [crime], to avoid making mistakes when dealing with it, and to instil a little more humanity and reality in our attitudes towards the phenomenon of crime and control ... The need for criminology is greater the more critical the condition of crime appears to be. One of the lessons which penal history teaches us is that it is almost always during such periods of tension, frustration and fear that solutions in the penological sphere are adopted primarily on emotional grounds or on opportunistic calculations. More often than not they prove to be regressive temporary short cuts of hardly any value. It is in times like these that criminology is particularly qualified to prove its uses. But penal history also reveals that at these very times the voice of criminology is too often silenced or ignored even in countries in an advanced state of civilisation.

(Radzinowicz 1999: 461)

His perception of the subject appears to have become more like Nils Christie's conception of the criminologist as critic rather than technocrat (Christie 1981: 110). He would have agreed with Christie that too much criminological research has been narrow, over-technical, pretentious and ephemeral (Christie 1997), but I do not think that he would, for this reason, have shared Christie's scepticism of scientific endeavour in the field. For all his interest in the intellectual substance of criminology, its historical development, and the sweep of its grand ideas – as can be seen from his *Ideology and Crime* (Radzinowicz 1966) – he held fast to the view that without well conducted empirical inquiry the subject would become moribund. If I can put it in my own words: *talking* about criminology is not the same thing as *doing* criminology. Both are necessary and both should support each other.

Criminological research and political agenda

Like so many others, and undoubtedly many of those who attended this colloquium, Sir Leon (as the penultimate chapter of *Adventures in Criminology* vividly displays) was dismayed by the 'profoundly disturbing gap' that had developed in recent years between the theories and evidence adduced by criminologists on how best to prevent or limit crime and the directions that public policy has taken in relation to the repression of and 'actual modes of controlling' crime (Radzinowicz 1999: 456, 468).

At the end of 1999, when I spoke on this theme at the Australian and

New Zealand Society of Criminology's Conference, I had no difficulty in finding statements to similar effect (Hood 2001: 1–2) from many leading Australasian scholars. The same can be said of Scandinavian (Bondeson 1998) and American criminologists. For example, six years ago Alfred Blumstein (1995: 68) declared that: 'The remarkable characteristic of the political debate [on the relationship between punishment and crime] has been total resistance to any consideration of what by now is reasonably well-developed criminological knowledge.'

David Garland (1996: 460) called this 'the politics of denial', where punitive policies are pursued 'in the face of evidence that crime does not readily respond to severe sentences or new police powers, or the greater use of imprisonment'. It has been powerfully argued that this development is, at least in part, a consequence of a perceived public demand for action, and action now, to deal with the problem of crime; and that politicians fear that failure to show they are acting decisively will be exploited by their political opponents.

In his scintillating new book, *The Culture of Crime Control*, Garland analyses the social-structural, cultural, mass communication, professional and political forces rooted in 'late twentieth-century modernity' that have led to the breakdown of penal-welfare ideology and lessened the influence of its associated criminological ideas. This, he argues, has produced two different responses in society's bid to control crime: what he calls the 'criminology of everyday life', concerned largely with ways of preventing crime through the management of opportunities and systems, and what he calls the 'criminology of the other', linked to exclusionary, punitive and risk-averse policies (Garland 2001: 167–92). It is fair to say that he does not contend that all the old social-welfare orientated ideas are dead and buried, far from it, but his emphasis is on the transformation of ideas and policies that has taken place in the last 25 years. This naturally raises the question of what place is left for criminology as an academic discipline, in particular for empirical criminological research in relation to policy concerned with controlling crime through the criminal justice and penal systems.

In their Introduction to the special issue of the *British Journal of Criminology* on 'Criminology and Social Theory', David Garland and Richard Sparks (2001: 196, 201) also note that: 'in the 1990s, as criminology flourishes in the academy, its influence in national penal policy appears to be diminishing.' They argue persuasively that: 'a criminology that disavows emotive and punitive policies ... has little affinity with the values and calculations that shape government decisions'. Furthermore, they note that criminologists are now perceived as having little to offer because, 'from the point of view of politicians, crime and punishment has become too important to leave to criminologists or to dominate the ways in which these issues are analysed', a point very similar in fact to the one made by Radzinowicz when he complained about the voice of criminology being silenced. Indeed, Garland and Sparks conclude their essay on a very pessimistic note: 'Whilst there continue to be institutional spaces in which criminologists can work, and policy audiences sometimes ready to listen to criminological evidence, the variance between the rationality proposed by modern criminology and the rationales for policing, punishment and control now in ascendancy is striking and perhaps irrevocable' (2000: 202).

Does this mean that criminologists can no longer hope that their research can have an impact on policy framers and governments? Not at all: rather, this analysis should be taken as a challenge. For, as David Garland says, in concluding his book, 'such policies are not inevitable … they are the outcome (partly planned, partly unintended) of political and cultural and policy choices – choices that could have been different and that can still be rethought and reversed'. In other words, structurally related changes are not the same as strictly determined changes (Garland 2001: 201–5). Indeed, Garland and Sparks insist that 'criminological knowledge – the insight and understanding that comes from close and critical study of crime and our institutional responses to it – has never been so relevant, however much governments resist its findings'.

Garland and Sparks's response to this challenge is to draw a distinction between the 'strategic choices' that the subject now faces:

'It can see itself as a kind of specialist underlabourer, a technical specialist … providing data and information for more lofty and wide ranging debates … Or it can embrace the world in which crime so loudly resonates and engage the discussion at this level too … a more critical, more public, more wide-ranging role' (2000: 21).

By this I understand them to mean that criminologists in pursuing empirical research, especially when it is related to the evaluation of criminal justice systems and policies, should recognise that the subject is far from 'value free'. In other words, it is not enough to contribute as technicians. I could not agree more and I applaud the call for criminologists to take cognisance of the impact of the many social, indeed, global, changes that have created, and will further create, new definitions, forms of and possibilities for criminality and its regulation and control. This may well bring with it new conceptions of the scope and subject matter of criminology (see, for example, Muncie 1998/1999).

Nevertheless, it is important, in my view, to stress that the voices of criminologists will be heard only if they can speak in their 'wider-ranging role' from a firm base of empirical research, and research that can make claims to be scientifically rigorous, in the sense that it is repeatable, reliable and valid. This is what distinguishes criminology from other types of discourse about crime. Unless legitimacy can be claimed for this view, the 'criminologist' will be treated as just another person with an 'opinion' on the subject.

As Garland points out, 'the criminology of the other' leads to policies of punitive exclusion. It is therefore vital that the assumptions of this kind of discourse about crime and criminals, and the way citizens react in certain contexts to attempts to control their conduct, should be subjected to rigorous criminological analysis and empirical research. We simply need to know a lot more about the nature of motivation to commit crimes and how the trajectories of persistence and desistance in criminal careers are affected by calculations of risk of punishment. As far as punitive policies are concerned we need also to know very much more about risks of re-offending, of what kind and with what intensity; what effects different levels of administered punishment have, if any, on rates of victimisation, reporting of crime, probability of conviction and on the institutions of punishment, especially the prison; on public confidence in the fairness of criminal justice, etc. Without evidence on such vital issues, the criminologist's voice will be muted, however strongly she or he feels about the social values involved in the pursuit of punitive policies.

Thus the 'two possibilities', the empirical and discursive, must not, as I know Garland and Sparks would agree, be regarded as a division of labour: for one cannot be done convincingly without the other. In this sense the term 'underlabourer' should not be interpreted as an inferior role. The problem for criminology lies in gaining the acceptance in the public and political sphere of the validity and usefulness of the scientific study of crime (broadly conceived to include historical scholarship) and society's response to it. We should therefore guard against being too pessimistic: indeed fight to counter pessimism. No one will want to pursue the criminological endeavour if we come to believe that the findings of criminological research are destined to be always dis-regarded in the late-modern world if they run counter to tendencies in popular political sentiment – which is, of course, often fuelled by distorted information in the mass media for purposes of increasing circulation and profit. As Jock Young (1999: 196–9) has reminded us in *The Exclusive Society*, the new technologies of social control may or may not be repressive, depending on the political context in which they are used, on the degree of public vigilance and on the purposes to which they are applied. And how they are used might depend, at least to some degree, on the evidence that can be gathered about their real effects. Thus there are many questions that remain as open as ever to scientific analysis, research and critique.

'Reductionism' runs hand in hand with risk-aversive measures. As we all know, the targets of the present government's 'Crime Reduction Strategy' (Home Office 1999) include 'crime prevention work with families and young people … more effective sentencing practices, and working with offenders [both within and outside of the prison system] to ensure that they do not re-offend … ' The 'what works agenda' which is invading the system at so many levels is, of course, supremely criminological in attempting to link the analysis of 'criminogenic' factors and risk indicators with programmes which aim to change attitudes and behaviour (Nuttall, Goldblatt and Lewis 1998). Furthermore, John Braithwaite's (1989) theory of reintegrative shaming has had a far-reaching impact on the 'restorative justice' movement, promising to harmonise several penal and social aims: disapproval of and blame for the offence, a voice for and restitution to the victim, and reintegration of the shamed offender into his or her community. This theory and the research it has inspired is a striking example of the role that crimino-logical analysis can play in the development of new approaches – approaches that Braithwaite (2000) conceives to be more in tune with the development of the 'new regulatory state'.

The problem of scientific legitimacy

David Garland (2001: 50) has identified 'the decline of the influence of social expertise' of social workers, psychiatrists and other professionals as one of the factors that led to the decline of the 'penal-welfare ideal', in which criminology had an accepted role. There is certainly a lot in this, but I would argue that, at least in part, the current crisis for criminology and the hopes for its future have something to do – perhaps ironically at a time when the government is seeking to introduce 'evidence-based policies' – with declining confidence in what criminology can deliver. On the whole it has not been very successful in establishing its legitimacy as a 'science' (a word I use here in its broad sense), or at least as an authoritative methodology or approach for providing analyses of problems that can help in the construction of effective solutions to the problems posed by criminality. It is not that science and social science in general are rejected in the analysis of other social problems. For example, if there is a crisis in health, such as an outbreak of disease, governments do not turn first to public opinion or react simply to demands based on perceived fears. They begin with medical science. I am not, of course, arguing that scientifically produced evidence will be conclusive. There may be a variety of different pieces of evidence to weigh up, and perhaps none of this evidence may be thought, in the end, to provide a sufficiently reliable or valid basis on which to decide policy. Nor will the scientific evidence be the only consideration: democratic accountability, economic and political considerations, legal and moral imperatives, will rightly play their part (see Ryan 1998/1999). I am merely arguing that criminologists should seek to gain the same respect for their theoretical and empirical contributions when questions of penal policy are debated.

Criminology's 'academic credentials are no longer in doubt', say Garland and Sparks (2000: 196). This is certainly true from an internal self-referential view, based on the number of academic departments, new students, journals and books published. But I wonder how far this is true when one considers either external academic judgement (criminology is widely accepted in the universities, but if we are honest can we really say that its standing is as high as we would wish it to be?) or a judgement at governmental or societal level. How many people do we come across who have any idea of what we do? And even if they have an inkling, how much credence do they give to it?

What criminology can deliver is obviously also affected by the resources made available to it, the training, imagination and ability of its practitioners, and the scientific agenda it pursues, or is able to pursue. But it also has something to do with how criminologists themselves conceive their subject, the scholarly and scientific credibility they are able to demonstrate, and their interest in pursuing theoretical development and empirical inquiry. Credibility is often undermined when positions that are clearly based on normative preferences alone are put forward as if they have the backing of scholarship or social science, even though they have neither, or the observer can find no way of disentangling one from the other. Thus I have been drawn to the conclusion that some of the problems that confront us as criminologists are due to our own failings.

As Max Travers (1997: 368) aptly put it, criminological research must, in particular, strive to avoid the accusation that it is merely 'preaching to the converted' by 'constructing an argument … by advancing a moral line and then supporting it with a number of "just so" illustrative examples'. It is also the case that academics themselves sometimes criticise research more because it challenges their own ideological stance or policy preferences rather than by demonstrating that the work has been conceptually or methodologically inadequate. The findings of Carolyn Hoyle's (1998) thorough study of the policing of domestic violence were, for example, immediately attacked by some for being 'anti-feminist' rather than on the basis of the authenticity of the methodology she had used to support them (Hoyle 2000: 396).

Clearly, there are many ways of pursuing criminological studies. But if the subject does not keep at its core the spirit of empirical inquiry, its distinctive voice and distinctive contribution will not be sustainable. Surely, this is precisely the time for us not to lose confidence, but to redouble our efforts to convince 'outsiders' that what empirical criminologists do is worthwhile. So, what might be done to improve the stock of criminology in the public sphere?

Criminological uncertainties

There is no doubt that as criminology developed, scholars found the connection of their subject to the pursuit of a particular penal or social control ideology very worrying. You will recall Professor Nigel Walker's (1965: i–ii) assertion that 'perhaps the hardest impression to eradicate is that the criminologist is a penal reformer'. Rather, he said, the criminologist is concerned 'to establish the truth or falsehood of some of the assertions upon which campaigns for penal reform are based'. Indeed, he went so far as to state that while the criminologist might test the assertion that the death penalty is not a deterrent, 'it is no more his function to attack or defend the death penalty than it is the function of a political scientist to take part in an election campaign.' In other words, political, legal and moral considerations would determine the aims and limits of penal policies, not criminological knowledge alone. The late Richard F. Sparks and I, introducing our book *Key Issues in Criminology* (1970: 8–9) thirty years ago, also tried to draw a distinction between criminology as a social science and criminal policy as a field of political activity. We said: '... there is plenty of scope for disinterested or purely scientific research on the operation of penal systems ...What [criminology] cannot do is to decide what the *aims* of penal policy should be ... [but] given certain aims, criminologists can try to discover by research the best means of accomplishing them'. In other words, criminological knowledge would provide a critique of policies rather than determine them as such.

Others held much more radical views. You will recall that the authors of *The New Criminology* (Taylor, Walton and Young 1973: 278–82) warned criminologists against becoming involved in what they stigmatised as 'correctionalism': dealing with crime by attempting to change offenders was a means of supporting a state that needed to be radically transformed. Stanley Cohen, in his much-admired *Visions of Social Control* (1985: 238), asserted that 'it is simply not our professional job to advise, consult, recommend or make decisions'.

In recent years, the argument that theory and research can be, indeed should be, completely disengaged from normative issues has been largely abandoned. Left realism (although it has rarely directly addressed the penal field) specifically connected the criminological enterprise with the need to deal with crime, especially that which disproportionately affected the lives of working people, *now*, rather than waiting for some hoped-for wider social transformations that would reduce the scale of criminality. Indeed, now most criminologists do not conceive of their activity as entirely value free. They engage in the subject (for the same reason as most medical researchers) in the ultimate hope that it will improve the condition of society. Stanley Cohen, for example, speaking to a conference in Australia seven years ago, posed the telling question 'If nothing works, what is our work?' and proclaimed: 'This is not the time for cynical impossibilism ... we have not lost all moral guidelines for recognising a progressive idea when we see one' (Cohen 1994).

Peter Young (1992: 427) put the dilemma facing many criminologists very well when he wrote:

> It is as if there is a wish to embrace the sort of project criminology amounts to, yet, at the same time, to show its limits; to be for criminology, but also to be against it; to wish to engage in the sort of action necessary, for example, to control crime but to be (rightly) suspicious of the very idea; to be against 'correctionalism', yet to want to see only correct action taken to control crime and to limit the use of arbitrary power.

Was the expectation that criminological insights and findings could play a crucial role in consideration of the likely effectiveness and propriety of prospective policies an entirely unrealistic, naive or indeed wrong-headed expectation? Maybe it was politically naive but it was not, in my view, fundamentally wrong-headed. Empirical research shorn of a normative direction is likely to be not only sterile but also open to abuse (see Braithwaite 2000: 235). On the other hand, given the level of resources made available for criminological research into one of society's most enduring and major problems, it was unrealistic to expect too much from it.

It has also to be admitted that the penological writings of the 'Nothing Works' school, despite their positive contribution in questioning the application of a 'medical model' to penal 'treatment', nevertheless had a negative and depressing effect on both criminologists and policy makers. And one should admit also that much of the lobbying by criminologists in favour of reducing the prison population has failed to convince policy makers. This is, at least in part, because the case has not been based on a full and careful analysis of the relationship between crime rates, conviction rates and sentencing practices, as well as the characteristics of that portion of the prison population that the lobbyists would wish to see dealt with by other means. Very few researchers have attempted to follow up systematically the lead given by Frank Zimring and Gordon Hawkins' path-breaking work on *The Scale of Imprisonment* (1991).

There has been, apparently often for ideological reasons or sheer distaste, a marked reluctance among British criminologists to engage empirically with some of the difficult subjects linked to punitive policies. Take general deterrence: a linchpin of penal policies round the world, especially as regards serious 'rational' crime. Leaving aside the conceptual clarification provided by Deryck Beyleveld (1979; see also Zimring and Hawkins 1973), the research effort and data pertaining to the United Kingdom remains appallingly thin (for an exception see Ross 1973). More has been accomplished in the United States, but even there few studies have been replicated and the conclusions drawn have often been suspect, as the recent Cambridge review of the subject has demonstrated (von Hirsch *et al* 1999). One must admit that the problems of proof are formidable. But much more effort and imagination needs to be put into inventing better research designs (for example, Buikhuisen 1974), rather than the mantra-like repetition of the obviously oversimplified refrain – which I heard not too long ago from a well-known professor – 'criminal sanctions have no deterrent effect'.

The same is largely true of risk assessment and accuracy of predicting the likelihood of serious harm, where far more progress has been made in the field of mental health than in relation to criminal offenders. There are, of course, some interesting findings. We know that it is hard to predict rare events, such as conviction for serious violence, that persons predicted to be high risks are more likely to be false positives than true positives and that the majority of serious crimes are committed by those predicted to have a low probability of doing so (see Monahan 1997; Brody and Tarling 1980). Given the salience of risk in public discourse, given the acceptance of criminologists that they live in a 'risk society', it is remarkable that a large body of knowledge has yet to be built up on this subject. For example, no place was found for it on the agenda of the recent large-scale Research Initiative on Violent Crime funded by the British Economic and Social Research Council. One can only assume that there was some ideological aversion to the subject. Yet there should be no place, to quote David Garland (1996: 6) again, for the 'dogmatic repetition of ideological positions that derive from a time when the field and its forces were quite differently constituted'.

Methodological disputations and confusions

Then there is the question of methodology. In *Adventures in Criminology*, Leon Radzinowicz (1999: 450) pointed out that there are fashions in methods, and that too often a methodology is regarded as sacrosanct, rather than one of several possible approaches. There are appropriate and inappropriate methodologies: depending on the question posed, the hypothesis framed, the behaviour, activities and institutional contexts to be observed, and the policies and practices to be evaluated. We can thank Tony (now Sir Anthony) Bottoms (2000) for his recent illuminating and wise discussion of these issues. There has, I fear, been a tendency in recent years to decry quantitative studies and to privilege 'qualitative' or 'appreciative' work. While a good deal of early quantitative work was indeed theoretically and conceptually naive, a dangerous and often false dichotomy appears to have been created between qualitative and quantitative approaches, as if some qualitatively gathered data cannot be quantified and all quantitative data are lacking in meaning. Furthermore, social science seeks not only an 'appreciation' of the actors' perspectives, but also an understanding of the social processes and structures that are linked to regularities in patterns of social behaviour, institutionalised responses and the predictability of various 'outcomes'.

There is a great deal of sophisticated quantitative work in the USA, much of it, I admit, hard to fathom; but elsewhere quite a number of criminologists have joined 'the anti-numbers brigade'. They regard crime as an entity that cannot be counted in any of its definitions or forms, or they simply decry 'number-crunching' as a far too simplistic approach to understanding the socially constituted and constructed phenomenon of crime. They are staunchly 'anti-positivist': a term often used for its damning – indeed stigmatising – effect, rather than denoting a wholesale rejection of scientific method. They insist that valid data can be obtained only through a 'qualitative' appreciation of the sentiments, actions and 'meanings' attached to actions by the participants. Such work has its place, but it is not always appropriate to the issue being researched. Nor can it provide the kind of evidence that would be regarded as convincing proof by those who require reliable, replicable observations, based on representative samples from which valid inferences can be drawn, before considering changing their policy or practices. Thus, to the extent that criminologists have rejected quantitative research methods, they have endangered their credibility in relation to some of the most important questions facing them. Think of the impact that epidemiological research has had on demonstrating the connection between smoking and lung cancer. That could not have been achieved through an 'appreciative account' of how smokers felt about their habit or viewed the effect of it on their health! However, that *would* be an appropriate methodology for providing data of value when considering the likely impact of preventive programmes. In other words, the appropriateness of the method depends on the issue being investigated. Often both quantitative and qualitative approaches need to be combined.

To take another disputed example: controlled trials. These involve many methodological problems of a kind that would challenge the ingenuity of any researcher, and care must be taken in drawing inferences from them. No doubt, as Pawson and Tilley have argued, evaluations should involve the collection of 'qualitative, contextual and process information.' But I cannot see that this is an argument against controlled trials *per se*. Why cannot this approach be combined with controlled trials so that some assessment can be made of influence of 'inputs' on the 'outputs' when comparisons are made (see Pawson and Tilley 1994; 1996; Bennett 1996; Sherman 1995; Stanko 1995)?

I remember Paul Rock commenting some time ago, in an address to the British Society of Criminology, on the fact that many criminologists and penologists had withdrawn from, or chosen not to become engaged with, empirical research in the field. Many of those who write on penology, including some of the best minds, have turned their attention to other worthy areas of related scholarship: such as sociological accounts of the influences behind changes in public policy – for example, the victims' movement, the jurisprudence of the 'just deserts' and 'penal communications' debate, or the sociology of penology, mapping trends in the shaping of the discourses and practices of modern 'penality' – and, of course, to social and penal history, as I have also done from time to time. Yet others have become engrossed in debates on various aspects of criminal policy.

This has undoubtedly broadened the perspective of penologists, and helped us to understand better the social forces and ideas that influence society's response to crime and to reflect on the development of our own subject. But I submit that it is important that the attractions of this broader area of scholarship – and the status accorded to it – do not divert attention from *doing* criminology: by which I mean critically addressing criminological theory and its jurisprudential and policy offshoots from the basis of knowledge gained through properly conducted empirical research. And, of course, to do that we need to ensure that there are scholars with the quantitative as well as the qualitative skills to do it (Wiles 1999/2000).

The responsibility of the state and other 'purse-holders'

How then can criminology establish the credibility which is vital if it is to be turned to by governments and others when seeking knowledge on the phenomenon of crime and on the ways of controlling and reacting to it? Two things have to happen. We as criminologists have to establish our scholarly and scientific credentials. And the authorities have to be persuaded to recognise their contribution to the problem.

As both Tony Bottoms (1987) and I (Hood 1987) noted some years ago, those who fund criminological research have gathered to themselves greater and greater power to set the agenda, to control access to information, to specify the scope of the work through tender documents and to approve the reports before final payment. Most of the research they promote and fund is 'policy relevant', often narrowly defined in administrative terms. The question usually posed is 'How does our system work?' And the answer usually looked for is 'How can we improve it to make it more cost effective and efficient in delivering its service?' The answer that the system itself is so fundamentally flawed that it inevitably produces undesirable consequences (youth prisons, for example) may be defined as 'beyond the terms of reference'.

In this, the criminologists are the 'weak' or 'supplicant' partner. Funding agencies have an obligation, especially in a supposedly 'knowledge-based policy environment', to ensure that adequate data can be collected from bodies over whom they have some control, and not to constrain the area of study, the resources and timing – for example, by not allowing sufficient time for controlled trials and adequate follow-up of outcomes – so as to make the validity of the findings questionable even before the work begins!

Criminology is, to use that ugly term, in danger of *commodification*:

another service to be bought under restricted contract by means of competitive tender. It seems incontestable, as a former head of Home Office research, John Croft (1996: 117), has said, that 'Given the limited resources, research strategy should not be at the mercy or – *pace* the customer/contractor principle introduced by Lord Rothschild – completely at the whim of the paymaster: researchers need to affirm their independence'. And it is not only a question of government-funded research in the universities. As we all know, by far the largest group of criminologists are direct employees of the government.

This lack of independence is another example of criminology's relatively low prestige. We have not, in my opinion, done enough in defence of our subject, either in terms of a high-level and prestigious professional organisation (the British Society of Criminology, for all the efforts of its recent presidents, is still too scattered and diffuse, in membership and organisation, to have yet successfully met this end), nor in terms of having any kind of professional solidarity about what standards should be demanded of a research contract before it is acceptable as a valid basis for a project. The demand to 'bring in research funds' – often under pressure to stave off unemployment so as to secure the continuation of the researcher's career – puts criminologists in a weak position. Large funds are to be welcomed but not as seduction.

We all meet colleagues who have succumbed to, and we ourselves in Oxford have on occasions fallen foul of, the temptation to do work which is known to be methodologically flawed, to be constructed on too short a timescale, to be 'quick and dirty' as some put it. Are we acting as responsible social scientists, or rather as people who are 'providing a product' in order to ensure employment? I wonder how many established medical researchers would agree to such research protocols, and if they did what it would do to their professional standing and reputation for integrity?

What can be done? In my view the academic and research community needs to find a way to promote and maintain its scientific integrity, which would mean, of course, that criminologists would have to put methodological integrity first. We might then see an end to the dispiriting sight of colleagues doing work which they believe to be far less good than it should be.

But, of course, professional integrity is inevitably, to some degree, undermined when so many researchers are employed on short-term contracts and moved swiftly from job to job, with far too little time to reflect on their findings. Often when a piece of research is completed the attitude seems to be that the subject as a whole has been 'done' and it is time to move on rather than build patiently on the knowledge obtained.

Furthermore, the fact that the prospects of future research contracts will depend on the value of the work as defined by the administrator, rather than on broader intellectual and academic criteria, is bound to have an effect on research initiative and freedom and on the quality of persons who can be attracted to criminological research.

In most sciences there would be a commitment to a long-term programme of work on a subject, moving from study to study as the body of evidence develops and new hypotheses emerge and are subjected to test and verification. There is, alas, virtually nothing like this in criminology in this country.

A (mini) research council?

In my view, the state as the major funder of research (as well as others who may wish to promote it) should create a new institutional structure. I have always agreed with Nils Christie that criminology needs to be 'institutionally and intellectually protected against the embracement by authorities' (Christie 1981:110) (although I would add, at least as far as is consistent with accountability for expenditure of public funds). Scientific research should not be part of the governmental apparatus – and indeed in most fields it is not. Government funding, as in other areas of research relevant to social policy, should be handled through an independent Criminological Research Council by which considerations of scientific advance and public utility can be weighed when deciding on the allocation of resources to the research community. This would mean that the Home Office would have to devolve at least a substantial part of the funding for its Research Unit to an independent body, on which it would naturally be represented.

This will not be easy to achieve. Michael Tonry (1998) has chronicled how, 30 years ago, the President's Commission Report *The Challenge of Crime in a Free Society*, recommended the establishment of an independent research agency for criminology, and how that proposal was 'still-born'. There is, I fear, not time to discuss the reasons why. But the American experience does not mean that we should give up. A mini research council (perhaps as part of the ESRC with a ring-fenced budget) is, in my view, essential if criminological research is to make a constructive yet critical contribution to the understanding of crime and its control in the twenty-first century. With new resources, a changed relationship to government, and a mandate to produce first class theoretical work and empirical inquiries, criminology could be revitalised and transformed rather than wither away in its social influence. If the *latter* were to happen, Sir Leon would really turn in his grave.

Notes

This contribution takes up the theme of two previous articles (Hood 1987 and Hood 2001), although this time more specifically in relation to Sir Leon's contribution to this subject. I am especially grateful to David Garland and Richard Sparks for the stimulating exchange of views we had after this talk was given, which helped me in preparing this text better to present their views.

References

Bennett, T. (1996) 'What's New in Evaluation Research? A Note on the Pawson and Tilley article', *British Journal of Criminology*, 36, 222–38.
Beyleveld, D. (1979) 'Identifying, Explaining and Predicting Deterrence', *British Journal of Criminology*, 19, 205–24.
Blumstein, A. (1995) 'Editorial: Probing the Connections between Crime and Punishment in the United States', *Criminal Behavior and Mental Health*, 5, 67–72.
Bondeson, U. (1998) 'Reflections on the Interplay between Criminological Research and Criminal Policy', in, H.-J. Albrecht *et al* (eds), *Internationale Perspektiven in Kriminologie und Strafrecht, Festschrift für Günther Kaiser*. Berlin: Dunker & Humbolt, vol. 1, pp. 57–69.
Bottoms, A.E. (1987) 'Reflections on the Criminological Enterprise', *Cambridge Law Journal*, 46, 240–63.
Bottoms, A.E. (2000) 'The Relationship between Theory and Research in Criminology', in R.D. King and E. Wincup (eds), *Doing Research in Crime and Justice*. Oxford: Oxford University Press, pp. 15–60.
Braithwaite, J. (1989) *Crime, Shame and Reintegration*. Cambridge: Cambridge University Press.
Braithwaite, J. (2000) 'The New Regulatory State and the Transformation of Criminology', *British Journal of Criminology*, 40, 222–38.
Brody, S. and Tarling, R. (1980) *Taking Offenders out of Circulation*, Home Office Research Study No. 51. London: HMSO.
Buikhuisen, W. (1974) 'General Deterrence: Research and Theory', *Abstracts on Criminology and Penology*, 14 (3), 285–98.
Butler, Lord (1974) 'The Foundation of the Institute of Criminology in Cambridge', in R.G. Hood (ed.), *Crime, Criminology and Public Policy: Essays in Honour of Sir Leon Radzinowicz*. London: Heinemann Educational Books, pp. 1–10.
Christie, N. (1981) *Limits to Pain*. Oslo: Universitetsforlaget.

Christie, N. (1997) 'Four Blocks against Insight: Notes on the Oversocialization of Criminologists', *Theoretical Criminology*, 1, 13–23.

Cohen, S. (1985) *Visions of Social Control*. Cambridge: Polity Press.

Cohen, S. (1994) 'If Nothing Works, What is our Work?', *Australian and New Zealand Journal of Criminology*, 27, 104–7.

Croft, J. (1996) 'Re-inventing the Wheel', *Vista*, September, 116–18.

Garland, D. (1996) 'The Limits of the Sovereign State: Strategies of Crime Control in Contemporary Society', *British Journal of Criminology*, 36, 445–71.

Garland, D. (2001) *The Culture of Control: Crime and Social Order in Contemporary Society*. Oxford: Oxford University Press.

Garland, D. and Sparks, R. (2000) 'Criminology, Social Theory and the Challenges of our Time', *British Journal of Criminology*, 40, 189–204.

Home Office (1959) *Penal Practice in a Changing Society*, Cmnd. 645. London: HMSO.

Home Office (1999) *The Government's Crime Reduction Strategy*. London: Home Office Communications Directorate.

Hood, R.G. (1987) 'Some Reflections on the Role of Criminology in Public Policy', *Criminal Law Review*, 527–38.

Hood, R.G. (2001) 'Penal Policy and Criminological Challenges in the New Millennium', *Australian and New Zealand Journal of Criminology*, 34, 1–16.

Hood, R.G. and Sparks, R.F. (1970) *Key Issues in Criminology*. London: Weidenfeld & Nicolson.

Hoyle, C. (1998) *Negotiating Domestic Violence: Police, Criminal Justice and Victims*. Oxford: Oxford University Press.

Hoyle, C. (2000) 'Being "a Nosy Bloody Cow": Ethical and Methodological Issues in Researching Domestic Violence', in R.D. King and E. Wincup (eds), *Doing Research in Crime and Justice*. Oxford: Oxford University Press, pp. 395–406.

Monahan, J. (1997) 'Clinical and Actuarial Predictions of Violence', in D. Faigman *et al* (eds), *Modern Scientific Evidence: the Law and Science of Expert Testimony*. St. Paul, Minn: West Publishing, vol. 1, pp. 300–18.

Muncie, J. (1998/99) 'Deconstructing Criminology', *Criminal Justice Matters*, No. 34, 4–5.

Nuttall, C., Goldblatt, P. and Lewis, C. (eds) (1998) *Reducing Offending: an Assessment of Research Evidence on Ways of Dealing with Offending Behaviour*, Home Office Research Study 187. London: Home Office.

Pawson, R. and Tilley, N. (1994) 'What Works in Evaluation Research', *British Journal of Criminology*, 34, 291–306.

Pawson, R. and Tilley, N. (1996) 'What's Crucial in Evaluation Research: a Reply to Bennett', *British Journal of Criminology*, 36, 574–8.

Radzinowicz, L. (1961) *In Search of Criminology*. London: Heinemann.

Radzinowicz, L. (1966) *Ideology and Crime*. London: Heinemann; New York: Columbia University Press.

Radzinowicz, L. (1988) *The Cambridge Institute of Criminology: Its Background and Scope*. London: HMSO.

Radzinowicz, L. (1999) *Adventures in Criminology*. London: Routledge.

Radzinowicz, L. and Turner, J.W.C. (1940a) 'The Language of Criminal Science', *Cambridge Law Journal*, 7, 224–37.

Radzinowicz, L. and Turner, J.W.C. (1940b) 'Introduction', in L. Radzinowicz and J.W.C. Turner (eds), *Penal Reform in England*. London: P.S. King & Son.

Ross, H.L. (1973) 'Law, Science and Accidents: the British Road Safety Act of 1967', *Journal of Legal Studies*, 2, 1–78.

Ryan, M. (1998/99), 'Criminology Re-engages the Public Voice', *Criminal Justice Matters*, 34, 10–12.

Sherman, L.W. (1995) 'The Truly Conceited: *Ex Cathedra* Doctrine and the Policing of Crime', *Australian and New Zealand Journal of Criminology*, 28 (Supplement), 45–51.

Stanko, E. (1995) 'A Rejoinder to Sherman: Only a Boys' Game', *Australian and New Zealand Journal of Criminology*, 28 (Supplement), 52–3.

Taylor, I., Walton, P. and Young, J. (1973) *The New Criminology*. London: Routledge.

Tonry, M. (1998) 'Building Better Policies on Better Knowledge', in *The Challenge of Crime in a Free Society: Looking Back, Looking Forward*. Washington, DC: US Department of Justice.

Travers, M. (1997) 'Preaching to the Converted? Improving the Persuasiveness of Criminological Research', *British Journal of Criminology*, 37, 359–77.

von Hirsch, A., Bottoms, A.E., Burney, E. and Wikström, P.-O. (1999) *Criminal Deterrence and Sentencing Severity: An Analysis of Recent Research*. Oxford: Hart Publishing.

Walker, N. (1965) *Crime and Punishment in Britain*. Edinburgh: Edinburgh University Press.

Wiles, P. (1999/2000) 'The Contribution of Research to Policy', *Criminal Justice Matters*, 38, 35–7.

Young, J. (1999) *The Exclusive Society: Social Exclusion, Crime and Difference in Late Modernity*. London: Sage.

Young, P. (1992) 'The Importance of Utopias in Criminological Thinking', *British Journal of Criminology*, 32, 423–37.

Zimring, F.E. and Hawkins, G. (1973) *Deterrence: The Legal Threat in Crime Control*. Chicago, IL: Chicago University Press.

Zimring, F.E. and Hawkins, G. (1991) *The Scale of Imprisonment*. Chicago, IL: University of Chicago Press.

Sir Leon Radzinowicz: a bibliography

1928   *Mesures de sûreté: étude de politique criminelle.* Paris: Les Ecrivains Réunis (Leon Rabinowicz).

1929   *La crise et l'avenir du droit penal.* Paris: Marcel Rivière (Leon Rabinowicz).

1929   Il problema delle misure di sicurezza e l'evoluzione moderna del diritto penale, Estratto dagli *Scritti in onore di Enrico Ferri*, pubblicati dal'Unione Tipografico-Editrice, Torinese (Leon Rabinowicz).

1930   La lutte moderne contre le crime. Brussels: Ferdinand Lascier (Leon Rabinowicz).

1931   *Le crime passionnel.* Paris: Marcel Rivière (Leon Rabinowicz).

1935   'Nowy ustrój penitencjarny we wloszech', *Odbitka 2, Archiwum Kryminologicznego*, 11 (1–2), 263–88.

1935   'L'antropologia criminale e l'esecuzione delle sanzioni detentive', *Rivista di diritto penitenziario*, 13 (2).

1937   'Variability of the Sex Ratio of Criminality', *Sociological Review*, 29, 76–102.

1939   'The After Conduct of Convicted Offenders in England', *Canadian Bar Review*, 17, 558–78. A revised article entitled 'The After Conduct of Discharged Offenders' appears in Radzinowicz (1940–78), vol. 4, pp. 142–61.

1939   'The Evolution of the Modern English Prison System', *Modern Law Review*, 3, 121–35. A revised article entitled 'English Prison System' appears in Radzinowicz (1940–78), vol. 4, pp. 123–41.

1939   'A Note on Methods of Establishing the Connection Between Economic Conditions and Crime', *Sociological Review*, 31, 260–80.

1939	'The Persistent Offender', *Cambridge Law Journal*, 7, 68–79. A revised article appears in Radzinowicz (1940–78), vol. 4, pp. 162–73.

1939   'The Present Trend of English Penal Policy', *Law Quarterly Review*, 55, 273–88. A revised article entitled 'The Assessment of Punishments by English Courts' appears in Radzinowicz (1940–78), vol. 4, pp. 110–22.

1940   'English Criminal Statistics: A Critical Analysis', *Law Quarterly Review*, 56, 483–503. A revised article appears in Radzinowicz (1940–78), vol. 4, pp. 174–94.

1940   Radzinowicz, L. and Turner, J.W.C. 'The Language of Criminal Science', *Cambridge Law Journal*, 7, 224–37.

1940–1978   Radzinowicz, L. (ed.) *Cambridge Studies in Criminology*, 52 vols. Volumes 1–19, London: Macmillan; Volumes 20–52, London: Heinemann. The first seven volumes were edited with J.W.C. Turner. The first ten volumes were published with the series title, *English Studies in Criminal Science*.

1941   *English Criminal Policy: an Attempt at Interpretation*. Edinburgh, 1941 (reprinted from *Juridical Review*, June 1941).

1941   'The Influence of Economic Conditions on Crime, 2 parts', *Sociological Review*, 33, 1–36, 139–53.

1941   'International Collaboration in Criminal Science', *Law Quarterly Review*, 58, 110–39.

1941   Radzinowicz, L. and Turner, J.W.C. 'Conviction and Probation', *Canadian Bar Review*, 19, 500–7.

1942   Radzinowicz, L. and Turner, J.W.C. 'International Commission for Penal Reconstruction and Development', *Canadian Bar Review*, 20, 503–4.

1943   'Some Sources of Modern English Criminal Legislation', *Cambridge Law Journal*, 8, 180–94.

1944   Radzinowicz, L. and Turner, J.W.C. 'A Study on Punishment', *Canadian Bar Review*, 21, 91–101. A revised article entitled 'Punishment: Outline of Developments Since the 18th Century' appears in Radzinowicz (1940–78), vol. 4, pp. 39–50.

1945   *Lombroso*, pp. 103–8 in *The Saturday Book*. London: Hutchison.

1945   'Present Trends of English Criminal Policy: An Attempt at Interpretation', in L. Radzinowicz and J.W.C. Turner (eds), *English Studies in Criminal Science*. Volume 4: *The Modern Approach to Criminal Law*. London: Macmillan, pp. 27–38. See Radzinowicz (1940–78).

1945   'The Waltham Black Act: A Study of the Legislative Attitude Towards Crime in the Eighteenth Century', *Cambridge Law Journal*, 9, 56–81.

1945   Radzinowicz, L. and Turner, J.W.C. 'The Social Problem Group', *Canadian Bar Review*, 23, 177–81.

1947	'An Early Stage in the Movement for the Reform of Criminal Law', *Law Quarterly Review*, 63, 94–111.
1948–68	*A History of English Criminal Law and Its Administration From 1750*, 4 vols. London: Stevens. Volume 1: *The Movement for Reform*, 1948. Volume 2: *The Clash Between Private Initiative and Public Interest in the Enforcement of the Law*, 1956. Volume 3: *Cross-currents in the Movement for the Reform of the Police*, 1956. Volume 4: *Grappling for Control*, 1968. (see also Radzinowicz and Hood 1986)
1952	'The Criminal Justice Act, 1948', in *Studi in memoria di Arturo Rocco*. Milan: Giuffré, vol. 2, pp. 405–18.
1954	'First Steps Towards Government Control over Police Before Peel', *Law Quarterly Review*, 70, 88–108.
1956	'The Ratcliffe Murders', *Cambridge Law Journal*, 14, 39–66.
1957	*Sir James Fitzjames Stephen 1829–1894 and His Contribution to the Development of Criminal Law*. London: Quaritch, The Selden Society Lecture.
1959	'Changing Attitudes Towards Crime and Punishment', *Law Quarterly Review*, 75, 381–400. Lecture delivered at the Royal Institute of Great Britain on 28 February 1958.
1959	Ancel, M. and Radzinowicz, L. (eds) *Introduction au droit criminel de l'Angleterre*. Paris: Les Editions de l'Epargne.
1960	'Criminal Law, Criminology and Forensic Science', *Medicine, Science and the Law*, 1, 7–15.
1960	Radzinowicz, L. and McClintock, F.H. 'Robbery in London', *Economist*, 197, 860–1.
1961	*In Search of Criminology*. Cambridge, MA: Harvard University Press, London: Heinemann.
1961	'New Departures in Maintaining Public Order in the Face of Chartist Disturbances', *Cambridge Law Journal*, 18, 51–88.
1961	'Public Opinion and Crime', *Medicine, Science and the Law*, 2 (1), 24–32.
1961	'The Study of Criminology in Cambridge', *Medico-legal Journal*, 29, 122–33.
1963	'Introduction', in Sidney and Beatrice Webb, *English Prisons Under Local Government*. London: Cass.
1963	'Report on Problems of Administration and Organisation of Criminological Research', Unpublished manuscript. Presented to the first European conference of directors of criminological research institutes in Strasbourg, 9–12 December 1963. Mimeo DPC/CDIR (64), pp. 5–26.
1963	*Judicial Attitudes: Punishment and Treatment*. Cambridge: Institute of Criminology
1963	'Problem of Counting Criminals', *The Times*, 12 August.

1964	'Cesare Beccaria and the English System of Criminal Justice: A Reciprocal Relationship', in *Estratto dagli atti del Convegno Internazionale su Cesare Beccaria*. Turin: Vencenzo Bona, pp. 57–66.
1964	'The Criminal in Society', *Journal of the Royal Society of Arts* 112, 916–29. The Peter le Neve Foster Lecture.
1964	*Criminology and the Climate of Social Responsibility*. Cambridge: Heffer. An address to the Howard League for Penal Reform, 7 May 1964.
1964	'Sentencing Policy in Criminal Cases', *The Times* (London), 30 May.
1965	'Ideology and Crime: The Deterministic Position', *Columbia Law Review*, 65, 1047–60.
1965	*The Need for Criminology*. London: Heinnemann.
1965	With M. Ancel. *Où en est la criminologie?* Paris: Éditions Cujas.
1966	*Ideology and Crime*. London: Heinemann; New York: Columbia University Press.
1968	'The Dangerous Offender', *Police Journal*, 41, 411–47. The Frank Newsam Memorial Lecture, given at the Police College, Bramshill, 1 August 1968.
1968	'Economic Conditions and Crime', Unpublished manuscript. Presented to the National Commission on the Causes and Prevention of Violence. Reprinted as 'Economic Pressures' in Radzinowicz and Wolfgang (1971), vol. 1, pp. 420–42.
1968	'Impressment into the Army and the Navy: A Rough and Ready Instrument of Preventive Police and Criminal Justice', in M.E. Wolfgang (ed.), *Crime and Culture: Essays in Honor of Thorsten Sellin*. New York: Wiley, pp. 287–313.
1969	'Hanging: Has Abolition Worked?', *Sunday Times*, 21 September.
1969	'Hanging: An All or Nothing Solution', *Burnley Evening Star*, 10 December.
1971	'A Foreseeable Failure', *Sunday Times*, 24 January.
1971	'The Police: Is the Get-tough School Right?', *Sunday Times*, 19 August.
1971	'Some Current Problems and Future Prospects of International Collaboration in Penal Matters', in J.P. Buhl *et al* (eds), *Liber Amicorum in Honour of Professor Stephen Hurwitz LL.D.* Copenhagen: Juristforbundets Forlag, pp. 387–406.
1971	'The Vision of Ramsey Clark', *Virginia Quarterly Review*, 71, 459–64.
1971	Radzinowicz, L. and Wolfgang, M.E. (eds) *Crime and Justice*, 3 vols, rev. edn. New York: Basic Books. Volume 1: *The Criminal in Society*. Volume 2: *The Criminal in the Arms of the Law*. Volume 3: *The Criminal in Confinement*.
1972	'The Criminal Law Explosion: Can It Be Controlled?', *Columbia Journal of Law and Social Problems*, 9, 88–130.

1972	'Them and Us', *Cambridge Law Journal*, 30, 260–79. A lecture given under the auspices of the New Bridge at the Mansion House, 26 April.
1976	Radzinowicz, L. and Hood, R. *Criminology and the Administration of Criminal Justice: a Bibliography.* London: Mansell. (Awarded the Joseph L. Andrews Award of the American Association of Law Libraries for the most significant legal bibliography published in 1976.)
1977	Radzinowicz, L. and King, J. *The Growth of Crime.* London: Hamish Hamilton; New York: Basic Books.
1978	Radzinowicz, L. and Hood, R. 'An English Attempt to Reshape the Sentencing Structure', *Columbia Law Review*, 78, 1145–58. Also published as 'A Dangerous Direction for Sentencing Reform', *Criminal Law Review* (1978), 713–24.
1979	Radzinowicz, L. and Hood, R. 'Judicial Discretion and Sentencing Standards: Victorian Attempts to Solve a Perennial Problem', *University of Pennsylvania Law Review*, 127, 1288–1349.
1979	Radzinowicz, L. and Hood, R. 'The Status of Political Prisoners in England: the Struggle for Recognition', *Virginia Law Review*, 65, 1421–48.
1980	Radzinowicz, L. and Hood, R. 'Incapacitating the Habitual Criminal: the English Experience', *Michigan Law Review*, 78, 1305–89.
1981	Radzinowicz, L. and Hood, R. 'The American Volte-Face in Sentencing Thought and Practice', in C. Tapper (ed.), *Crime, Proof and Punishment: Essays in Memory of Sir Rupert Cross.* London: Butterworth, pp. 127–43.
1981	Radzinowicz, L. and Hood, R. 'Sir Rupert Cross 1912–1980', *British Journal of Criminology*, 21, 176.
1981	Radzinowicz, L. and Hood, R. 'Dangerousness and Criminal Justice: a Few Reflections', *Criminal Law Review*, 756–61.
1981	With J. King. *La spirale del crimine: L'esperienza internazionale.* Milan: Giuffré.
1983	'Herbert Wechsler's Role in the Development of American Criminal Law and Penal Policy', *Virginia Law Review*, 69, 1–10.
1986	'Hermann Mannheim', *Dictionary of National Biography 1971–80.* Oxford: Oxford University Press, pp. 543–4.
1986	Radzinowicz, L. and Hood, R. *A History of English Criminal Law and its Administration from 1750, Vol. 5, The Emergence of Penal Policy.* London: Stevens. Republished as *The Emergence of Penal Policy in Victorian and Edwardian England.* Oxford: Oxford University Press, 1990.
1988	*The Cambridge Institute of Criminology: Its Background and Scope.* London: HMSO.

1991   'Penal Regressions', *Cambridge Law Journal*, 50, 422–44.
1991   *The roots of the International Association of Criminal Law and their significance: A tribute and a re-assessment on the centenary of the IKV.* Freiburg: Max Planck Institute for Foreign and International Criminal Law.
1994   'Reflections on the State of Criminology', *British Journal of Criminology*, 34, 99–104.
1995   'Revisiting the American Society of Criminology: 1976–1994', *The Criminologist*, 20 (1), 22–3.
1995   'Kristian Geogevich Rakovsky: A Criminological Interlude: Born 13 August 1873. Executed 11 September 1941, Rehabilitated 1988', in F. Adler and W. Laufer (eds), *Advances in Criminological Theory*, 6, 287–302.
1999   *Adventures in Criminology.* London, Routledge.

Index

Long Lartin, 104–5, 107, 109
McManus, Terence Bellew, 63
Macpherson Report, 43, 44
MacSwiney, Terence, 69
managerialist approach, tackling crime, 44
maréchaussée, 87
Martin, John, 63
maximum-security prisons, 104
methodological disputations, 165–7
Metropolitan Police, 82, 83, 86, 87, 89–90
Middlesex Justices Act (1792), 75
military police, Europe, 87
minor offences, changed attitude towards, 14–15
Mitchel, John, 61, 62–3, 63–4
moral judgements, 22
moral neglect, Prison Service, 43
morality
    rule-related behaviour, 26, 27–8
    social contexts, 42
    see also critical morality; positive morality
Mountbatten, Lord, 101, 102, 111–19
Movement for Reform, The, xv
Municipal Corporations Act (1835), 90

Narey, Martin, 43, 44
negative labelling, prisoners, 135
negotiation model, order, 109
New Criminology, The, 162
night watches, 77
normative compliance, 30f, 31, 33–9
normative factors
    criminal policy, 42–5
    criminology, 24–8
'Nothing Works' school, 163

O'Brien, William Smith, 60, 62, 63
O'Connell, Daniel, 60
offenders
    prison-community border, 12
    rehabilitation of, 10–11, 14
    risk factors of persistent, 39
    see also political offenders; society-offender relation

Offending Behaviour Programmes, 131–5
order, dispersal prisons, 109

paedophile registers, 14
parish constables, 78
Parkhurst, 105, 111–19
Peel, Robert, 83, 85
penal ideology
    changes in, 8–9
    first modern, 4
penal measures, welfare state values, 7
penal policy
    criminology and, 153–69
    'What Works' movement, 10
penal practice, late twentieth century, 97–140
Penal Practice in a Changing Society, 154
Penal Regressions, 7, 8
penal-welfarism
    culture of crime control, 157
    individualisation, 12
    prisons, 11
    probation, 11
    progressive measures, 7
    recoding of, 9–10
    society-offender relation, 13
    stigma, 14
persistent offenders, risk factors, 39
physical constraints, 30
police, development of English, 74–91
Police Act (1856), 91
Police Law (1850), 91
policy
    changes, dispersal prisons, 127t
    see also criminal policy; penal policy; public policy
political agenda, criminological research, 156–60
political offenders
    history of, 56–7
    Irish, 60–72
political policing, 76, 89
'politics of denial', 157
Popay, Sergeant, 90
positive morality, 23, 24–5, 26, 43
positivism, 5, 21–2, 155